MEDIA LAW
for
PRODUCERS

2nd Edition

Philip Miller

Focal Press

Boston   Oxford   Johannesburg   Melbourne   New Delhi   Singapore

Focal Press is an imprint of Butterworth–Heinemann.

Copyright © 1996 by Butterworth–Heinemann

℞ A member of the Reed Elsevier group

∞ Recognizing the importance of preserving what has been written, Butterworth–Heinemann prints its book on acid-free paper whenever possible.

Library of Congress Cataloging-in-Publication Data

Miller, Philip.
    Media law for producers / Philip Miller. — 2nd ed.
      p. Cm.
    Orginally published: 2nd ed. White Plains, NY : Knowledge Industry Publications, c1993.
    Includes bibliographical reference and index.
    ISBN 0-240-80246-2
    1. Motion pictures—Law and legislation—United States. 2. Video recordings—Law and legislation—United States. 3. Copyright—United States. I. Title.
KF4298.M55   1996
343.7309'9—dc20
[347.30399]

        96-5083
        CIP

British Library Cataloguing-in-Publication Data
A catalogue record for this book is available from the British Library.

The publisher offers special discounts on bulk orders of this book.
For information, please contact:
Manager of Special Sales
Butterworth–Heinemann
313 Washington Street
Newton, MA 02158–1626
Tel: 617-928-2500
Fax: 617-933-2620

For information on all Focal Press publications available, contact our World Wide Web home page at:
http://www.bh.com/bh/

10 9 8 7 6 5 4 3 2 1

Printed in the United States of America

Foreword

As media productions have become more sophisticated, so have the legal issues that can affect their development and distribution. From performer contracts to copyright registration, producers need to be able to recognize the legal questions that can come up during production projects and to be ready with the appropriate responses. This is true not only for producers of major film and television projects, but also for independent and corporate producers involved with industrial and other non-broadcast programs.

Media Law for Producers helps producers and other production professionals meet this need. The book can work in two ways: as a general overview of media law that helps you anticipate and head off legal problems, and as a handy reference that you can pull off the shelf when questions and problems do arise. This mix of background material and practical information also makes *Media Law for Producers* appropriate as a text for courses on media production and law.

Before readers proceed any farther, a word of caution is in order. Although *Media Law for Producers* provides important information, it is not intended as a substitute for professional legal counsel. Turn to this book for a general understanding of the basic principles underlying media law, descriptions and examples of the various legal questions that can come up during production, and sample forms and agreements that can help you anticipate and avoid legal snags. Turn to an attorney for answers to legal questions not covered in this text, for information about laws and regulations that are specific to individual states and municipalities, and for detailed advice on contracts and other legal matters that do arise during production.

Media Law for Producers begins with an introduction to the sources and basic principles of media law. This is followed by chapters that address key areas of concern for media production professionals: establishing contracts and production agreements; using public domain and copyrighted materials; securing appropriate releases and permissions; avoiding libel and right of privacy challenges; licensing music; working with unions; registering copyright and trademarks; understanding the laws affecting programs that will be broadcast; and negotiating licensing and distribution agreements. The book ends with a glossary that defines important legal terms, a bibliography that lists useful references, and appendices that provide the names and addresses of important organizations.

Most of the chapters begin by reviewing the basic concepts that form the foundation for a specific aspect of media law. This background information is followed by examples that show how this area of media law applies to various production situations and contexts, precautions that producers can take to avoid legal entanglements, and suggestions for dealing with problems when they do appear. Wherever possible, the chapters provide sample forms and agreements that producers can use to set the framework for documents tailored to their particular needs.

Readers should also be aware of what *Media Law for Producers* does not cover. Because the book focuses on legal aspects of the production process, it does not deal with many of the policy and technical issues that are generally considered part of communications law. For example, *Media Law for Producers* does not discuss the public policy issues raised by the manner in which the Federal Communications Commission assigns broadcast licenses, the technical standards that are imposed on broadcasters, or the ongoing debate over concentration of ownership in the communications industry. While these are all important issues, they are not among the day-to-day concerns of most media production professionals.

Media Law for Producers also does not examine, in depth, many of the more intricate financial and ethical aspects of negotiating deals and doing business as a media producer. Because media production and distribution deals are often very complex business transactions, and because what is "standard practice" in the industry can vary from year to year, many producers choose to have an experienced attorney, agent or other knowledgeable and trusted adviser review all of their deals before they commit to a binding agreement.

As readers will discover, many of the examples used in *Media Law for Producers* refer to video productions developed for non-broadcast distribution. However, most of the legal principles covered in the chapters apply with equal validity to a wide range of production situations—from the preparation of slide-tape presentations that will be shown to a small group of corporate clients to the development of a television series scheduled for broadcast on a major network.

Earlier in this forward, I was careful to point out that *Media Law for Producers* is not intended as a substitute for professional legal counsel. However, after reading the chapters that follow, media producers should be familiar with enough of the legal landscape to make their way around and through many of the minor legal entanglements that can slow the production process. Just as important, readers should end up knowing enough law to know when they need to call a lawyer and what questions they need to ask.

Barbara J. Shulman
Stroock & Stroock & Lavan
New York, New York

iv

ACKNOWLEDGEMENTS

Barbara Shulman reviewed each section of the first edition of this book and provided very patient and valuable counsel. Without her expertise and guidance, *Media Law for Producers* would never have made the transition from rough drafts to finished work. Any errors or omissions that remain in the book are my responsibility, not hers.

I am also indebted to Kit Laybourne of Noyes and Laybourne Productions. As I began my work on *Media Law*, Kit provided sample contracts and materials that helped focus my research. Joan Greenspan of the Screen Actor's Guild provided materials that helped me with Chapter 7, the chapter on working with guilds and unions. Joan also reviewed sections of that chapter.

Ellen Lazer, senior editor at Knowledge Industry Publications, encouraged me to write *Media Law for Producers*, and Laurie Nevin, the editor for the book, encouraged me to keep going when the writing took longer than originally planned. Thanks, also, to John LeBaron, my original mentor in the book-writing business.

I am especially grateful to my wife Anne and son Christopher (and, for the second edition, to our new daughter Rosemary) for their understanding during the many hours that I spent behind closed doors with my word processor. The doors are open now, and the weekends are yours again. Thanks, also, to Robert and Roey for providing babysitting services at several critical times during the development of this manuscript.

Finally, my appreciation to my former colleagues at Scholastic Inc., a very professional and special place where I learned that writers and editors can never care too much about their work.

NOTICE

Table of Contents

List of Figures

1

MEDIA LAW: AN OVERVIEW

Media law is a very broad body of law that incorporates elements from a variety of legal disciplines. Those disciplines include copyright and trademark law, contract law, labor law, the laws and regulations concerned with privacy and defamation, telecommunications law and policy, and the many legal issues and interpretations that arise from the First Amendment's guarantees of free speech and freedom of the press.

To protect themselves from lawsuits and legal entanglements, media producers need to be familiar with these key areas of law. Just as important, media professionals must be able to recognize the various guises under which legal issues can appear during the production process. Consider this fictional account of the legal roadblocks that confronted one unwary producer:

> **Richard Newman is the director of video production in the corporate media department of a large financial firm. At the request of the firm's training division, Newman produced a 45-minute videotape on management communication skills titled *Listen While You Work*. Newman assumed that, like all of the other programs that he had produced for the firm, *Listen While You Work* would be limited to internal distribution.**
>
> **In producing the program, Newman faced a familiar battle. He wanted to create an engaging, effective training tape, but has constrained by a limited production budget. As a result, Newman found himself "borrowing" from a variety of sources and resources. To illustrate the effects of poor communication, he used footage from a vintage theatrical film he had rented from his neighborhood video store. To add some punch to the audio track, he dubbed clips from several popular rock-and-roll recordings. He taped most of the original video material in the company's headquarters, using employees as his talent.**
>
> **Newman prepared the script himself, with some help from a friend who is a professional script-writer. The script included dialogue adapted from several case**

1

studies published in a popular management text, plus material taken from videotaped interviews with management consultants. Portions of the script were read by an announcer who Newman hired on a flat-fee basis.

Because *Listen While You Work* was intended for internal use only and because deadlines were pressing, Newman did not bother to negotiate formal contracts with the scriptwriter or announcer. He also did not bother to ask for signed releases from the employees who appeared in the tape or the management consultants who had participated in the videotaped interviews.

Newman put a great deal of his own time into the tape, completing the final edits himself on the weekend before the program was scheduled to premiere at the company's annual management training conference. His hard work paid off. The program played to a packed house and received rave reviews from company officials.

The program also received something that Newman had not expected—an offer to distribute the tape outside the company. The offer came from a group that was established to find new markets for the firm's internal resources.

Although Newman was flattered by the offer, he realized that his haste in producing the program might have left some legal strings untied. A call to the corporate legal office confirmed that there were indeed many questions that needed to be resolved before the tape could be cleared for external distribution. Faced with the prospect of having to wait for answers to those questions, the marketing group withdrew its offer to distribute the tape.

Although Newman was wise to contact his corporate legal department, it does not take a trained legal mind to recognize many of the matters that were cause for concern. A partial list follows:

•Use of copyrighted film footage from a motion picture without seeking permission from the individual, group or organization that owns or controls the film's copyright.

•Use of copyrighted music recordings for a soundtrack, without seeking clearances from the appropriate individuals, music licensing groups and record companies.

•Use of copyrighted print material without seeking permission from the book's author or publisher.

•Failure to secure releases from employees featured in the production. Because of this oversight, employees who might feel that the program depicts them in an unfavorable light are free to sue Newman or the firm for which Newman works for invasion of privacy or libel. Employees featured in the film could also sue to collect a portion of the revenues that the program generates through outside distribution.

•Failure to secure written contracts or release forms from the scriptwriter and announcer who worked on the program. Although the scriptwriter and announcer apparently agreed to participate on a flat fee basis that would not provide them with any ownership in the program, they might change their minds now that the program has the potential to generate revenues through outside sales. Because the copyright law stipulates that work-for-hire agreements must be placed in writing, Newman would have nothing to support his contention that the pair performed on a flat-fee basis.

•Violation of union agreements. If the scriptwriter and announcer were members of a union or guild, Newman and his firm might also find themselves in trouble for not complying with union contracts. However, as discussed in Chapter 7, this would not be the case if the firm was not a signatory to the union agreements. In that case, it would be the writer and announcer themselves who might face sanctions from their own unions.

Newman's case also raises another key issue. Who would actually own *Listen While You Work*, Newman or his company? Under the current copyright law, the company would have the most legitimate claim to ownership of the finished production, unless Newman's employment contract states otherwise. This would be the case because Newman produced the program within the normal scope of his employment—even though he spent some of his own time on the project. To avoid disputes over the ownership of materials produced on the job, many companies require employees to sign release forms as part of their employment agreement.

Another very important question needs to be addressed. Would Newman's actions have been legal if, as he had originally assumed, *Listen While You Work* had been limited to internal distribution? As subsequent chapters will show, the answer to that question is no—even though limiting distribution of the program would certainly have reduced his exposure and the risk of litigation.

HOW MUCH LAW DO YOU NEED TO KNOW?

Although the *Listen While You Work* scenario was stretched to make a point, it does indicate some of the very real legal troubles that can afflict unwary producers. This is not to suggest, though, that producers should become paranoid, paralyzed by fears that any action they take will leave them open to lawsuits or other litigation. Instead, producers should seek the creative freedom that comes from understanding when it is necessary to take steps to protect their work. Leave the heavy worrying—and the paranoia—to the lawyers.

Media professionals do not need to be lawyers. You do not need to know how to draft a legal document, how to conduct a copyright or trademark search or how to defend a case in court. However, as someone responsible for a media production, you should know the following:

•when it would be prudent for the parties in a production deal to sign legally binding agreements;

•what permissions, permits and releases producers need to secure during the course of a production;

•when it is legal or illegal to incorporate copyrighted materials in a production;

•what special steps producers must take to license music used in a production;

•what legal issues are involved in working with, and working without, union employees;

•what statements or portrayals may constitute libel or an invasion of privacy;

•what special precautions producers need to take on productions that will be used to advertise a product or service, or programs that will be broadcast or cablecast; and

•how copyright and trademark registration can help producers protect their finished productions.

This book examines how these and other practical legal matters can come up during media production, and how producers can resolve these matters in a manner that protects both them and their media properties. First, though, it helps to understand just who it is that creates, interprets and enforces "media law."

WHO CREATES MEDIA LAW?

According to most high school civics texts, federal laws are created in a fairly straightforward manner. The Congress, responding to a public need, drafts and passes a piece of legislation. Congress then sends the legislation to the President, who either signs or vetoes it. Once the President signs the legislation, or once Congress overrides the President's veto, responsibility for interpreting and enforcing the new law falls to the federal court system. If the law is challenged on constitutional grounds, the federal courts are also responsible for determining whether the new law is legal under the United States Constitution—the venerable document that establishes the scope and structure of the federal government, and that defines and delineates the government's lawmaking powers.

Although the textbook model is essentially accurate, it does not tell the whole story. In drafting legislation for example, Congress is often responding as much to private and political pressure as public need. Private lobbying groups, including many groups representing media interests, work overtime to promote or prevent the passage of legislation that affects their industries. In addition, before bills appear before the full Senate and House of Representatives, they must make their way through a gauntlet of committee meetings and hearings. Figure 1.1 illustrates the process through which a bill becomes law. While this process may help ensure that all evidence for and against a bill is heard, it also opens almost limitless opportunities for backstage deals and political trade-offs. The result is often a piece of legislation that resembles a patchwork quilt of conflicting aims and interests rather than a clear, coherent law.

The Role of the Courts

Civics texts also tend to simplify the role of the courts in the lawmaking process. As most texts point out, the Constitution assumes a primarily reactive, interpretive role for the federal judiciary in the lawmaking and governing process. In truth, however, the courts have a very active role in shaping both the scope and impact of federal statutes. This is especially true for the U.S. Supreme Court and the federal appeals courts, whose rulings serve as legal precedents that lower federal courts are obliged to follow. In fact, these higher court rulings often have the effect of law, particularly in areas where legislative statutes are vague or incomplete. This "judge-made" law is discussed more fully in the section on types and categories of law that follows.

Figure 1.1: An Overview of How Federal Laws Are Made

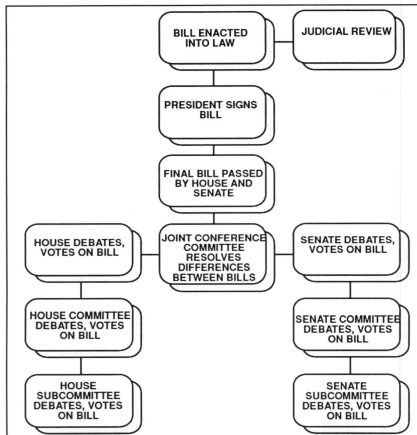

Once a representative or senator introduces a bill, it is usually referred to the appropriate standing committee for action. Most bills are then passed down to one or more subcommittees. If the subcommittee reports favorably on the bill, it moves to the full committee. If the full committee votes favorably on the bill, it is brought before the House or Senate, where it is debated and then voted on or referred back to committee. If the House and Senate vote favorably, the bill's next stop may be a joint conference committee, where any differences between the House and Senate versions of the bill are resolved. Assuming that the House and Senate approve identical versions of the bill, it is sent to the president. Once the president signs the bill, or once a two-thirds vote of Congress overrides the president's veto, the bill is enacted into law. The new law is then subject to judicial review by the federal courts.

The Role of Regulatory and Administrative Agencies

Another issue that many texts tend to downplay is the power that regulatory and administrative agencies exercise in creating and enforcing laws. Federal agencies and commissions create many rules that are as forceful as laws. This would come as quite a surprise to the framers of the Constitution, who never defined a formal role for federal bureaucracies in the system of checks and balances that is supposed to govern lawmaking.

State and Local Governments

State and local governments add more layers of complexity to the lawmaking process. Every state has its own executive, legislative and judicial branches of government—and its own bureaucracy. Although the U.S. Constitution dictates that no state law can contradict federal law in areas where the federal government has exclusive jurisdiction, the states are free to extend and enhance federal statutes and to establish laws in areas where there is limited federal legislation or jurisdiction. County and city governments also get into the lawmaking act, passing laws and ordinances designed to protect the safety and well-being of their residents.

Media Law—A Combination of Elements

Like most bodies of law, media law includes a mix of elements from all these levels of government. For example, while most of the key regulations affecting copyrights and trademarks stem from federal legislation, many aspects of contract law are based on state statutes and *common law*. Federal agencies such as the Federal Communications Commission (FCC), also play an important role in media law, particularly in the regulations of broadcasting and advertising. Media producers must be aware of municipal and county laws too, especially those ordinances that require production crews to acquire shooting permits and adhere to safety codes.

Lawyers who specialize in media law must be able to navigate their way through all of these legal nooks and crannies. For most media professionals, it is enough to know that these different sources and layers of law exist.

TYPES AND CATEGORIES OF MEDIA LAW

As the preceding section suggests, laws and regulations come from a variety of sources. They also come in various types, shapes and sizes. Fortunately, this is not as confusing as it might seem, since most types of law

fit rather neatly into one of four categories: constitutional law, statutory law, common law and regulatory law.

Constitutional Law

Federal Constitutional Law

Constitutional law is based on the articles and amendments that comprise the U.S. Constitution. Because the Constitution is the supreme law of the United States, any law or regulation that contradicts the Constitution is invalid. As mentioned earlier, the federal courts, particularly the supreme court and the federal appeals courts, are responsible for determining whether a federal, state or local law is constitutional. For that reason, the category of constitutional law includes both the articles and amendments of the Constitution (the "letter" of the Constitution) and the key federal court decisions and opinions that determine how the Constitution is applied in specific cases.

Because it incorporates opinions and precedents issued by the courts, and because the Constitution itself is subject to amendment, constitutional law is continually growing and changing. This is a characteristic that constitutional law shares with all categories of law—particularly the category of *common law* described later.

State Constitutional Law

Like the federal government, each state government has a constitution that serves as the supreme law of that state. The court systems in each state interpret and apply the constitution of that state. Often, this involves determining whether a law passed by the state legislature or a county or city government is valid under the provisions of the state constitution. Many counties and cities also have constitutions or charters that define their governing and lawmaking powers. Keep in mind, though, that no provision of a state, county or city constitution can contradict the U.S. Constitution.

Media and Constitutional Law

Many elements of media law are directly tied to constitutional law. For example, the right of media professionals to ply their craft free from government censorship is guaranteed by the First Amendment to the Constitution, which declares that "Congress shall make no law...abridging the freedom of speech or of the press...." In addition, the copyright laws that protect producers' rights to profit from sale of their media properties are based on Article 1,

Section 8, of the Constitution, which states that Congress is empowered to establish laws that give "authors and inventors the exclusive right to their respective writings and discoveries."

Statutory Law

Statutory law consists of legislative acts (or statutes) passed by Congress, state legislatures and local governments. Much statutory law is organized into *codes*, which are indexed compilations of laws arranged around specific subjects (the penal code, the motor vehicle code, etc.). One widely distributed code is the United States Code which includes most federal statutes. The Communications Act of 1934 and the Copyright Act of 1976 are two examples of federal statutes that are part of media law and the United States Code.

Federal Statutes Governing Media Law

The Communications Act of 1934 and the Copyright Act of 1976 are fundamental federal statutes that govern two key areas of media law. The Communications Act of 1934 lays the ground rules for broadcast, telephone and cable communications in the United States. In particular, the act determines who controls the broadcast airwaves by defining procedures for allocating television and radio frequency assignments in the United States. The act also created the Federal Communications Commission to administer and enforce those procedures.

In contrast to the Communications Act of 1934, which determines who controls broadcast channels, the Copyright Act of 1976 addresses the question of who owns and controls the programs that are transmitted on those channels. The Copyright Act of 1976 also defines who owns industrial training programs, educational videotapes and other forms of nonbroadcast programming. In fact, the act establishes rights of ownership in all forms of "intellectual property," including books, feature films and audio recordings. Because of its importance to all media producers, the Copyright Act of 1976 is discussed in detail in Chapter 4.

Statutory Law and the Courts

As mentioned earlier, the responsibility for interpreting and applying statutory law falls to the courts. Generally, the federal courts interpret federal statutes, state courts interpret state statutes and municipal courts interpret municipal statutes. In interpreting statutory law, the courts establish precedents that influence how the law will be applied in the future. That is why many statutory codes are published in annotated versions that list how various courts have interpreted statutes in specific cases.

In more than a few cases, the courts have declared that a federal, state or local statute is invalid. As discussed in the section on common law that follows, this generally happens only when a law is found to be in conflict with a pre-existing statute, or when the law appears to contradict one or more provisions of the U.S. Constitution. A state court may also declare a state statute invalid if it is found to be in conflict with the constitution of that state.

Common Law

Also called case law or judge-made law, common law is law based on judicial precedents. Each time judges issue decisions and opinions that establish legal precedents, they are contributing to the body of common law.[1]

Common law tends to be most important at the state level. Each state has its own court system and its own body of case law. As a result, common law often varies from state to state. However, no state common law can contradict federal constitutional law, federal legislation or rulings of the federal courts.

Common law serves a vital function in the American legal system. When statutory law lags behind social changes or important social needs, common law can help fill in the gaps. In cases where a clear injustice has occurred, the courts will first look to existing statutes for a remedy. If the present body of statutory law offers no obvious remedy, a judge might extend or reinterpret the existing laws to cover the current case. In some cases, judges will actually establish new legal rights in this manner.

Privacy and Copyright

Privacy and copyright are two areas of media law where courts have frequently had to interpret and extend existing statutes to accommodate new technological developments. In *Sony Corp. of America v. Universal City Studios*, for example, the Supreme Court was called on in 1984 to decide if manufacturers of home video recorders could be held liable for contributory copyright infringement because their machines facilitate the taping and duplication of broadcast television programs. Reading the Copyright Act of 1976 broadly, the court concluded that there was no contributory infringement because

---

[1]Like many areas of United States law, our common law is based in part on the English legal system. When state and federal courts first began in the new nation, they adopted many of the English judicial traditions that had been the basis for common law in the American colonies.

home video recording of TV programs was, for the most part, a non-infringing "fair use" under the copyright law. Similarly, in the area of privacy law, courts have had to determine whether existing statutes and regulations can be expanded to cover new surveillance technologies.

The Interaction of Judge-Made and Statutory Law

Some who study the lawmaking process argue that the courts have been much too willing to reinterpret and modify statutory law. According to these analysts, it is Congress and the state legislatures that should be making laws, not federal and state judges. Defenders of our judicial traditions point out that judge-made law is often just a temporary fix that allows statutory law to catch up. If precedent-setting court decisions raise important public policy issues, Congress and state legislatures can and often do pass laws that either incorporate or correct elements of judge-made law. This was true for copyright law, when decades of judicial interpretations applied to the Copyright Act of 1909 were finally pulled together, revised and refined in the Copyright Act of 1976. As discussed in Chapter 4, the Copyright Law of 1976 is now the subject of much judicial review and interpretation, particularly in the area of works-made-for-hire. And so the process of judicial review and interpretation of statutory law begins anew.

Distinguishing Cases

Although common law is based on precedents, judges do not always abide by those precedents. Faced with changing social circumstances, or with a legal proceeding that presents new conditions or issues, a judge may decide to distinguish a case by showing that an old precedent no longer applies. When judges issue decisions that they distinguish from previous precedents, they establish new precedents that other judges may either accept or further distinguish in their decisions.

Regulatory Law

Regulatory or administrative law is bureaucratic law—the vast inventory of rules, regulations and procedures promulgated by agencies at all levels of government. These regulatory agencies are often empowered both to write and enforce laws. For example, an agency that is responsible for worker safety might write codes that apply to specific industries, seek out employers who violate those codes, hold hearings to evaluate the evidence and issue civil or criminal penalties to "convicted" violators.

Legislative Oversight of Government Agencies

With all of this authority, many government agencies wield considerable power. Fortunately, there are some checks on this power. Since most government agencies are created through legislation, they are subject to legislative scrutiny. In fact, the same statute that creates an agency often places strict limits on its jurisdiction. In addition, because the legislature gives power to an agency, it can also take it away—either through additional legislation or reductions in an agency's funding.

Judicial Supervision of Regulatory Agencies

Regulatory agencies are also subject to judicial supervision through the appeals process. Most regulatory decisions can be appealed either to special administrative courts or to the state or federal courts, depending on whether the agency involved is a state or federal agency. One noteworthy example of this process is the case known as *Midwest Video II*, a 1978 case involving the appeal of an FCC ruling. In that ruling, the FCC had issued a regulation that required local cable television companies to provide public access channels. The FCC based this public access ruling in part on constitutional grounds, citing its belief that these publicly programmed cable channels would facilitate the free exchange of ideas that is both promoted and protected in the First Amendment.

Although the federal appeals court acknowledged the noble objectives of the public access requirements, it found that the FCC had exceeded its authority by requiring cable television operators to offer these channels. Specifically, the court found that the FCC's public access requirements exceeded its mandate under the Communication Act of 1934, the federal statute that created the FCC:

> **...we deal here with the Federal Communications Commission, not the Federal First Amendment Commission. We are aware of nothing in the Act... which places with the Commission an affirmative duty or power to advance First Amendment goals by its own tour de force, through getting everyone on cable television or otherwise. Rhetoric in praise of objectives cannot confer jurisdiction.[2]**

In other words, the court was reminding the FCC that it is the federal

---

[2] *Midwest Video Corp. v. FCC*, 571 F.2d 1025 (1978).

courts, not federal regulatory agencies, that are ultimately responsible for interpreting the Constitution.

Other Regulatory Agencies That Affect Media Law

In addition to the Federal Communications Commission, several other government agencies create regulations, policies and procedures that are of interest to media producers. Those government groups include:

•the Federal Trade Commission (FTC), which regulates advertising practices;

•the federal Copyright Office, which establishes procedures for registering copyright; and

•the Patent and Trademark Office, an agency of the U.S. Department of Commerce, which establishes procedures for registering trademarks and applying for patents.

Media professionals should also be aware of the various state, county and municipal agencies that issue regulations related to media production. For example, many states have offices that help producers find shooting locations for film and television, and also check that production companies conduct their businesses safely and with the proper permits and insurance.

CIVIL CASES VERSUS CRIMINAL CASES

When a case comes to court, it is categorized as either a *criminal case* or a *civil case*.

Criminal Cases

Criminal cases include burglary, robbery, murder, manslaughter and other crimes that threaten the safety or well-being of society as a whole. These cases are prosecuted by the state, with taxpayers picking up the bill for the cost of the prosecution. When defendants are convicted in a criminal case, they can face punishments that range from fines and parole to jail sentences and the death penalty. That is why the prosecutor must prove guilt "beyond a reasonable doubt" in criminal cases.

Media producers rarely find themselves caught up in criminal cases. This did happen, however, to a film producer John Landis, who was accused of involuntary manslaughter in the July, 1982 deaths of actor Vic Morrow and two children during the filming of the *Twilight Zone*. Although Landis was acquitted of this criminal charge in 1987, he and his production company may still face civil litigation brought by the families of the victims.

Civil Cases

Civil cases are usually considered less severe than criminal cases, and the standard of proof is less stringent. In civil cases, one party (an individual, group, corporation and so on) claims that another party has caused it physical, emotional or financial injury. The result is a dispute between the two parties, rather than between an accused criminal and the state, with the courts serving as arbitrator. If the "preponderance of evidence" proves that the party who brought the lawsuit (the *plaintiff*) was indeed injured by the second party, the judge may award *damages* in the form of money or some other appropriate compensation. In some cases, the judge may also award *punitive damages* as a way of punishing the guilty party.

Media Producers and Civil Litigation

When media producers find themselves involved in litigation, it is most

Figure 1.2: The Federal and State Judicial Systems and the Appeals Process

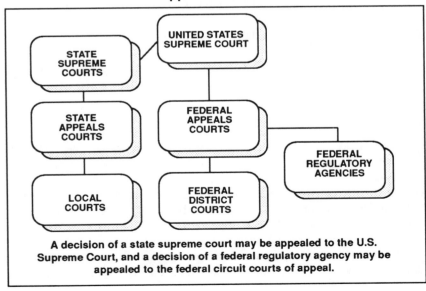

A decision of a state supreme court may be appealed to the U.S. Supreme Court, and a decision of a federal regulatory agency may be appealed to the federal circuit courts of appeal.

probably a civil case. For example, a television producer might sue a production company for failing to deliver promised services; a motion picture producer might sue a film distribution company for not living up to the terms of a distribution contract; or a video producer might sue another video producer over the rights to market a program that they co-produced. These kinds of civil cases are very common in the world of media production, where the many deals that make up any major project may sometimes turn sour. Most civil cases of this type are settled out of court, with lawyers for the parties working out a compromise.

Breach of Contract and Torts

Most civil litigation that grows out of media production is based on one of two types of "wrongs": a breach of a contract or a tort. A breach of contract is a wrong that occurs when one or more parties to a contract fail to perform an act that was required by the contract. A tort is almost any wrong other other than a breach of contract in which a party claims injury by another party. When a producer sues a subcontractor for failing to deliver an agreed upon service, the suit is a breach of contract action. When a subcontractor sues a producer for an injury that occurred on the production set, the suit is a tort action.

THE COURT SYSTEM

No overview of media law would be complete without a quick description of the court system. In the United States there are actually two court systems: the federal courts and the state courts. Within both the federal and state systems, there are also several types and levels of courts. Figure 1.2 shows the types of courts and where they fit within the federal and state systems.

The figure also shows the hierarchy a case passes through during the trial and appeals process. When the case is an appeal from a federal regulatory agency decision, it is brought before a U.S. Court of Appeals.

Federal Jurisdiction vs. State Jurisdiction

What determines whether a case falls under state or federal jurisdiction? For the most part, the state courts retain jurisdiction unless the case involves matters of federal law. The framers of the Constitution were very careful to grant the federal government authority over specific legal matters, with the remaining powers left to the states.

Federal Jurisdiction: Copyright and Interstate Commerce

One of the powers that the Constitution gives to the federal government is the authority to pass laws in the areas of copyright and interstate commerce. That is why most cases that involve copyright and broadcasting, which is considered a form of interstate commerce, fall under federal jurisdiction. The federal courts also have primary jurisdiction over all other cases that hinge on constitutional questions, including those cases that raise "free speech" and "free press" issues. In some instances, a federal court may intervene to overturn a ruling of a state court because, in the opinion of the federal court, the state court has failed to interpret properly a constitutional question.

Diversity of Citizenship

Federal courts may also assume jurisdiction in cases that involve "diversity of citizenship." This situation occurs when a citizen of one state initiates legal action against a citizen of another state. Because the court in either state might be prejudiced in favor of its own citizen, a federal court may agree to hear the case. By serving in this capacity, the federal court prevents either party in the case from gaining a "home court advantage." Diversity of citizenship can be important in lawsuits that grow out of media productions, since productions are often partnerships that involve several companies from different states. It can also be important in legal action that grows out of location work performed in one state by a production company based in another state.

Shared Jurisdiction

In many areas of law, the federal courts share jurisdiction with the state courts. This is true for cases that grow out of trademark regulation, for example, where certain types of proceedings can be brought in either state or federal court. In areas such as these, the federal and state courts are said to have *concurrent jurisdiction*. In addition, in lawsuits involving claims of $50,000 or more, a party can move to have the case heard in federal court under the diversity jurisdiction described above.

The Federal Court System

Cases that fall under federal jurisdiction enter the federal court system. As Figure 1.3 shows, the federal court system is divided into 13 circuits. The

Figure 1.3: The Federal Judicial Circuits

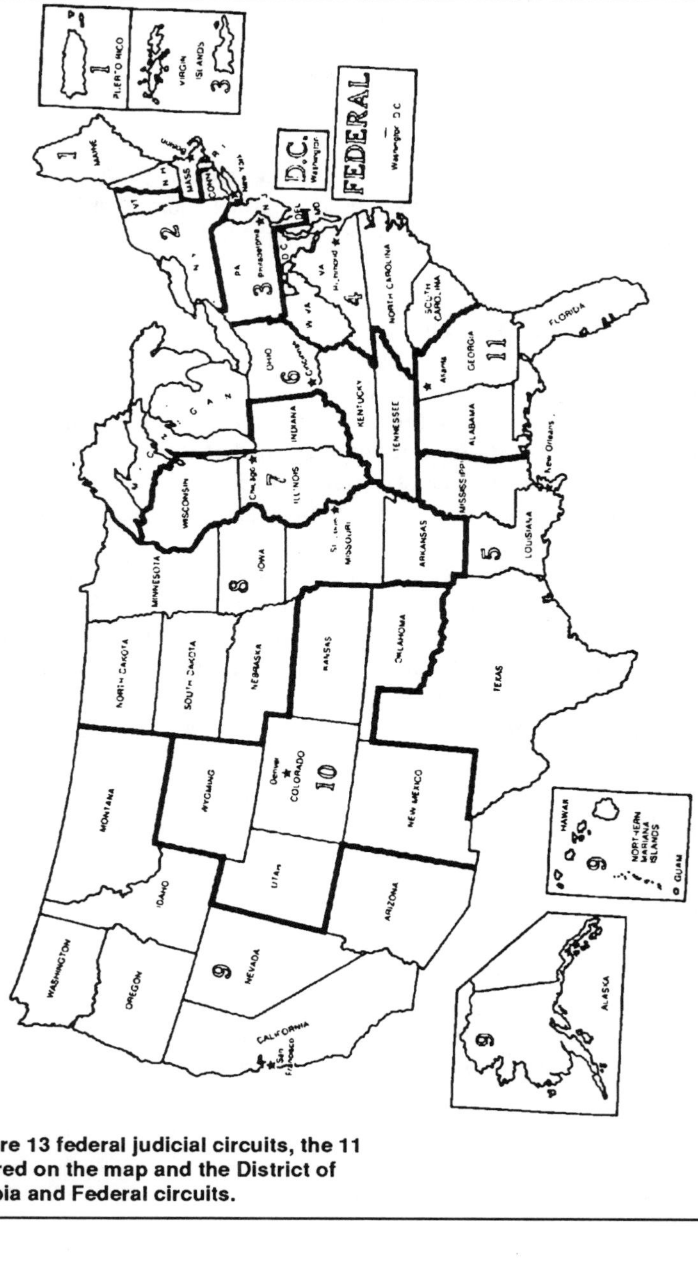

There are 13 federal judicial circuits, the 11 numbered on the map and the District of Columbia and Federal circuits.

term *circuit* is a throwback to the frontier era, when judges would "make the rounds" by traveling from town to town on horseback. Today, each circuit includes one court of appeals (also called "circuit courts") and a number of district courts.

The U. S. District Courts

The first stop for a case coming into the federal court system is usually one of the U.S. District Courts. These are trials courts that handle both civil and criminal cases. There are a total of 90 U.S. District Courts, with at least one in each state.

The U. S. Court of Appeals

If you lose your case in the district court, you can appeal to the circuit court for your region. Formally called the U.S. Courts of Appeals, the circuit courts are responsible for determining whether the case under appeal was handled properly at the U.S. District Court level. In hearing an appeal, the circuit court judges focus on matters of law and interpretation, not on matters of guilt or innocence.

Most appeals are heard by a panel of three judges. The appeal is decided when at least two of the three judges form a majority. Usually, the judges who form the majority will issue an opinion in which they explain the legal logic that led to their decision. These majority opinions are important since they often carry considerable weight as legal precedents.

Along with hearing appeals that come up from district courts, the circuit courts also handle the appeals of decisions made by federal regulatory agencies (the Federal Communications Commission, the Federal Trade Commission, etc.). For this reason, the D.C. circuit and the Federal circuit are among the busiest of the circuit courts of appeal.

The U.S. Supreme Court

If you lose your appeal at the circuit court level, the next stop is the U.S. Supreme Court, but only if the Supreme Court agrees to hear your case. Out of the thousands of petitions that are submitted to it each year, the Supreme Court agrees to hear only a few dozen cases. Generally, the Supreme Court gives preference to those cases that involve important or far-reaching legal issues, or cases in which two or more lower courts have interpreted a legal issue in conflicting ways.

At least four of the nine Supreme Court justices must vote in favor of hearing a case for it to be placed on the court's calendar. If a petition does not receive the necessary votes, the decision of the lower court is allowed to stand. This means that the justices have decided that the case does not warrant a full hearing before the nation's highest court. It does not necessarily mean that they agree with the original decision.

Although this petitioning process is the most common way for cases from the circuit courts to reach the Supreme Court, it is not the only way for a case to be scheduled on the Court's calendar. The Supreme Court will hear cases that involve disputes between two states. It is also the court of first appeal for cases that come out of certain special courts, including the U.S. Court of Claims. In addition, the U.S. Supreme Court will sometimes accept appeals of cases that state supreme courts have either ruled on or refused to hear, particularly when those cases involve important federal issues.

The Supreme Court truly is the supreme court of the United States. The opinions issues by the justices often capture headlines nationwide, and the Supreme Court's decisions are binding on all lower courts. As mentioned earlier, the Supreme Court is also responsible for determining whether federal laws and regulations are constitutional—a responsibility that often casts the justices as key players in the legislative process.

State Courts

Like the federal court system, the 50 state court systems are divided into tiers: lower courts and upper courts. The lower courts are trial courts that hear cases involving violations of state laws. The upper courts are appellate bodies that hear appeals from the lower courts.

In large states, the appellate courts are themselves divided into two tiers: state courts of appeals and the state supreme court. Cases from the lower courts are appealed first to the state appeals court and then to the state supreme court. States that feature this two-tier appeals system include California, Illinois, Michigan, New York, Ohio and Pennsylvania. In New York, though, the highest court is called the Court of Appeals, and district courts with the power to hear some kinds of appeals are called supreme courts.

In some small states, there is no intermediate appeals court. Instead, cases from the trial courts are appealed directly to the state supreme court. In recent years, however, the crush of litigation and appeals has moved many of these small states to introduce intermediate appellate courts.

The trial courts that make up the lower court system are often divided into civil courts, which hear civil cases, and criminal courts, which hear criminal cases. Along with these trial courts, the lower court systems in many states include various special jurisdiction courts: probate courts, family courts, juvenile courts, and so on.

Local and Municipal Courts

The lowest of the lower courts are the local and municipal courts that rule on matters involving county, city, town and village ordinances. Included in this category are traffic courts, police courts, small claims courts and justices of the peace. Generally, state statutes limit these local courts to ruling on civil cases involving relatively small sums and criminal cases involving only minor offenses. Because the cases tried in these courts are so minor, they are rarely appealed—even though most states do make provisions for such appeals through their appellate court systems.

ARBITRATION

Media professionals should also be aware of an important alternative to conventional courtroom litigation: the process of arbitration. In arbitration, a dispute between parties is brought before one or more independent arbitrators, rather than before a judge and jury. Arbitration has recently become a more attractive way of resolving disputes in certain civil cases, particularly as the number of lawsuits has grown and the cost of trial lawyers has reached several hundred dollars an hour plus expenses.

Along with saving money and reducing the need for a lawyer, arbitration can also save a great deal of time. Conventional litigation can drag on for years, but cases placed in arbitration are often resolved in a matter of weeks. To media professionals, the time saved can be critical, particularly when a contract dispute threatens to tie up the completion of a project.

Of course, there are also some limitations to arbitration. First, the type of arbitration described here only works in civil cases, and only in cases that involve claims that grow out of contract or other commercial disputes. Second, for the process to work at all, both parties must agree to submit the matter to arbitration. Usually, this means that an *arbitration clause* must be part of the original contract or agreement between the parties. Here is an example of how this provision might look:

> **If disputes to this agreement arise among the parties, any party may request the other party or parties to submit the dispute to binding arbitration. This arbitration will take place in (name of city) under the rules of the American Arbitration Association.**

In the United States, most arbitration cases are conducted under the auspices of the American Arbitration Association (AAA). The AAA furnishes forms for the parties to complete, arranges for a place to hold the arbitration sessions and proposes a list of arbitrators who have expertise in the disputed matter. Once both parties have had the option of reviewing the list and striking off names, the AAA chooses the arbitrators from the names that remain.

The arbitration procedure is similar to trying a case before a judge. You have the opportunity to state your case, to present evidence and witnesses, and to respond to the accusations and claims made by the other party. The rules that govern the arbitration sessions are relatively relaxed compared to courtroom proceedings. This makes it easier for you to present evidence, to cross-examine witnesses and to present affidavits that contain the sworn testimony of witnesses who cannot appear in person. It also makes it easier for you to serve as your own lawyer—although many parties still prefer to hire a lawyer.

Once the hearing is completed, the AAA guidelines allow the arbitrators up to six months to announce their decision, although the decision usually comes much sooner. Assuming that all parties involved agreed to binding arbitration in the original contract, the decision of the arbitrators has the same impact and authority as a judgment of the courts. The decision becomes a true judgment once it is filed in a state court. Appeals are possible, but only if one of the parties can convince the appellate court that the arbitration was conducted improperly.[3]

SUMMARY

What is media law?

Media law is a very broad body of law that incorporates elements from a variety of legal disciplines. Those disciplines include copyright and trademark law, contract law, labor law, the laws and regulations concerned with privacy and defamation, telecommunications law and policy, and the many legal issues and interpretations that arise from the First Amendment's guarantees of free speech and freedom of the press.

How much law must media producers know?

Producers and other media professionals do not need to be lawyers. However, producers should be able to anticipate and identify the many legal

---

[3]For more information about arbitration contact the American Arbitration Association at 140 West 51st Street, New York, NY 10020. The telephone number is 212-977-2070. On the west coast, AAA can be reached at 443 Shatto Place, Los Angeles, CA 90020. The phone number there is 213-383-6516.

issues that can come up during production and to recognize when it is necessary to call in a lawyer. Producers should also know when it is necessary to secure licenses, releases, permits and permissions for a particular production.

Who makes media law?

Media law is created by Congress and state legislatures, federal and state courts, and federal, state and municipal regulatory agencies. The courts create law by establishing legal precedents (case law) that determine how laws and regulations are interpreted and enforced. Federal offices and regulatory agencies involved in media law include the Federal Communications Commission, the Federal Trade Commission and the U.S. Copyright Office.

What are the types and categories of law?

In the United States, there are four major categories of law: constitutional law (law based directly on the U.S. Constitution) statutory law (laws passed by Congress and state and local legislatures), common law or case law (law established by the courts through judicial precedents), and regulatory or administrative law (rules and regulations passed by regulatory agencies).

What is the difference between civil cases and criminal cases?

Criminal cases involve crimes such as burglary and murder that threaten the safety of society as a whole. Civil cases are typically private lawsuits in which one party claims that another party has broken a contract or caused physical, emotional or financial harm. Most cases that grow out of media production are civil cases.

What is the court system?

In the United States, there are two court systems: the federal system and the state system. The federal system includes the federal district courts, the U.S. Circuit Courts of Appeals and the U.S. Supreme Court. The state system includes the municipal and county courts, trial courts, appeals courts and supreme court located in each state.

Must all legal disputes be settled in court?

Binding arbitration is one way the the parties in a civil suit can avoid the cost of going to court. If arbitration is to serve as an option, a clause to that effect should be written into the contract between the parties. Many cases are also settled out of court by mutual agreement of the parties involved.

2

Managing Relationships: Contracts and the Media Production Process

Like any business, the business of media production involves managing many working relationships. In a typical video production for example, a producer must manage relationships with the talent, the writer, the production crew, the post-production crew, the client who has commissioned the project and any subcontractors who are supplying music, stock footage, title sequences and other production materials. In addition, once the project is finished, many producers are responsible for negotiating relationships with program distributors. The success of any production project depends, to a significant degree, on the producer's success in coordinating these relationships.

In an ideal world, all production relationships could be based solely on trust. The producer would explain what he expected of an actor or editor for example, and what the actor or editor could expect in return. Then the producer could sit back and relax, confident that the agreed upon services would be delivered on time and in an acceptable form. The actor and editor could also relax, assured by the knowledge that they would receive the agreed upon compensation for their work.

Unfortunately, the world of media production is rarely ideal. As a result, producers can rarely afford to rely solely on the good faith of performers, crew members and subcontractors to guarantee that the services needed to complete a project will be delivered. Instead, experienced producers will usually seek more formal, contractual assurance that the promised goods and services will show up on time and in suitable shape.

PRODUCTION CONTRACTS

Production contracts provide a formal legal foundation on which to build production relationships. Although they cannot guarantee the success of those relationships, production contracts can do the following:

•specify the responsibilities of the various individuals and groups involved in the production;

23

•designate delivery dates for goods and services that these parties will provide;

•describe the quality and condition of "deliverable" goods and services;

•delineate the compensation that parties will receive in return for delivering the specified goods and services; and

•provide for what happens should any of the parties breach the terms of the agreement.

Above all, contracts can help because they require the parties to a production relationship to agree on the terms of their relationship up front, before deadlines are pressing and tempers are short. Just as important, because they require the parties to put terms in writing, contracts can help deter disagreements during a production—and the lawsuits that can sometimes follow.

WHAT IS A CONTRACT?

When most people hear the word "contract," they think of a thick document printed in tiny type and filled with legal jargon. However, as Figure 2.1 shows, contracts are often fairly brief documents written in the form of business letters. Many are also written in relatively plain English. As a matter of fact, contracts do not necessarily have to be written at all—although all media production contracts should be.

In its most basic sense, a contract is simply a legally binding agreement between two or more parties. A lawyer might prefer a more formal definition, such as that provided by *Black's Law Dictionary*:

> **An agreement between two or more persons which creates an obligation to do or not to do a particular thing [and] the writing which contains the agreement of parties, with the terms and conditions, and which serves as proof of the obligation.[1]**

As this definition indicates, a contract creates legal obligations between two or more parties. In addition, once the contract is written and signed by the parties, the document serves as proof of those obligations. That is why, even though oral contracts are considered valid under many circumstances, all media production contracts should be in writing. Should there be a dispute

---

[1] Henry Campbell Black, *Black's Law Dictionary*, 5th ed. (St. Paul, MN: West Publishing Co., 1979), 291.

Figure 2.1: A Contract in the Form of a Letter

Corporate Video Center
Advanced Technologies, Inc.
4400 Industrial Drive
Houston, TX 77061

November 6, 1989

Mr. Jason MacDonald
Voices of Experience, Inc.
737 Stadium St.
Houston, TX 77056

Dear Jason:

I am writing to confirm the offer that I made to you during our telephone conversation on November 3.

Advanced Technologies Inc. ("the Company") would like to hire you to provide voice-over narration for a training videotape titled "Better Systems/Better Management" (the "Project") that is currently under production in our corporate video center. The voice-over recording session will take place on December 4, 1989, at Soundsgood Studios located at 47 Halford Highway, Houston, TX. We will need you for the full session, which will run from 9:00 a.m. to 5:00 p.m. I will send you a complete script at least one week before the session.

As full and complete consideration for your services, the Company will pay you a one-time fee of $1250. Should the recording session require you to be present beyond 5:00 p.m. on December 4, the Company will pay you $100 for each additional hour or part-hour of your time. The Company's terms are net 30 days from the date that you complete your work on the Project.

This offer will be held open for 10 calendar days from the date of this letter. Should you not accept by that date, the offer will be withdrawn.

Your work on the Project will be deemed a "work-made-for-hire" within the meaning of the U.S. Copyright Act of 1976. You agree to transfer all rights of ownership to your services on the Project to the Company.

Figure 2.1: A Contract in the Form of a Letter (cont'd.)

The Company will own and hold the copyright to the Project and your work on it as its sole and exclusive property. In addition, as an independent contractor, you acknowledge that you will be solely responsible for all taxes, fees and assessments due with respect to your compensation hereunder. As an independent contractor, you also agree not to make any claims against the Company for insurance, worker's compensation or any other benefits offered by the Company.

In the event that you fail to provide the full services specified in the offer described above, the contract will be void and no payment will be due to you.

If you agree to the terms set forth in this contract, please sign both copies and return them to me.

I look forward to working with you.

Sincerely,   AGREED AND ACCEPTED:

_____   _____

Advanced Technologies, Inc.

_____   _____

Date   Date

                                                         _____

                                                         Social Security Number

among the parties, the written contract provides immediate proof of the terms and conditions to which they agreed.

The "terms and conditions" written into a contract are important, since these provisions often place qualifications on the core agreement that the contract covers. For example, a video producer in a corporate communications department and an outside production facility might sign a contract that obligates the outside facility to deliver an opening title and graphics sequence. In return for this work, the corporate video producer agrees to pay the facility the fee designated in the contract, subject to the following terms and conditions:

•the title and graphics sequence is delivered by a designated date;

•the sequence runs for the exact time specified; and

•the sequence meets defined technical standards.

Depending on the situation, the video producer and outside facility might also want to specify other terms and conditions in the contract. For example, the video producer might decide to designate several checkpoint dates for reviewing preliminary versions of the title sequence. The outside facility might decide to specify, in turn, that the video producer must deliver an approval within 24 hours of receiving the preview versions. In fact, in many media production contracts, the list of terms and conditions included in the contract runs much longer than the basic agreement itself.

Some media producers prefer not to bother with formal contracts for many production matters. This is particularly true in the world of corporate communications, where business is often based on promises made during last-minute phone calls to talent, production crews and subcontractors. Producers should understand that, under the law, a promise is not the same as a contract—even when the promise is made in writing. As the section that follows explains, a contract must contain at least three key components to be legally binding.

THE COMPONENTS OF A CONTRACT

A contract must contain three components: the *offer*, the *consideration* and the *acceptance*. If a contract is missing any of these elements, it may not be enforceable under the law. Of course, a contract can also contain other components, including the conditions and provisions mentioned earlier. Often though, these additional elements are contained as part of the offer, the consideration or the acceptance. Figure 2.1 shows a simple contract that contains these three key components plus several additional provisions. (For greater detail, see the media production contract checklist and sample contracts in Chapter 3.)

The Offer

The *offer* is the fundamental proposal that forms the core of any contract. In its most basic form, the offer says "We want you to do this for us." In a contract between a video production company and a songwriter, for example, the basic offer might be "We want you to write and produce a theme song for our current production." Typically, the offer would also indicate how much the company is willing to pay, although technically, this is part of the consideration.

In actual practice, most offers are subject to a number of terms and conditions. Here are some sample conditions that might be attached to the theme song offer described in the preceding paragraph:

• The offer must be accepted within one week of its issuance.

• The songwriter must agree to relinquish all copyright claims to the song, so the video production company becomes the sole owner of both the lyrics and the music.

• The songwriter must deliver the lyrics and tune for preliminary approval by a specified date.

• The songwriter must deliver the completed song by a specified date.

• The songwriter must deliver the song in a specified form (for example, two audiocassette copies plus the master studio tape).

• The completed song must meet specified time requirements, for example, one minute, 90 seconds.

• The completed song must meet certain technical specifications.

What this full offer really says is, "If you meet all of these requirements, we agree to live up to our end of the deal." Of course, before deciding whether to accept the offer, the songwriter should take a close look at the part of the contract that describes what he or she will get in return for performing the work. This "what's in it for me" part of a contract is called the consideration.

The Consideration

The *consideration* is the component of a contract that describes in detail what the accepting party will receive in return for meeting the terms of the offer. In most contracts, the consideration is entirely or mostly money. However, consideration in media contracts can also involve other sorts of compensation, including the following:

• credits at the beginning or end of the program for the songwriter, scriptwriter, performer, production crew or subcontractor (something that is specified in some union contracts);

• a provision to provide performers, writers and crew members with residual (royalty) payments from revenue generated through certain types of distribution (again, something that is often specified in union contracts);

•the "right of first refusal" to perform similar work for subsequent projects; and

• copies of the completed production.

Some producers also include bartered services as part of the consideration. For example, a contract between a video production company and a songwriter might call for the production company to provide the songwriter with access to its sound studio as full or partial consideration for the songwriter's work on a soundtrack.

Under contract law, consideration actually cuts both ways. For the party that has made the offer, the consideration is the goods or services that they will receive from the party that accepts the offer. For the accepting party, the consideration is the payment that they will receive for delivering those goods and services.

The consideration is a critical component of any contract. By specifying what each party will receive in return for fulfilling its end of the contract, consideration establishes a "mutuality of obligation" between the parties. It is this mutuality of obligation that distinguishes a contract from a promise or other non-binding agreement.

Needless to say, both the offer and consideration portions of a contract are often subject to lengthy negotiation. For example, a songwriter might prefer to retain certain rights to the song, to be paid more for the song than the production company has offered or to take longer to complete the project than the offer specifies. Because making changes to contracts can be costly and time consuming, many of these disagreements should be worked out before the contract is put in writing. That way, once the contract is issued, acceptance is likely to follow quickly.

The Acceptance

Acceptance occurs when the parties agree to be bound by the terms of the contract. Although the exact manner of acceptance can change from one contract to the next, almost all written contracts call for the parties to indicate acceptance by signing in the space or spaces provided in the contract. In cases where a party is a group or corporation, an authorized representative of the group will sign the contract. It is also possible to indicate acceptance orally, although this rarely happens with written business contracts.

By signing a contract, you are accepting all of the terms of the contract. As a result, you should make sure that all of the terms are indeed acceptable before signing. With deadlines pressing, some parties to media production contracts make the mistake of signing a contract containing vague or questionable provisions and simply assuming that "things will work out." Unfortunately, things left unresolved often do not work out.

It is also a mistake to assume that you can simply mark a few changes in the margins of a contract and then accept it. Under the law, making even small modifications to an offer can be interpreted as constituting a rejection of the offer. To arrive at a final contract, you will need to renegotiate with the party that made the offer, receive a new written offer that includes the renegotiated terms and then accept that new offer.

Amendments

One way to get around rewriting the entire contract after resolving disputed matters is to attach a list of amendments to the offer. Assuming that both parties agree with the amendments, the list can become part of the final contract. This option works well when the matters under dispute are relatively minor, or when one or both of the parties wish to clarify a provision of the offer. However, if the disputed items include basic terms of the offer, renegotiating and rewriting the contract may be the only safe alternative.

Sunset Provisions

Although you should take the time to review all of the terms and conditions of an offer, be careful not to take too long. Many offers contain a *sunset* provision that requires you to respond to an offer by a specified date. If you do not respond in time, the offer is automatically withdrawn. If the offer calls for you to respond through the mail, your acceptance will usually become effective on the day that you mailed it, provided that the contract does not say that the acceptance must actually reach the party that has made the offer by a specified time.

Offer versus Contract

Keep in mind that an offer and contract are not necessarily the same thing. Often, a media producer may make an informal offer to a performer or writer, for example, with the understanding that a written contract will follow if the the performer or writer is interested in considering the offer. It is the written contract that contains the complete terms of the offer and consideration, and that the performer or writer must sign to signal acceptance.

Other Issues and Concerns

As a media professional, you should also be aware of several other issues related to the creation of legally enforceable contracts.

Mental Competence

The law assumes that all of the parties to a contract were mentally competent and sober at the time of acceptance, and that none of the parties was accepting the contract under physical or psychological duress. For most contracts, the law also assumes that the parties are adults, although the exact age at which a person reaches legal majority can differ from one state to the next. If a media producer wishes to place a child performer under contract, a parent or legal guardian must sign for the child.

Illegal Acts

It is not legal to enter into a contract that requires someone to perform an illegal act. For example, a contract that calls for a stunt person to drive a car down a busy city street at 100 miles per hour would not be legal, since it requires the stunt person to break to law. Contracts can also be declared invalid if they require a party to perform actions that run counter to public moral standards—although those standards are often difficult to define.

Fraud

A contract can be declared invalid if one of the parties is proven guilty of fraud or misrepresentation, or if a party can prove in court that the contract is based on a fundamental misunderstanding or "mutual mistake." However, because it is difficult to prove that there was a misunderstanding or mutual mistake at the time that the agreement was signed, few contracts are actually invalidated on these grounds.

SOURCES OF CONTRACT LAW

Unlike copyright law, which is governed by the Copyright Act of 1976, contract law is not governed by a single, overriding federal statute. Instead, most contract law is based on common law and statutes enacted by individual states. To provide some consistency across state boundaries, all states except Louisiana have adopted the Uniform Commercial Code (UCC), a standardized body of laws governing the sale of goods and various other commercial transactions. Most states have also adopted the Statute of Frauds, a body of rules that determine whether a particular type of contract must be placed in writing. In all states, the law gives individuals the right to enter into legally binding contracts, to go to court when necessary to have those contracts enforced and to receive some form of compensation or redress when a contract is breached.

CATEGORIES OF CONTRACTS

There are many different types and categories of contracts, including many that are specific to certain types of businesses and transactions. For media producers the distinctions between express and implied contracts and between oral and written contracts are especially important.

Express Contracts versus Implied Contracts

An *express contract* is a written or oral agreement that is expressly declared at the time that it is made. In other words, an express contract is one in which the terms are made explicit and clear, and in which all parties are clearly aware that they are agreeing to those terms. All of the sample media production contracts provided in Chapter 3 are express contracts.

In contrast, an *implied contract* is an agreement that is not expressly stated, but that is instead implicit in a transaction between parties. Like all contracts, an implied contract obligates the parties to perform certain responsibilities. In an implied contract, however, those obligations are not made explicit through a formal agreement. For example, when you order out for a pizza, you are entering into an implied contract that obligates you to pay for the pizza once it arrives—even though you did not expressly state, "I will pay for the pizza once it arrives," when you placed the order. The pizza vendor is obligated, in turn, to deliver the pizza that you ordered within a reasonable amount of time. If the wrong pizza arrives six hours later, the vendor has breached the terms of the implied contract, and you are not obligated to pay. On the other hand, if the pizza vendor fulfills its obligations but you refuse to pay, the vendor could initiate legal action against you for breaching the implied contract.

Of course, neither you nor the pizza vendor is likely to initiate formal legal action over the price of one pizza. However, as a matter of justice, the law does allow individuals and corporations to seek redress against parties that violate implied contracts. This doctrine evolved as a way to establish equitable rights and responsibilities in the innumerable business and personal transactions that occur every day, but that are not covered by express contracts. If an implied contract dispute reaches the litigation stage, it is up to the court to determine what rights and responsibilities were implied through the transaction in question.

As the examples provided in Chapter 3 show, the business transactions that grow out of media production should be covered by some sort of express contract. However, you should be aware that, even when no express contract exists, a media production transaction still creates rights and responsibilities under the doctrine of implied contracts. For example, when you sell video footage to a producer with knowledge that it will be used in an upcoming production, you imply that you have full rights to the footage. If the buyer discovers that this was not the case, you could find yourself caught up in an implied contract dispute. In this instance, the best protection for all parties would have been to create an express contract that defined what rights you had to the video footage and what rights you were transferring to the other party. In fact, one of the best reasons for drawing up an express contract is to anticipate and avoid the conflict and confusion that can arise from implied contract disputes. For this reason alone, all of the relationships in media productions should be covered by express contracts.

Oral versus Written Contracts

Many media professionals are surprised to learn that a contract does not always have to be written to be legal. For many types of transactions, oral agreements can constitute a legally binding contract, as long as the three key components of a contract (offer, consideration and acceptance) are present. However, state statutes and the Uniform Commercial Code do require certain types of contracts to be placed in writing. In most states, this includes contracts that cover:

• Transactions for the sale of goods that exceed a certain price ($500 under the Uniform Commercial Code).

• Agreements that cannot be completed within one year (or within some other period of time defined by state statute). Under this provision, a multi-year production contract would not be legal unless it was placed in writing.

• Transactions that involve the sale of real estate or the lease of property for more than one year (three years in some states). Under this provision, a four-year leasing agreement for video production facilities must be placed in writing.

• Agreements in which you assume another person's obligations (for example, an agreement in which you agree to take over a production contract that another party could not complete).

Many state statutes regarding written and oral contracts are based on the Statute of Frauds, a British law enacted in 1677 that was eventually adopted, in whole or part, by most of the United States. Where the Uniform Commercial Code covers only transactions involving the sale of goods, the Statute of Frauds applies to contracts for both goods and services.

Because the laws and regulations governing contracts can vary from state to state, it is important to check with a lawyer to determine what written contracts are required in your area. The safest and recommended route is to place all media production contracts in writing—even if the written contract is a brief document that serves only to confirm an oral agreement. This is particularly important in media production agreements that involve *work-for-hire* arrangements, which are discussed in more detail in Chapter 4.

As mentioned earlier in this chapter, a properly written contract can help deter disputes and disagreements during the production process, since it provides tangible proof of the terms that the parties are obligated to honor. If a transaction involves both a written and oral contract, and if the two contracts contain conflicting terms, the courts will usually give precedence to the written version.

WHEN DO YOU NEED A LAWYER?

With lawyers' fees reaching several hundred dollars an hour, many media producers have begun looking for ways to limit the number of occasions that they seek professional help on contract matters. Unfortunately, there is no simple set of guidelines that can tell you when a call to your lawyer is required. As a general rule, however, you should always seek a lawyer's advice under the following circumstances:

• When you are drafting a standard contract that you will use as a model for the contracts offered to talent, writers, crew members, subcontractors, and so on.

• When you are being asked to sign a contract that contains terms that you do not fully understand.

• When you are being asked to sign a contract that commits you or your company to a long-term obligation.

• When you are negotiating a contract for a deal that is vital to the success or survival of your company.

•Whenever you feel uneasy or unsure about a contract matter.

Many media producers work with their lawyers to prepare standard contracts that cover a variety of production relationships (hiring performers, writers and crew members; subcontracting production services; renting production facilities and equipment, etc.). The producers then tailor the contracts to particular productions by "filling in the blanks" with the appropriate names, dates and amounts. After their initial involvement, the lawyers are called in only when circumstances require a producer to make major modifications to a standard contract. Even then, it usually takes much less time for a lawyer to review changes to a standard contract than it does to draft individual contracts to cover each new production relationship.

A growing number of producers prepare and store their standard contracts on microcomputers. This makes it easy for them to call up the standard document; add names, dates and amounts; make minor modifications; and print a legible and professional-looking copy.

As a safety measure, some production companies bring a lawyer back into the process whenever the amount of money involved in a pending contract exceeds a predetermined threshold. The exact figure used for this threshold varies from company to company, depending on how much risk the organization is willing to take with a contract to save on up-front legal fees. Of course, having a lawyer review a contract does not provide any guarantee that the agreement is risk-free. However, a qualified lawyer can point out areas of the contract that appear to contain risks and that may result in considerable legal expense down the road.

If you work in a corporate setting, you should also be aware of your company's policy on contracts. In many companies, all contracts must subscribe to a specific format and pass through the corporate legal office. In fact, in some organizations, only one or two officers of the corporation are permitted to sign contracts. However, even in companies with the strictest contract policies, the legal department may be willing to work with you to create standard agreements that cover many production situations. No corporation wants to see its high-powered legal staff drown in the stream of small contracts that can flow from a corporate media production facility.

BROKEN CONTRACTS

As mentioned earlier, contracts establish a "mutuality of obligation" between parties. In fact, one of the main benefits of a carefully written contract is that it defines exactly what each party's obligations are. Once all involved parties accept the terms of a legally binding contract, they can be required by law to fulfill their obligations.

But what happens when one party fails to live up to its end of the deal? For example, what happens if an animation facility that you hired to create an opening for a video production fails to deliver the finished footage by the date specified in the contract? Or what happens when a performer who signed a contract to appear in a TV program never bothers to show up for the production?

In both of these examples, one party to a contract has breached the terms of the agreement. Once that happens, the other party is no longer obligated to honor its end of the contract. For example, if the contract called for you to pay the animation facility $10,000 if it delivered the opening sequence by a specified date, you are no longer obligated to pay the $10,000 if the the material is not delivered by that date. Similarly, you would not be required to pay the performer who failed to show up for work.

Seeking Compensation

Unfortunately, the fact that you are not obligated to pay for an undelivered product or service may be little consolation if an important project is delayed by an unfulfilled contract—particularly when the main purpose for entering into the contract was to ensure that the product or service would be delivered on time and in acceptable condition. If you find yourself in this situation, you may want to seek compensation from the offending party. How you go about doing this depends on what kind of compensation you are after and what sort of remedy was written into the original contract.

When a key production contract is broken, the immediate goal of most media producers is to find a way to keep the project moving. With this in mind, they will often look for a way to "work something out" with the offending party. For example, in the case of the missing animation sequence described earlier, you or your lawyer might contact the animation facility to work out a revised deal for delivering the sequence. The new deal might call for the facility to deliver the finished footage at a later date for reduced compensation. For instance, if the original contract specified that the animation facility would receive $10,000 for delivering the sequence by May 15, a revised arrangement might call for you to pay $9000 if the facility delivers the finished goods by May 22. To obtain leverage as the new deal is negotiated, you or your lawyer might also drop some hints about taking the animation facility to court for breach of contract if the company fails to meet the revised delivery date. Finally, if the company still fails to deliver, you may ask your lawyer to initiate a lawsuit against the company.

Of course, the last thing that most media professionals really want is to get caught up in an extended court battle over an unfulfilled contract. That is why many media production contracts contain a schedule of payments that calls for subcontractors to be paid in stages as they deliver sections or preliminary versions of a product or service. The partial payment dates then serve as checkpoints that let the producer know how the subcontractor is progressing. Just as important, these intermediate dates also serve as incentives to keep a subcontractor's attention focused on a particular project.

Remedies and Damages

Many media production contracts also include clauses that specify what forms of remedies and damages are available if a party defaults on its obligations. For example, if the contract calls for a film production company to receive a down payment upon signing a contract, it might also require the company to return the payment and all interim payments should it fail to deliver the final product specified in the contract. Another remedy might give the producer the option to fix the final product at the subcontractor's expense if, when the product arrives, it does not meet the specifications detailed in the contract. In this case, the repair costs would probably be deducted from the payments due to the subcontractor.

Arbitration and Litigation

If your efforts to settle a contract dispute out of court fail, and if the remedy language written into the contract does not provide for an adequate resolution, the next step may be to initiate formal proceedings against the offending party. As mentioned in Chapter 1, contracts can include a provision that calls for disputes to be settled through arbitration. However, unless the contract in question contains this provision, or unless both parties agree to arbitration, the only alternative may be litigation. In all but the smallest matters, this usually means having a lawyer conduct the case.

At this point, you should stop to ask yourself if litigation is really worth it. Is the amount of money that you might recover worth all of the time, effort and lawyers' fees that a lawsuit can involve? Or are you acting out of a desire to "get back" at the other party? When revenge is your primary motivation, litigation is never really worth the time and money involved.

Keep in mind that, if you do decide to proceed with litigation, your claim will be treated as a civil action. As a result, the burden of proof will be on you and your lawyer. You must prove that the party in question did indeed violate the terms of a legally binding contract, and you must show that you incurred losses as a result. You must also disprove any claims or counter-allegations that the party offers as a defense. For example, the party could claim that, for one or more of the reasons discussed earlier in this chapter, the contract in question was not a legally binding agreement. Or the party could show that its failure to fulfill its obligations was due to an "act of God" or some other reasons beyond its control.

Despite all of these considerations, breach of contract cases can be worth pursuing. In fact, if the contract was carefully written and the evidence is strong enough to convince a jury, the payoff can be substantial. At a minimum, the jury will usually award *actual damages*—compensation for losses that you can document. Typically, this means that you will receive any money that you paid to the party under the unfulfilled contract—minus, in some instances, the value of any products or services that were delivered in partial fulfillment of the contract. You might also recover consequential damages, or damages that, while not tied to specific out-of-pocket expenses, were reasonably foreseeable when the parties entered into the contract. In addition, if you can prove that the breach of contract caused additional expenses on a production project, you could be awarded actual or *incidental* damages to cover those costs.

SUMMARY

What is a contract?

A contract is a legally binding agreement that establishes mutual obligations between two or more parties.

What are the key components of a contract?

The key components of a contract are the offer, the consideration and the acceptance. If a contract is missing any of these elements, it may not be enforceable under the law.

What happens when a contract is broken?

Many contracts include remedies or damages clauses that describe the compensation due to the parties should one or more of the parties fail to live up to its obligations. In most cases, the parties will try to reach a quick settlement or compromise. If this fails, a breach-of-contract dispute may go to the courts.

What are the sources of contract law?

Contract law is not governed by a single, overriding federal statute. Instead, much contract law is based on common law and statutes enacted by individual states. All states except Louisiana have also adopted the Uniform Commercial Code, a standardized body of laws governing the sale of goods and various other commercial transactions.

What is the difference between an express and an implied contract?

An express contract is an agreement in which the terms are made explicit and clear at the time that the contract is made, and in which all parties are clearly aware that they are agreeing to those terms. An implied contract is a binding agreement that is not expressly stated, but that is implied in the transaction between parties.

Must all contracts be placed in writing?

Contracts do not have to be placed in writing to be binding under the law, although all media production contracts should be. Written contracts can help deter and resolve disputes, since they provide tangible proof of the conditions and terms that the parties are obligated to honor. Under the Uniform Commercial Code and statutes in many states, some contracts must be placed in writing, including contracts for the sale of goods worth $500 or more.

When should a lawyer review contract matters?

There is no simple set of guidelines that can determine when a lawyer's help is required to review or resolve contract matters. As a general rule, you should always seek a lawyer's advice when you are drafting a standard contract that will be used as a model for various business contracts; when you are being asked to sign a contract that contains terms that you do not fully understand or that commits you to a long term obligation; or whenever you feel uneasy or unsure about a contract matter. If you are working in a corporate setting, you should also inquire about your company's contract review policy.

3

Getting It In Writing: Sample Media Production Contracts

Chapter 2 described the basic components of contracts, the fundamental principles of contract law and ways that you can use contracts to manage many production relationships. In this chapter, you will see how the general guidelines and principles introduced in Chapter 2 have been put to use in sample contracts that define four production relationships. The samples include:

- A crew contract that describes the rights and responsibilities of a crew member hired as a camera operator for a production.

- A writer's contract that defines the relationship between a production company and a freelance researcher and writer.

- A facilities contract that establishes the terms of a daily rental agreement between a producer and a studio facility.

- A project contract that details an agreement between a production company and a client that has commissioned the company to produce a program.

Of course, the samples do not cover all of the contracts that you might initiate or be asked to sign during the course of a production. Several other types of media production contracts—including union agreements, music contracts and publishing agreements—are discussed in Chapters 6, 7 and 8.

In each case, the sample contract is intended to serve as a model that suggests the structure and scope of a typical production agreements. Because each media production is unique, you should not assume that the sample agreements can serve without considerable modification as the basis for your own production contracts. You also should not assume that you can simply pick and mix clauses from the sample agreements to create a contract that covers all of the requirements of a particular production. If you are not sure which terms and provisions apply to a particular production situation, be sure to consult a competent contract lawyer.

41

CONTRACTING FOR THE RIGHT RIGHTS: WORK-MADE-FOR-HIRE

When subcontractors supply materials and services for a production, you must make sure that you receive all of the rights necessary to use those materials and services. For example, if you are a staff producer who has hired a freelance writer to prepare a script for a production that will be part of your company's sales training effort, you must make sure that you have the right to distribute the program based on the script within your company. You may also want to obtain the rights to distribute the program based on the writer's script to other companies, to the general public and perhaps even to cable television or some other distribution channel.

The best place to guarantee these rights is in your contract with the individual or group that is supplying the goods or services. In most cases, the contract should include a clause stipulating that the subcontractor is transferring ownership of the materials to the producer or production company. This frees you from having to go back to the subcontractor and renegotiate for the right to reuse the materials. However, as discussed in Chapter 7, this sort of buyout is not always possible when you are dealing with writers, performers or technicians who are union members. At a minimum, however, however, the contract must guarantee you the right to use the materials in the manner that you intend on this particular production.

In the past, some producers assumed that they automatically obtained full ownership and control of the materials because arrangements with subcontractors were considered work-made-for-hire relationships. but this practice has been called into question by a 1989 U.S. Supreme Court ruling that took a close look at the work-made-for-hire provisions of the Copyright Act of 1976. Briefly, the 1976 law states that an employer or person who commissions a work is the copyright holder in cases where the work is "prepared by an employee within the scope of his or her employment" or when the work is "specially ordered or commissioned for use as a contribution to a collective work (or) as part of a motion picture or other audiovisual work. . . if the parties expressly agree in a signed writing that the work is to be considered a work-made-for-hire."[1] In other words, you own the copyright on materials that are prepared by your employees as part of their jobs or by independent subcontractors that are contributing materials to a production—as long as your written agreements with the subcontractors expressly state that they are producing the materials as works-made-for-hire.

The 1989 Supreme Court ruling concerned a case in which the group that was paying for the work, an advocacy group for the homeless that had com-

[1]Copyright Revision Act of 1976 (P.L. 94-553). (90 Stat. 2541) Sec. 101.

missioned a sculptor to create a depiction of a homeless family, did not have a contract that clearly defined who would own the completed work. The Supreme Court ruled that, in the absence of such an agreement, the sculptor retained the copyright to the work.

For media producers the implication is clear. Although the Copyright Act states that contributions to audiovisual works will in most cases be considered works-made-for-hire, it is a good idea nonetheless to include a clause in contracts specifying this. As the sample contracts in this chapter show, it is also advisable to go further and to specify that, as the producer, you will hold full ownership and control of the materials.

MEDIA PRODUCTION CONTRACT CHECKLIST

The media production contract checklist (see Figure 3.1) can be used as a quick reference when you are reviewing or participating in the development of a media production contract. As the checklist shows, you should always begin

Figure 3.1 Media Production Contract Checklist

Use the following eleven-step checklist as a general guide when you are preparing or reviewing a media production contract. If you are not sure whether a provision listed in the checklist should be part of the agreement, consult a contract lawyer. A lawyer can also determine if your contract should contain special terms and conditions that are not shown.

1. Does the contract include a clear and definite offer?

Does the contract describe, in detail, the goods or services that will be delivered under the agreement? Does the contract state when and where these materials must be delivered? Is it clear to whom the offer is being made? Is the offer transferable or assignable to another party?

2. Does the contract specify, in detail, the consideration that the party or parties will receive for delivering the goods or services?

Exactly how and how much will the party or parties be paid for fulfilling the terms of the contract? Are the contracted services being performed for a flat fee, or will the consideration include royalty or residual payments? Will the party be listed in the credits?

Figure 3.1: Media Production Contract Checklist (cont'd.)

3. Does the contract specify how the parties will indicate their acceptance of the agreement?

Will the parties indicate their acceptance by signing the contract? If so, who will sign and where will they sign? Must the parties accept the agreement by a specified date?

4. Does the contract include delivery and payment schedules?

Will the products or services be delivered in stages? If so, when are the partial products (treatments, storyboards, rough cuts, etc.) due? Are payments tied to these delivery dates? How and when will the party receive final and full payment for its work?

5. Does the contract establish guidelines for reviewing and approving deliverables?

Who has creative control over the contracted goods or services? Who has the right to approve or reject the deliverables? What criteria will he or she use? Does the delivery schedule provide for approvals of partial products? Must the approvals be in writing? If the final product is rejected, who is responsible for fixing it? Who pays for the remedies?

6. Does the contract indicate who will own the goods and services delivered under the agreement?

Is the contract being performed on a work-made-for-hire basis? Will the party that produces the deliverables retain some right of ownership in the finished production? Who will retain the right to use the deliverables in future productions? Does the contract provide for reuse fees?

7. Does the contract include warranty and indemnity clauses?

These two clauses work together and are sometimes combined as a single section of the contract. Warranty clauses specify that the party that has agreed to deliver goods under the contract has full rights to those materials and that there is no other contract or obligation that prohibits the party from entering into the agreement. Indemnity clauses stipu-

Figure 3.1: Media Production Contract Checklist (cont'd.)

late which party will be held responsible for any judgment and legal fees, if ownership of the materials or some other term of the contract should become the source of litigation initiated by an outside party.

8. Does the contract define the working relationships between the parties?

Will the work be performed on a guild or union basis? (See Chapter 7.) If the parties are performing the work as independent contractors, do they agree to waive all rights to claims against the company for insurance, worker's compensation and other benefits of employment?

9. Does the contract offer the right of first refusal to perform similar work on related projects?

Will the party who is performing services under the contract be given the right of first refusal to perform similar work on related or derivative projects? If so, what are the terms and limitations of that right?

10. Does the contract stipulate the circumstances under which the agreement can be terminated?

Under what conditions and circumstances can the contract be cancelled? What violations will result in the automatic termination of the agreement? How and when must the parties receive notification of the termination?

11. Does the contract provide for remedies if either or both parties violate terms of the agreement?

If the contract is terminated, or if terms of the agreement are violated, what remedies will be available to the parties? Will the parties be required to return any payments that they have already received? Who will own the work that has already been completed? Will the parties receive partial compensation for this work? Can the contracting company repair materials that arrive in unacceptable condition at the other party's expense? Do the parties agree to submit all disputes to binding arbitration?

by making sure that the agreement includes a clear and definite *offer*, a thorough description of the *consideration* and a way for the parties to indicate their *acceptance*. The checklist also lists various terms and provisions that should be part of most media production contracts, including provisions that define who will own the products or services delivered under the terms of the agreement. To see these terms and provisions at work in actual contracts, examine the sample agreements shown in Figures 3..2, 3.3, 3.4 and 3.5.

Of course, not every item on the checklist will be appropriate for all types of production contracts. However, when any of the criteria from the checklist are missing from a contract, you should always pause and ask why. If the answer is not clear, consult a lawyer.

Finally, be careful *not* to rely on this checklist as your sole means of evaluating a contract. Even when a contract meets all of the criteria specified in the checklist, it may still not be in your best interest to offer or accept it. Be sure to read all of the terms of a contract carefully and seek a lawyer's advice if something seems to be missing or out of place.

A SAMPLE CREW CONTRACT

Figure 3.2 is a sample contract that defines the relationship between a production company and a camera operator. Although the contract is relatively brief, it does contain the three key components of a legally binding agreement: *offer, consideration*, and *acceptance*.

The *offer* is presented in paragraph 1. It describes what the contractor's responsibilities will be, when and where he will discharge those responsibilities, and how long his services will be required.

Paragraph 2 defines the *consideration* that the contractor will receive. For fulfilling the terms of the offer, the contractor will be paid a single fee of $750. The contractor is responsible for submitting an invoice for his work, and the company is obligated to pay him within 30 days of receiving the invoice. However, as paragraph 3 points out, the production company does retain the right to dismiss the contractor if his work proves unsatisfactory. If the production company exercises this right, it must pay only for the work that the contractor performed up to the point of dismissal.

Paragraphs 4 through 6 detail other conditions placed on the basic agreement defined in paragraphs 1 and 2. One particularly important condition appears in paragraph 4, where the contract establishes that the camera operator's work and services on the project will be considered a "work-made-for-hire," as that term is defined in the U.S. Copyright Act of 1976, and that the camera operator will transfer all rights of ownership in his or her work on the project to the production company. By including this clause, the production company prevents the camera operator from claiming that, through his work

Figure 3.2: Sample Crew Contract

November 8, 1989

The following terms and conditions will constitute an agreement between RoBo Productions, Inc. (hereafter "RP" and Christopher Barnaby, a freelance video camera operator.

1. RP offers Christopher Barnaby (hereafter the "Contractor"), and the Contractor accepts, a position as a video camera operator on "Infrequent Flier," a television commercial production. The Contractor's work on the production will not be subject to the terms of any guild or union contract. The Contractor's services will be required for three shooting days scheduled for November 22, 23 and 24. The Contractor will report to the RP offices at 167 Leland Ave., Los Angeles, CA, at 8:30 a.m. on each of these days. Each shooting day will run from 8:30 a.m. to 5:30 p.m., with one hour off for lunch. Should the Contractor's services be required beyond 5:30 p.m., RP agrees to pay the Contractor $50 for each hour or part-hour of additional time.

2. As full and complete consideration for the work performed under this agreement, RP will pay the Contractor $750. Payment will be mailed to the Contractor within 30 days upon receipt of an invoice.

3. If RP determines that the Contractor's work is unsatisfactory, RP can terminate the contract and pay the contractor for work completed to that point, with payment calculated on a pro rata basis.

4. The Contractor's work on this Project will be considered a "work-made-for-hire" as defined in the U.S. Copyright Act of 1976. The Contractor will assign all rights to services provided under this agreement to RP. RP will own all right, title and interest in and to the results of the Contractor's services.

5. This offer must be accepted by 5:00 p.m.on November 15, 1989. Should the Contractor not accept by that date, the offer will be withdrawn.

6. This agreement will be governed by the laws and courts of the State of California.

Figure 3.2: Sample Crew Contract (cont'd.)

To indicate acceptance of these terms and conditions, the Contractor should sign in the space indicated below. The Contractor should sign and return both
copies to RP.

Very truly yours,

ROBO PRODUCTIONS INC.

By _____

Title _____

Agreed and Accepted as of the _____
Day of _____, 19_____

_____
Christopher Barnaby

_____
Federal ID or Social Security #

on the project, he has the right to share in the ownership of the finished program.

Another important condition appears in paragraph 6, where the contract
states that the agreement will be governed by the laws of the State of
California. This statement of jurisdiction is especially significant when the
parties to a contract reside in different states or countries, since the laws governing contracts can vary from one jurisdiction to the next. When you are
entering into an agreement with a party from another state, it is almost
always in your best interest to have the agreement governed by the laws and
courts of your state. That way, should there be a contract dispute, you will
not be forced to travel to another state for any legal proceedings (including
depositions and a possible trial) and to find a lawyer who is licensed to practice in that state.

The contract ends by describing how the parties will indicate their acceptance of the agreement. In this case, and in most written contracts, the parties
will accept the terms and conditions of the agreement by signing in the space
provided at the end of the contract.

Significantly, this crew contract is being offered to a nonunion camera operator for work on a nonunion production. If the work was to be performed on a union basis, the relationship between the camera operator and the production company would be covered, instead, by the current union agreements. These agreements are discussed in detail in Chapter 7.

A SAMPLE WRITER'S CONTRACT

Figure 3.3 is a contract in the form of a business letter that defines the relationship between a company that is producing a corporate video program and a freelance writer/researcher. In contrast to the camera operator in the previous contract, who was hired to deliver a relatively narrow service over a relatively short period, the writer/researcher in this contract is responsible for performing and producing a much wider range of services and products over a much longer period of time. That is the main reason that the writer's contract in Figure 3.3 is much more detailed than the camera operator's contract presented in Figure 3.2.

The *offer* is defined in paragraphs 1 through 5. Corporate Media Corporation, the hiring company, begins by dividing the writer's job into a series of tasks and responsibilities, each of which is listed in paragraph 1. In paragraphs 2 through 5, the company goes on to indicate who will evaluate and approve the materials that the writer submits, what those materials are and when they are due, and what responsibility the writer will have for revising the materials and meeting with the production staff.

In return for all of this work, the writer will receive the *consideration* described in paragraphs 6 through 9. The writer's total compensation will be $14,000. That fee will be paid in three installments, each of which is tied to the delivery of one of the materials that the writer is responsible for producing. As mentioned earlier in the chapter, this installment plan provides the hiring party with a series of checkpoints that can be used to assess the contractor's progress and performance.

Paragraph 7 provides the hiring company with a way to terminate the contract if the writer's work proves inadequate. If the company does cancel the contract, it must pay the writer for all work performed and expenses incurred up to that time, plus a penalty of $1000.

As part of the consideration, the writer will also receive the screen credit described in paragraph 9, provided that her work on the project proves satisfactory. This type of credit can be very important, particularly for young writers or performers who are trying to establish a reputation and build a portfolio of their work.

Paragraphs 10 through 14 place several conditions on the writer's work. First, by accepting the terms of the agreement, the writer will be agreeing to

FIGURE 3.3 Sample Writer's Contract

September 7, 1989

Ms. Maria Oster
47 Palmetto St.
Atlanta, GA 30301

Dear Maria,

This letter, when signed by you in the space provided below, will constitute a binding agreement between you and Corporate Media Corporation (the "Company"), a Georgia-based corporation.

The Company engages your services as a writer on "Future Flight," a 30 minute video production that the Company is producing for its client, Johnson Aviation Systems. The terms of the agreement are contained in the numbered sections that follow:

1. You will be responsible for performing and/or delivering the following:

    a.)   interviews and site visits;
    b.)   background research and preparation;
          of a 20-page minimum, typed,
          double-spaced background report;
    c.)   attending research and script meetings;
    d.)   writing a detailed treatment based on
          your research materials;
    e.)   writing a script based on the treatment.

The background report, treatment and script comprise the Materials that you will be required to deliver under this agreement, and that are discussed in the following sections.

2. You will coordinate your work with Ms. Karyn Mariano (the "Producer"). The Producer must evaluate and approve each of the Materials listed in paragraph 1.

3. The Term of this agreement will begin October 2, 1989, and end January 26, 1990.

FIGURE 3.3 Sample Writer's Contract (cont'd.)

4. The schedule for delivering the Materials is as follows:

MATERIALS	DUE TO PRODUCER
Background Report	November 6, 1989
Detailed Treatment	December 4, 1989
Finished Script	January 12, 1990

The last two weeks of the Term (January 16-26,
1990) will be reserved for making final changes and
adjustments to the script. During this time, you may
also be asked to meet with the Director, crew and
performers to discuss the production of the script.

5. Upon receiving the materials listed in steps 1 and
4, the Producer will have five working days to evaluate each item and to return it to you with comments.
If the Producer requests revisions to any of the
Materials, you will have five working days to make
the changes and to return a revised
copy.

6. As full and complete compensation for your services and for all the rights therein granted by you for
the Materials, the Company will pay you the total
sum of $14,000. The total sum will be paid out in
three installments tied to the delivery and acceptance
of the Materials:

Delivery and Acceptance of Research Report
$3000
Delivery and Acceptance of Detailed Treatment
$4000
Delivery and Acceptance of Finished Script $7000

These payments will be made upon delivery and
acceptance of the scheduled Materials, and upon the
Producer's receipt of an invoice for each payment.

7. If at any time the Company determines that your
performance is unsatisfactory, it may terminate this
contract and pay you only for work completed and

FIGURE 3.3 Sample Writer's Contract (cont'd.)

expenses incurred at the time, plus a $1000 termination fee.

8. The Company agrees to reimburse you for all reasonable expenses you incur during your work on the project, provided that all expenses over $50.00 are approved, in advance, by the Producer. All expenses must be submitted to the Company with appropriate documentation, including receipts for and written descriptions of each expense. Expense reports and requests for reimbursing expenses to date should be submitted at each of the deliverable dates described in section 4.

9. Provided that all of the Materials are accepted by the Company, you will receive screen credit as Researcher and Writer. If the Company rejects any or all of the Materials, the Company will be under no obligation to provide you with screen credit. You also have the right to remove your name from the credits, provided that a written request to that effect is received by the Company on or before February 1, 1990.

10. Your work under this agreement will not be subject to the terms and conditions of any guild or union contract. In addition, your work under this agreement will be considered a work-made-for-hire as that term is defined in the U.S. Copyright Act of 1976. This agreement shall be deemed to be an assignment of all rights in and to the materials to the Company. The Company will retain all copyright, title and interest in and to the Materials. You also agree that the Materials are not to be reproduced or used by you in any manner without the Company's express written permission.

11. The Company will have complete creative control of the Materials and of the production that will be based upon the Materials. The Company may, at any time and at its sole discretion, revise or rewrite any part or parts of the Materials delivered under the terms of this agreement.

FIGURE 3.3 Sample Writer's Contract (cont'd.)

12. You warrant and represent to the Company as follows:

(a) The Materials are original with you and you are the sole author of the Materials.

(b) You have not made, authorized, or consented to and will not make, authorize or consent to any commitment, agreement, obligation, grant, assignment, encumbrance or other disposition of any rights in the Materials or otherwise perform any act that would conflict with any rights granted to the Company hereunder.

(c) As of the date hereof, there are no adverse claims of which you are aware, and you know of no possible claims relating to the Materials.

(d) You have the right to enter into this agreement and to assign the rights granted herein, and you have not authorized the exploitation of any rights in the Materials other than as set forth herein.

(e) The exercise of the rights granted herein will not infringe on any rights of any third party, including but not limited to copyright, trademark, unfair competition, defamation, privacy and publicity rights.

13. You agree to indemnify to the Company at all times and hold it harmless from and against any and all claims, damages, liabilities, costs, and expenses, including but not limited to legal expenses and reasonable counsel fees arising out of 1) the use by the Company of any material provided by you under this agreement, or 2) any breach by you of any representation, warranty, or covenant made by you in this agreement. In the event that the Company receives notice of any claim or service or process involving the foregoing indemnification, the Company shall promptly notify you thereof. You will promptly adjust, settle, defend, or otherwise dispose of such claim at your sole cost. If you have been so notified and you do not diligently pursue such matter, the Company may take such action on its own behalf to adjust, settle, defend, or otherwise dispose of such claim. In this event, you shall, upon being billed therefor, reimburse the Company in the amount thereof.

The Company agrees to indemnify you at all times

FIGURE 3.3 Sample Writer's Contract (cont'd.)

and hold you harmless from and against any and all claims, damages, liabilities, costs, and expenses, including but not limited to legal expenses and reasonable counsel fees arising out of 1) the use by you of any material provided by the Company under this agreement, or 2) any breach by the Company of any representation, warranty, or covenant made by the Company in this agreement. In the event that you receive notice of any claim or service of process involving the foregoing indemnification, you shall promptly notify the company thereof. The Company will promptly adjust, settle, defend, or otherwise dispose of such claim at its sole cost. If the Company has been so notified and it does not diligently pursue such matter, you may take such action on your own behalf to adjust, settle, defend, or otherwise dispose of such claim. In this event, the Company shall, upon being billed therefor, reimburse you in the amount thereof.

14. You will regard all the ideas, concepts, technical information and market data divulged to you by the Company or its client to be strictly confidential during the term of this agreement and thereafter. You shall not reveal to any third party or use any such ideas, concepts and data without the Company's express written permission.

15. The Company may use and authorize others to use your name, likeness and biographical information to publicize the production. However, no direct endorsement by you of any product or service shall be made or implied without your written consent.

16. You are being engaged as an independent contractor. As such, you shall make no claims against the Company for insurance, worker's compensation or any other employee benefits offered by the Company. You also acknowledge that you will be solely responsible for all taxes, fees and assessments due with respect to your compensation hereunder.

FIGURE 3.3 Sample Writer's Contract (cont'd.)

17. This document contains the entire understanding between you and the Company. No amendment, waiver, consent, variation or modification shall be made to this agreement unless it is set forth in a document signed by the Company and you.

18. Should any dispute arise between you and the Company, you and the Company agree that, at either's request, the dispute will be submitted to binding arbitration in Atlanta, Georgia, under the auspices of the American Arbitration Association.

19. This agreement shall be governed by the laws of the State of Georgia.

20. If you are in accordance with the foregoing terms and conditions, please indicate your acceptance by signing in the space below and returning the signed agreement to the Company by September 22, 1989. If the signed agreement is not received in the Company's office by 5:00 p.m. on September 22, this offer will be withdrawn.

Very truly yours,

Corporate Media Corporation, Inc.

By: _____

AGREED AND ACCEPTED:

By:_____
  Maria Oster

Date_____

Social Security Number _____

provide her services on a nonunion and work-made-for-hire basis. This means that Corporate Media Corporation, the hiring company, will own the copyright and all other rights to the materials that the writer will deliver under the contract and that the writer will not receive any of the profit from the sale of the videotape that is based on those materials. As paragraph 10 indicates, the company will also retain complete creative control over the materials and may revise or edit them in any way.

Most contracts that involve the delivery of creative materials require contractors to warrant that they actually own the materials that they are being paid to deliver. As paragraph 12 shows, this sample writer's contract is no exception. Along with guaranteeing that the work is entirely her own, the writer in the sample contract is accepting full responsibility for any legal action or judgments that arise from disputes over ownership of the materials.

In paragraph 13, the writer is agreeing not to disclose any confidential information and market data that she receives through her work under the contract. This sort of confidentiality clause is common in contracts that cover corporate media projects, since these projects often include sensitive information about new products, services and technology.

Paragraph 18 stipulates that any disputes arising out of the agreement will be submitted to binding arbitration. As mentioned in Chapter 1, with the costs of courtroom litigation continuing to rise, arbitration has become an increasingly attractive alternative for resolving contract disputes.

The contract closes by describing how the parties will indicate their acceptance of the agreement. Like the camera operator in Figure 3.2, the writer must return the signed agreement by the date specified or the offer will be withdrawn.

A SAMPLE FACILITIES RENTAL CONTRACT

Figure 3.4 is a facilities rental contract between Mag Media Corporation, a video production company, and Lakeshore Studios, a television production facility. Like most well-constructed contracts, this agreement benefits both parties. For Mag Media, the agreement guarantees that the equipment, crew and studio space that it needs will be available at the designated time and for the specified price. For Lakeshore Studios, the agreement provides written proof of the crew, equipment and services that the production company has hired and the price that it has agreed to pay.

It is significant that the sample contract also requires Mag Media to pay a fairly stiff penalty if it cancels the deal after the date designated in paragraph 8. This termination clause helps protect Lakeshore Studios from a last-minute cancellation that might leave its valuable facilities idle for the period covered by the contract. The presence of this penalty clause also helps guarantee that Mag Media is a serious client committed to using the facilities on the designated dates, rather than a production company that is simply reserving studio time on the hope that a program deal that is under negotiation might come through.

Figure 3.4: Sample Facilities Rental Contract

June 23, 1989

The terms described below will define the agreement between Mag Media Corporation (the "Company"), an Illinois-based corporation, and Lakeshore Studios. The terms and conditions of that agreement are as follows:

1. The Company will hire Studio 2 at Lakeshore Studios for three working days commencing July 19, 1989 and ending July 21, 1989.

2. Included in this rental agreement are Studio 2 and its facilities and the following additional equipment: 4 lavalier microphones, 1 beta video recorder and monitor, and supplemental studio lights as required.

3. Also included in this agreement are the following crew: lighting director, 2 camera operators, video engineer, tape operator, audio engineer, gaffer/grip and studio manager.

4. The length of each shooting day will be 9 hours (1 hour setup, 1 hour lunch and 7 hours shooting). The first half of the shooting day on July 19 will be devoted to assembling the set and setting up and testing lighting, sound and video. Principal photography will begin after lunch on July 19 and continue through July 20 and July 21. The last two hours of the shooting day on July 21 will be devoted to striking the set.

5. As total compensation for the facilities, services and crew described above, the Company agrees to pay Lakeshore Studios $8925.

6. July 22 will be reserved as a bumper day. If the Company requires the studio on July 22, an extra charge of $2975 will apply.

7. The Company will supply its own videotape stock. The Company understands that, should bulbs burn out in the studio lights during the shooting days, it will

Figure 3.4: Sample Facilities Rental Contract (cont'd.)

be assessed the replacement fee listed on Lakeshore Studios' standard rate card.

8. This agreement can be terminated by the Company without penalty through written notice received by Lakeshore Studios on or before 5:00 p.m. on July 15. If termination occurs after that date, Lakeshore Studios reserves the right to assess the Company a single cancellation fee of $2975.

9. At all times, Lakeshore Studios will be responsible for providing reasonable security and reasonable care for the studio, storage areas and any other areas where the Company's personnel or property may at any or all times be located.

10. Lakeshore Studios will maintain fire, theft and comprehensive general personal and property liability insurance (under which the Company is named as an additional insured) in a form and in reasonable amounts satisfactory to the Company. Such insurance will cover the personnel and property of the Company on Lakeshore Studio's premises.

11. In the event that the equipment provided by Lakeshore Studios fails to operate properly and that this equipment failure causes a delay in production, or delays in production occur due to Lakeshore Studios personnel that are not a normal part of production, then the Company may at its option:

(a) extend the term of the agreement by the amount of time equal to the time lost at no additional cost to the Company; or

(b) continue production activities into overtime provided that the amount of overtime shall not exceed the amount of time lost due to the delays, and provided that such overtime will be at no additional cost to the Company for services provided by Lakeshore Studios.

12. The terms and conditions described above com-

Figure 3.4: Sample Facilities Rental Contract (cont'd.)

---

prise the entire agreement between the Company

and Lakeshore Studios. No amendment, waiver, variation or modification will be made to this agreement unless set forth in a document signed by both the Company and Lakeshore Studios.

13. This agreement will be governed by the laws of the State of Illinois.

If you are in accordance with the foregoing, please indicate your acceptance by signing in the space indicated below and returning the signed agreement to the Company.

AGREED TO:

_____   _____
For Mag Media Corporation   For Lakeshore Studios

_____   _____
Title   Title

_____   _____
Date   Date

In many cases, the rental of production facilities is not covered by express contracts like the sample shown in Figure 3.4. Many production companies use the same facility on all of their projects and routinely make last-minute arrangements as production needs come up.

While these informal agreements may work well in certain cases, they also carry considerable risks. With no express contract between the parties, there is no assurance that the production facility will deliver the equipment, crew and services that the production company requires. There is also no assurance that, once it does deliver, the production facility will receive the full payment that it deserves. Even more important, with no written contract to verify the terms of their agreement, there is no quick and clear way to resolve any disputes that might arise between the parties—disputes that can cause damaging delays on tightly scheduled production projects.

PROJECT CONTRACT

Figure 3.5 is a project contract between Bayside Distributors, a video distribution company that has commissioned a 30-minute exercise program, and Meyer Video, the production company that has agreed to produce the program.

In this type of contract, it is especially important to spell out who will own the completed program and whether the production company will retain a royalty interest in the project. The sample contract indicates that the idea for this particular project originated with Bayside Distributors, and Bayside is paying Meyer Video to produce the program on a work-made-for-hire basis. Under this arrangement, Bayside will keep all rights of ownership to the program, including the right to copyright the production under its name. However, as part of the deal, Bayside has agreed to pay Meyer royalties on a percentage of gross sales after the first 1000 copies of the program are sold. The details of this royalty payout appear in paragraph 4.3.

Many of the other provisions of the production agreement should be familiar from the sample contracts presented earlier, particularly the writer's contract shown in Figure 3.3. Like that contract, the production agreement in Figure 3.5 begins by describing the materials that the contractor will be responsible for delivering, defining a delivery schedule for the materials and delineating an approval process that will be followed once Bayside receives the materials. As in the writer's contract, the consideration will be paid in installments tied to the delivery schedule, and the contractor will receive a termination fee if the hiring company elects to cancel the project.

Paragraph 6 of the project contract contains a warranty clause similar to the warranty provisions included in the writer's contract. In this case, however, the warranty is coupled with an indemnification clause (see paragraph 7) in which both companies agree to protect each other from certain types of outside legal actions brought against the project. This clause would protect Bayside if, for example, the materials that Meyer delivers contain segments stolen from another copyrighted production. It would also protect Meyer if certain materials that Bayside provides for inclusion in the production are the source of a lawsuit.

The project contract in Figure 3.5 also includes a number of other clauses and provisions worth studying, including the following:

• A "no obligation to publish" clause (paragraph 9) that frees Bayside from any obligation to publish or distribute the finished production. This sort of "pay or play" clause can be particularly significant in contracts that provide

Figure 3.5: Production Agreement

Agreement made this 11th day of April, 1989 by and between BAYSIDE DISTRIBUTORS CORP., a Massachusetts-based corporation with its principal offices located at 343 Hastings Street, Boston, Massachusetts 02140 (hereafter "Bayside") and MEYER VIDEO PRODUCTIONS, INC., a Massachusetts-based corporation with its principal offices located at 1186 Newton Boulevard, Boston, Massachusetts 02151 (hereafter "Meyer").

WHEREAS Bayside has a concept and preliminary treatment for the production of one thirty (30) minute video program tentatively titled "The Execucise Executive Workout," and

WHEREAS Bayside desires to engage Meyer to produce and deliver this program, pursuant to the terms and conditions set forth herein;

NOW, THEREFORE, the parties agree as follows:

1. Description of the Project

Meyer will produce one thirty (30) minute videotape tentatively titled "The Execucise Executive Workout." This videotape will be hereinafter called "the Project."

The Project will be marketed as a videocassette through video retailers and direct mail solicitations.

The Project will be produced on one-inch videotape. Meyer will deliver to Bayside three (3) copies of the finished 1-inch master tape and three (3) 3/4-inch copies of the master tape.

The Project will be suitable for broadcast use and reproduction.

The Project will feature opening and background music created and supplied by Meyer.

The Project will be based on a treatment supplied by Bayside. Bayside will also provide an opening logo

Figure 3.5: Production Agreement (cont'd.)

sequence. All other planning and production materials (including scripts, storyboards and music) will be created or supplied by Meyer.

2. Project Phases and Delivery Dates

A preliminary schedule for delivery of the Project Materials follows.

PHASE 1

Delivery Items: Rough storyboards and rough script based on the treatment supplied by Bayside.
Delivery Date: May 22, 1989

PHASE 2

Delivery Items: Final storyboards and shooting script.
Delivery Date: June 16, 1989

PHASE 3

Delivery Items: Offline edited workprint of the Project, including music.
Delivery Date: August 29, 1989

PHASE 4

Delivery Items: Final edited program, including all music, titles, and credits.
Delivery date: October 6, 1989

Once Meyer receives Bayside's written approval of the final edited program delivered in Phase 4, Meyer will have two weeks from that date to deliver to Bayside's offices three (3) copies of the finished one-inch master tape and three (3) 3/4-inch copies of the master tape.

Meyer will use all reasonable efforts to conform to this schedule and any revisions to the schedule, as approved by Bayside.

Figure 3.5: Production Agreement (cont'd.)

3. Approvals.

Once Bayside receives the Materials described in Paragraph 2 of this agreement, Bayside will use reasonable efforts to review the Materials immediately and either:

3.1. Approve the Materials, thereby enabling Meyer to proceed to the next scheduled phase.

3.2. Request specific changes and corrections, made in writing, that will permit the Project to proceed to the next scheduled phase once Meyer has made the requested changes and corrections.

3.3. Reject the Materials and terminate the Project.

All approvals related to the Materials delivered in the various phases will be made in writing in a letter addressed to the Project producer at Meyer's offices.

If Meyer does not receive a response from Bayside within 10 working days of Bayside's receipt of the materials, the materials will be deemed approved.

Bayside shall be the sole judge as to whether the Project Materials are satisfactory, and Bayside shall have the sole and exclusive right to reject the Materials and terminate the agreement.

However, if Bayside exercises the option described in Paragraph 3.3 and terminates the Project, or if Bayside terminates the Project for any reason other than gross breach of contract, Meyer is entitled to a $20,000 fee plus reimbursement of all expenses related to the Project that have been incurred or committed at the date of termination.

Should Bayside wish to make changes to the Materials completed in a particular phase after Bayside has approved the Materials, such changes will be made at Bayside's sole expense. Meyer will

Figure 3.5: Production Agreement (cont'd.)

provide cost projections for such changes.

4. Consideration

4.1. For producing the Project and delivering the Materials described in sections 1 and 2 of this agreement, Bayside will pay Meyer the total sum of $58,000. The payment schedule is as follows.

DATE OR ACTION	PAYMENT
Signing of this production agreement	$13,000
Delivery and approval of Phase 2 Materials	10,000
Delivery and approval of Phase 3 Materials	10,000
Delivery and approval of Phase 4 Materials	25,000

Meyer will submit an invoice to Bayside for each payment, and Bayside will issue payment within ten (10) working days of its receipt of eacy invoice. None of these payments are refundable in whole or in part.

4.2. Any payments for additional work performed on the Project at the request of Bayside will be paid in a single, lump sum due upon the completion and delivery of such work.

4.3. Meyer will be entitled to royalty compensation for the Project based on the following schedule:

First 1000 units sold	0% of gross revenue
Second 1000 units sold	8% of gross revenue
All sales after 2000 units sold	10% of gross revenue

Bayside will provide Meyer with quarterly statements showing, in summary form, the appropriate calculations under this agreement. These statements and royalty payments due (if any) will be issued on April 30, July 31, September 30 and January 31 for each preceding calendar quarter. The statements rendered by Bayside may be changed from time to time

Figure 3.5: Production Agreement (cont'd.)

to reflect year-end adjustments made by Bayside's accounting department, returned merchandise or corrections to errors. If Bayside shall extend credit to any party with respect to distribution of the Project, and if such credit has been included in the gross receipts, and if, in the opinion of Bayside, any such indebtedness shall be uncollectible, the uncollected amount may be deducted in any subsequent earnings statement. Should Bayside make any overpayment to Meyer for any reason, Bayside shall have the right to deduct and to retain for its own account an amount equal to such overpayment from any sums that may thereafter become due or payable to Meyer, or Bayside may demand repayment from Meyer, in which event Meyer shall repay the same when such demand is made.

All amounts payable to Meyer hereunder shall be subject to all laws and regulations now or hereafter in existence requiring deductions or withholdings for income or other taxes payable by or assessable against Meyer. Bayside shall have the right to make such deductions and withholdings and the payment thereof to the appropriate government agency in accordance with its interpretation in good faith of such laws and regulations. However, Bayside shall not be liable to Meyer for the making of such deductions or withholdings or the payment thereof to the appropriate government agency.

Bayside shall keep books of account relating to the distribution of the Project, together with vouchers, exhibition contracts and similar records supporting the same (all of which are hereinafter referred to as "records"). To verify earning statements rendered hereunder, Meyer may, at its own expense, audit the applicable records at the place where Bayside maintains the records. Any such audit shall be conducted only by a public accountant during reasonable business hours and in such a manner as not to interfere with Meyer's normal business activities. In no event shall an audit with respect to any earnings statement commence later than 24 months from the rendition of the earnings statement involved; nor shall any audit

Figure 3.5: Production Agreement (cont'd.)

continue for longer than 30 consecutive business days; nor shall such audits be made more frequently than once annually; nor shall the records supporting any earnings statement be audited more than once. All earnings statements rendered hereunder shall be binding upon Meyer and not subject to objection for any reason unless such objection is made in writing, stating the basis thereof and delivered to Bayside within 24 months from the rendition of the earnings statement, or if an audit is commenced prior thereto, within 30 days of completion of the audit. Meyer's right to examine Bayside's records is limited to the Project, and Meyer shall have no right to examine records related to Bayside's business generally or with respect to any other project for purposes of comparison or otherwise.

4.4. Should the Project be licensed for broadcast or cable distribution or any other form of exhibition, Meyer will be entitled to 10% of the gross receipts for such licenses. Notice of and payment for all broadcast and cable licensing shall be included with the royalty statements for the Project, a schedule for which is included in Paragraph 4.3.

4.5. If at any time, for any reason, Bayside decides to discontinue promoting or distributing the Project, Bayside shall be responsible only for that compensation earned to date based on the above payment and royalty schedules. Meyer is not entitled to any of the anticipated royalty or licensing revenue had the Project been promoted further.

5. Ownership of Materials and Copyright

Upon payment of all fees set forth above, Meyer will irrevocably grant, convey, and assign to Bayside and its successors, licensees, and assigns exclusively and forever all rights of any kind whatsoever in the Project, including but not limited to the following:

Figure 3.5: Production Agreement (cont'd.)

(a) the exclusive right to reproduce and sell the Project in all markets. Bayside may use, deal with, or exploit the Project, or any element or portion thereof, throughout the world, in perpetuity, in any manner, in any or all means or media, now known or hereafter devised.

(b) the right to secure copyright and renewal of copyright for the Project and for any version of the Project that Bayside may produce hereunder, throughout the world in our name or otherwise.

(c) the right to use the name of the Project, the character or characters contained therein, or any material contained in and/or based upon the Project, for any commercial tie-ups or for merchandising any commodity, product or service.

All rights, licenses, privileges and property herein granted to Bayside shall be cumulative. Bayside may exercise or use any or all of said rights, licenses, or privileges, or property simultaneously with or in connection with or separate and apart from the exercise of any other of said rights, licenses, privileges and property.

The Project shall be considered a work-made-for-hire by Meyer for Bayside, as that term is defined and used in United States copyright law. Meyer will not have any rights in or to the project, or any element thereof or any related Materials. If, for any reason, the project or the Materials are determined not to be a work-made-for-hire, then the project or Materials, as applicable, will hereby be deemed assigned to Meyer together with all rights therein.

Meyer agrees that it will execute and deliver to Bayside any documents that Bayside may deem necessary or appropriate to record, attest, or confirm that Bayside is the owner of all right, title and interest, including the copyright, in the Project.

6. Meyer's Warranties

Meyer warrants that neither the Project nor any

Figure 3.5: Production Agreement (cont'd.)

Materials furnished or selected by Meyer will violate any law or infringe upon or violate the rights of any person or entity.

In the event that Meyer incorporates into the Project any materials that are protected by copyright, Meyer will notify Bayside of such protections, and will present for approval to Bayside and its counsel releases, permissions or other evidence of right to use for the protected materials.

Meyer further represents, warrants and covenants that it has all necessary rights and power to enter into and fully perform this agreement and that its product will be free of liens, claims or encumbrances whatsoever in favor of any other party, and that the Project, and all elements thereof, will be Meyer's own and original creation, except for matter in the public domain, or matter provided to Meyer by Bayside.

Meyer also warrants that it will comply with all laws, rules, and regulations applicable to the production of the Project and the employment of individuals therefor, including, but not limited to, employment and immigration laws.

7. Indemnification

Meyer agrees to indemnify Bayside at all times and hold it harmless from and against any and all claims, damages, liabilities, costs and expenses, including legal expenses and reasonable counsel fees arising out of 1) the use by Bayside of any material produced by Meyer under this agreement; or 2) any breach by Meyer of any representation, warranty, or covenant made by Meyer in this Agreement. In the event that Bayside receives notice of any claim or service of process involving the foregoing indemnification, Bayside shall promptly notify Meyer thereof. Meyer will promptly adjust, settle, defend or otherwise dispose of such claim at Meyer's sole cost. If Meyer has been so notified and does not diligently pursue such matter, Bayside may take such action on its own behalf to adjust, settle, defend or otherwise dispose of such claim. In this event, Meyer

Figure 3.5: Production Agreement (cont'd.)

shall, upon being billed therefor, reimburse Bayside in the amount thereof.

Bayside agrees to indemnify Meyer at all times and hold it harmless from and against any and all claims, damages, liabilities, costs and expenses, including legal expenses and reasonable counsel fees arising out of 1) the use by Meyer of any material provided to Meyer by Bayside; or 2) any breach by Bayside of any representation, warranty, or covenant made by Bayside in this Agreement. In the event that Meyer receives notice of any claim or service of process involving the foregoing indemnification, Meyer shall promptly notify Bayside thereof. Bayside will promptly adjust, settle, defend, or otherwise dispose of such claim at Bayside's sole cost. If Bayside has been so notified and does not diligently pursue such matter, Meyer may take such action on its own behalf to adjust, settle, defend, or otherwise dispose of such claim. In this event, Bayside shall, upon being billed therefor, reimburse Meyer in the amount thereof.

8. Credits

Bayside agrees that the published work shall, in an appropriate place and in a separate frame, display the words:

> Produced by Meyer Video Productions
> Boston, Massachusetts

Bayside agrees that these words will also be displayed in all print and television advertising for the Project.

Bayside also agrees that, upon receipt of a written request from Meyer, it will remove Meyer's credit from all newly manufactured copies of the published work and all new advertising for the work.

9. No Obligation to Publish

Nothing in this agreement shall be deemed to obligate Bayside to publish, distribute or exhibit the Project. Meyer agrees that, upon payment of the compensation described in Paragraph 4 above, Bayside shall have fully performed its obligations under this agreement.

Figure 3.5: Production Agreement (cont'd.)

10. Independent Contractor Status

Meyer shall have the entire responsibility as an independent contractor to discharge all of its obligations under any federal, state, or local laws, regulations or orders now or hereafter in force, including, without limitation, those relating to taxes, unemployment compensation or insurance, social security, worker's compensation, disability benefits, tax withholding, and employment of minors, and including the filing of all returns and reports required of independent contractors, and the payment of all taxes, assessments, contributions and other sums required of them.

Nothing in this agreement shall be construed as making Bayside and Meyer partners, or making either entity an employee of the other.

11. Right of First Refusal

Meyer will retain a Right of First Refusal to serve as producers of any sequel to or spin-off from the Project. Bayside and Meyer will negotiate in good faith with respect to such engagement. If the parties are unable to reach an agreement, Bayside will be free to negotiate with a third party with respect thereto, provided, however, that prior to entering into any such third party agreement, Bayside will notify Meyer in writing of the terms of such agreement. Meyer will have 30 days from receipt of such notice to accept the engagement as producer on the terms set forth therein. If Meyer fails to accept such offer, Bayside will be free to enter into the third-party agreement, but only on the terms set forth in the notice.

12. Insurance

Upon execution of this agreement, Meyer shall promptly secure a policy of producer's errors and omissions insurance applicable to the production of the Project. Such policy shall have a limit of at least $1 million per occurrence with respect to each loss or claim involving the same act of failure to act. Such policy shall be secured at Meyer's own expense and

Figure 3.5: Production Agreement (cont'd.)

shall be maintained by Meyer at least until Bayside's approval and acceptance of the Phase Four materials, shall name Bayside as an additional insured, shall include a provision requiring the insurance company to notify Bayside of any material diminution or cancellation thereof, and shall be deemed primary insurance covering any claims arising at any time (whether prior to or after the delivery of the Phase Four materials) in connection with the production of the Project. Before proceeding with production, Meyer shall promptly furnish to Bayside a certificate attesting to such insurance and describing its terms and limits.

13. Force Majeure

If Meyer or Bayside fail to perform any obligation hereunder due to unavailability of services or materials, labor disputes, governmental restrictions, or any other circumstances beyond their control, such failure shall not be deemed a breach of this Agreement, and if any time period for performance is specified, such period shall be deemed extended accordingly.

14. Miscellaneous Provisions

14.1. Applicable Law. This agreement shall be construed in accordance with the laws of the Commonwealth of Massachusetts.

14.2. Modification, Waiver or Change. No modifications, waiver or change shall be made in the terms and conditions of this agreement, except as may be mutually agreed upon in writing by all parties hereto.

14.3. Successors and Assigns. This agreement shall inure to the benefit of and be binding upon the successors and assigns of each of the parties hereto.

14.4. Entire Understanding. This agreement, together with all exhibits attached hereto, if any, represent the entire understanding of the parties, and neither party is relying upon any representation not contained herein.

Figure 3.5: Production Agreement cont'd.

14.5. <u>Severability.</u> In the event that any provision of this agreement shall be deemed invalid, unreasonable or unenforceable by any court of competent jurisdiction, such provision shall be stricken from the agreement or modified so as to render it reasonable, and the remaining provisions of this agreement or the modified provision as provided above, shall continue in full force and effect and be binding upon the parties so long as such remaining or modified provisions reflect the intent of the parties at the date of this agreement.

14.6. <u>Notices.</u> Any and all notices and written approvals required to be given under this agreement shall be deemed to be made if they are mailed postage prepaid by certified mail, return receipt requested, to the party at the respective address set forth above, or at such address as may from time to time be designated by the party as a change of address. Any notice period shall begin running as of the date provided on the return receipt.

14.7. <u>Marginal Headings.</u> The marginal headings used in this agreement are for convenience only and shall not be deemed to be a binding portion of the agreement.

IN WITNESS WHEREOF, the parties have hereunto set their hands and seals the day and year first above written.

In the presence of: BAYSIDE DISTRIBUTORS, INC.

_____

Donald E. Sweeney
  Its President
Meyer Video Productions, Inc.

_____

Cheryl S. Meyer
  Its President

for royalty payments, since withdrawing a project from distribution would cut off the flow of royalty revenues to the production company.

• An "independent contractor clause" (see paragraph 10) that reminds Meyer of its obligations as an independent contractor, and that reminds the world that the agreement between Meyer and Bayside does not place the two companies in a partnership or employer-employee relationship.

• A "right of first refusal" clause (see paragraph 11) that requires Bayside to offer Meyer the chance to produce any sequels to or spinoffs from the project.

• A "force majeure" clause (see paragraph 13) that protects the parties if they fail to deliver on their contractual obligations due to circumstances beyond their control.

The project contract ends with a list of miscellaneous provisions that further define the scope and limits of the agreement. Included in those provisions are terms that define the jurisdiction of the contract and the manner in which the agreement may be amended and modified.

Like the other sample contracts, this project contract is a nonunion agreement. For information about union agreements, see Chapter 7.

SUMMARY

What is the first step in drafting a media production contract?
You should always begin by making sure that the contract includes a clear and definite *offer*, a thorough description of the *consideration* and a way for the parties to indicate their *acceptance*. Once you have built this basic framework, you can add the other terms and provisions that will further define the production relationship covered by the contract.

What are some of the other terms and provisions that should be included in media production contracts?
Media production contracts should always include schedules that indicate when and how the contractor will deliver the goods and services covered by the agreement. Production contracts should also establish guidelines for approving the deliverables and procedures for paying the contractor. In addition, the contracts should define the working relationships between the production parties. Will the contract work be performed on a guild or union basis? If the party that is performing the work is acting as an independent contractor, does it agree to waive all rights to claims against the company for

insurance, worker's compensation and other benefits of employment?

How should issues of ownership be addressed in media production contracts?

All production contracts should include language that clearly defines who will own the materials that will be delivered under the agreement and who will own the finished program. In most cases, the producer should obtain full ownership of the materials and services delivered by the contractor. The producer should also retain complete ownership of the finished production. In addition, the contract should stipulate what rights the producer will have to reuse the materials delivered by the subcontractor.

What role should warranty and indemnity clauses play in production contracts?

Warranty clauses specify that the party that has agreed to deliver goods under the contract has full rights to the material and that there is no other contract that prevents the party from entering into the agreement. Indemnity clauses stipulate which party will be held responsible for any judgment and legal fees if ownership of the materials or some other term of the contract should come into dispute.

What is a statement of jurisdiction?

Through the statement of jurisdiction, the parties to a contract agree that the contract will be governed by the laws of a specific state or, in the case of an international production, by the laws of a specific nation. The statement of jurisdiction is especially significant when the parties to the contract reside in different states or countries, since the laws governing contracts can vary from one jurisdiction to the next. As the producer, it is almost always in your best interest to have the agreement governed by the laws of your home state.

What is a termination clause?

Termination clauses define the conditions under which a contract can be cancelled; thus they prevent one of the parties from canceling the contract arbitrarily. In most cases, the option to terminate is tied to the failure of one or more parties to live up to their obligations under the agreement.

What is a remedy clause?

Remedy clauses define what happens when one or both of the parties violate the terms of the agreement, or when the contract is canceled. Will the violating party be required to return any payments that it has already received? Which party will won the work that has already been completed? Do the parties agree to submit all disputes to binding arbitration?

4

Getting Permission: Copyright Concerns During Media Production

Most media productions are actually a mix of materials that a producer has pulled together from a variety of sources. In preparing a video documentary, for example, the producer might commission a freelance writer to write the script, an animation house to prepare a title sequence and an outside video facility to produce several special effects segments. The producer might also buy or "borrow" existing materials to enhance the production: stock footage, still photographs, music, excerpts from other video or television programs, and so on.

Chapters 2 and 3 examined how contracts can help define the relationships between a producer and the various performers, writers and crew members commissioned to provide services or original materials for a production project.

In contrast, this chapter focuses on the many legal issues involved in incorporating *existing* materials such as film clips and photographs in a production. These are materials that already exist in one form or another, and that were not created as contract items for the production in question.

Some producers make the mistake of assuming that it is okay to incorporate existing materials in a production as long as they use only a brief excerpt, or as long as they acknowledge the source of the materials in the production credits. The following discussion will show that this is a very dangerous assumption to make. To understand why, it helps to begin with an introduction to the fundamental concepts underlying copyright law.

AN INTRODUCTION TO COPYRIGHT LAW

For media producers, copyright cuts two ways. On one hand, copyright *protects* a producer's right to profit from the sale of his or her work. On the

75

other hand, copyright *prevents* producers from using the work of others without their permission. This chapter will discuss the preventive role that copyright plays during the media production process. For information about the ways that copyright can protect a producer's right to control and profit from a completed work, see Chapter 8.

What Is Copyright?

Copyright is actually a series of rights granted to the creators of literary, artistic, musical, dramatic and audiovisual works. Under United States law, copyright gives the creators of these "intellectual properties" the exclusive right to:

•reproduce and distribute copies of the copyrighted works (in other words, the "right to copy");

•create derivative works based on the copyrighted work; and

•perform and display the copyrighted work publicly.

Above all, copyright gives authors, artists, musicians and media producers the right to own and control their completed works. Significantly, as part of that control, the owners of copyrighted materials can authorize others to copy, distribute and adapt their work. This happens all the time in the world of media production, where video and film producers regularly assign publishers and distributors the right to reproduce and distribute copies of their work in return for royalty payments. It also happens when the owners of video, film, photographic and music materials authorize their work to be used in media productions, and when authors allow their works to be adapted for the stage, cinema or television.

Although copyright gives authors, artists and media producers the power to control their creative properties, federal copyright law does place some restrictions on that power. First, copyright is limited to a defined period of time—currently the author's life plus 50 years for most works. In addition, under the *compulsory licensing* provisions of the U.S. copyright law, the creators of published musical compositions must make their work available for licensing by others. Under certain circumstances, U.S. copyright law also allows media producers and others to use and adapt copyrighted materials without securing permission from the copyright owner. This *fair use* provision is discussed in detail later in this chapter.

Sources of Copyright Law

Like much U.S. law, federal copyright law is rooted in English common and statutory law. In England, copyright first emerged as a legal issue with the development of movable type and related printing technologies in the fifteenth and sixteenth centuries. In 1709, after more than a century of government attempts to license printing and publishing rights, the English Parliament passed the first comprehensive copyright law. Known as the Statute of Anne, the 1709 law gave authors the exclusive right to own and profit from their works for a period of 14 years.

The notion that individual authors— not guilds or printers—should retain control of their creative works eventually made its way into Article I, Section 8 of the U.S Constitution:

The Congress shall have the power to promote the progress of science and the useful arts, by securing for limited times to authors and inventors the exclusive right to their respective writings and discoveries.

As this language suggests, the framers of the Constitution—several of whom were authors— believed that copyright involved both individual rights and a national need. By granting Congress the power to pass copyright legislation, they hoped to protect the rights of individual authors to control and to profit from their creative works. In doing so, they also anticipated that copyright legislation would help promote "the progress of science and the useful arts" in the new nation.

Just three years after the Constitution was completed, Congress exercised its powers under Article I, Section 8 by passing the Copyright Act of 1790. This first federal copyright statute covered books, maps and charts. Like the Statute of Anne, the Copyright Act of 1790 granted authors the exclusive right to publish and profit from their work for 14 years. Under the 1790 Act, however, this initial grant of copyright could be renewed for an additional 14 years.

Federal copyright law has been revised many times since 1790, usually in response to the emergence of new recording, image reproduction and transmission technologies (photography, phonograph records, motion pictures, photocopying, radio and television, videotaping, etc.). Major revisions occurred in 1831, 1870, 1909 and, most recently and most significantly, in the Copyright Act of 1976. Copyright has also been the subject of much common law, particularly when new technologies have raised issues that were not yet addressed in federal copyright statutes.

It is important to note that, unlike many areas of media production law, copyright law is governed by a single, preemptive federal statute. This means that the individual states are restricted to playing only a minor, secondary role in regulating copyright. It also means that common law in the area of copyright is primarily federal common law—law that is based on judgments rendered in federal courts. In the United States, copyright procedures are administered by the U.S. Copyright Office, an office of the Library of Congress.

The federal statute that currently dominates the copyright landscape is the Copyright Act of 1976. Passed after more than two decades of research and debate, the Copyright Act of 1976 became fully effective on January 1, 1978. The 1976 act supersedes the Copyright Act of 1909, a statute that was the subject of many amendments and much federal common law over the years.

The Copyright Act of 1976 set down new rules governing what can and cannot be copyrighted, the scope and duration of copyright, and the steps involved in establishing copyright. The 1976 Act was also the first federal copyright statute to include provisions for the fair use of copyright materials—a doctrine that was an established component of common law, but that had never been formally recognized in federal statutory law. As discussed later in this chapter, fair use is of particular interest to media producers.

What Can be Copyrighted

Under the Copyright Act of 1976, almost any creative work can be protected by copyright. A partial list incudes:

•books of fiction, non-fiction and poetry;

•films, television programs, radio programs and other audiovisual works;

•scripts for films, television programs, radio programs and other audiovisual works;

•photographs;

•paintings, illustrations, sculptures and other works of art;

•dramatic works;

•music and sound recordings;

•choreographic works and pantomimes; and

•computer software.

As this list suggests, most media properties can be copyrighted, as long as those properties are "fixed" in tangible form.

Although copyright law is quite broad, it does not cover all types and categories of materials. For example, an idea or concept for a television program is not eligible for copyright, even when the idea is expressed in tangible form. However, a treatment or script developed from the idea could be copyrighted, as could the television show that is based on one or more of those materials. In other words, it is the particular form in which an idea is expressed that is eligible for copyright protection, not the idea itself.

In addition to ideas, other items and materials that cannot be copyrighted include:

•information and materials produced by federal government employees as part of their jobs;

•scientific, historical and other factual information, including the news (although a specific selection and arrangement of factual information can be copyrighted);

•inventions and industrial processes; and

•titles of products or services.

Although these items cannot be copyrighted, they may be eligible for other forms of protection. For example, inventions and certain industrial processes can be protected by patents, and titles can be protected by trademarks and service marks. Patents, trademarks and service marks are discussed in Chapter 8.

HOW IS COPYRIGHT ESTABLISHED?

Under the Copyright Act of 1976, copyright is established as soon as you create, in fixed form, a work that is eligible for copyright protection. To help preserve your copyright, you should also add a copyright notice to the work. If you have created a television program or slide tape show, for example, you would display a notice that looks like this:

Copyright 1988 by Magic Media, Inc.

Unlike the Copyright Act of 1909, the 1976 law is fairly flexible in its rules regarding the form and placement of the copyright notice. However,

Section 401 of the 1976 law does stipulate that the copyright notice on "visually perceptible works" should include the following:

1. the symbol © (the letter C in a circle) or p (for sound recordings), the word "Copyright" or the abbreviation "Copr.,"
2. the first year of publication of the work, and
3. the name of the owner of the copyright in the work, or an abbreviation by which the name can be recognized or a generally known alternative designation of the owner.[1]

Section 401 of the law also requires that the notice "shall be affixed to the copies in such a manner and location as to give reasonable notice of the claim of copyright." In other words, the notice should be displayed in a prominent position, rather than buried deep inside the work. In most films and television programs, the copyright notice appears as part of the opening titles or closing credits. On videocassettes, a copyright notice usually appears on both the program material and the cassette label.

Significantly, as part of the change made to the 1976 act in advance of the United States joining the Berne Convention in 1989, a copyright notice is no longer required as a condition of copyright protection—although it is still strongly recommended. For more information, see the section on the Berne Convention that appears later in this chapter.

Registering with the U.S. Copyright Office

Displaying the proper copyright notice on fixed copies of a creative work is the first recommended step in securing copyright. The second step is registering the work in the U.S. Copyright Office. This involves filling out the appropriate application and returning the completed forms, together with a small fee and two copies of the completed work, to the Copyright Office.

Under the current law, registering a work with the Copyright Office is not required as a condition of copyright protection. In other words, if you fail to register a work that you created, you will still retain the copyright for that work. However, there are several significant advantages to registering with the Copyright Office, particularly if your work becomes the subject of a copyright dispute. First, registration establishes a public record for a copyrighted work—a record that can come in very handy in the event of legal proceedings. In addition, if someone has violated your copyright, you must register the work before you can bring a suit for copyright infringement before a court of law. Although it is possible to register the work after the

---

[1]Copyright Act of 1976, 17 U.S.C. § 401(b).

infringement has occurred, this will limit you to suing for actual damages—monetary losses that you can actually prove. If you had taken the time to register before the infringement occurred or within the first three months after the work was published, you would be eligible to sue for attorney's fees and statutory damages—damages awarded by the court when the actual monetary loss is either difficult to prove or very small. Because the actual monetary loss from a copyright infringement often is very difficult to prove, being able to sue for statutory damages is a definite advantage.

Special Cautions for Incorporating Existing Works into Media Productions

Media professionals who are planning to incorporate existing works into a production should be also be aware that, under the Copyright Act of 1976, and international law copyright is established by the author as soon as a work is created in a fixed form. In other words, it is the act of creating a work that establishes copyright, not the act of displaying a copyright notice or registering the work with the Copyright Office. As a result, media producers who assume that a work is in the public domain simply because it does not include a copyright notice may discover that the work is copyrighted after all. Unfortunately, if they have used the work in a production without the proper permissions, they may also discover that they are the subject of an infringement action brought by the copyright owner. In this case, the producers would probably not be held liable for damages, as long as they could show that they were innocent infringers who were misled by the absence of the copyright notice. However, a court could require the producers to remove the copyrighted material from the production, or to pay licensing fees for continuing to use the material. For more information about securing copyright protection for completed media productions, see Chapter 8.

DURATION OF COPYRIGHT

Under the Copyright Act of 1909, an author's copyright began the day that a work was published and extended for 28 years. At the end of this initial period, the author could renew the copyright for an additional 28 years. If the author failed to renew the copyright, the work fell into the public domain.

All this changed on January 1, 1978, when the Copyright Act of 1976 went into effect. With the new law, copyright now extends for the life of the author plus 50 years. For works with joint authors, the term of copyright is the life of the last surviving author plus 50 years. For anonymous works, the term is 75 years from the date of publication (the day when the work was first distributed to the public) or 100 years from the date that the work was created, whichever comes first. If the author is listed as a group or organization, as is often the case with media productions, the 75-year term for anonymous or pseudonymous works applies. This is also the case with works-made-for-hire.

For works created before 1978, the following changes apply under the new law:

•If the work was still in its initial 28-year copyright period as of January 1, 1978 the copyright will continue to the original expiration date. At that point, the copyright can be renewed for 47 years, rather than for the 28 years that were allowed under the old law. This results in a total copyright term of 75 years.

•If the work had already been renewed before January 1, 1978, the copyright term changes to 75 years from the date that the original copyright first became effective.

In other words, the new copyright law gave existing copyright owners an additional 19 years of protection—as long as they remembered to renew their copyright after the original 28-year period. Significantly, a 1992 amendment to the copyright law eliminated the renewal requirement for all works that came or will come up for renewal after the amendment became effective. For these works, the copyright term will automatically be extended to 75 years.

COPYRIGHT INFRINGEMENT

Copyright infringement occurs when someone uses copyrighted work in a manner that violates the copyright owner's exclusive rights to the work. As described earlier in this chapter, those exclusive rights include the right to reproduce and distribute copies of the work, to create derivative works and to perform and display the work publicly. When someone exercises one of more of these rights without the express permission of the copyright owner, he or she is committing copyright infringement.

Significantly, one of the rights reserved for copyright owners is the right to determine whether all or part of their works are used in another work. For media producers, this means that it is illegal to incorporate a copyrighted work in a production without securing the copyright owner's permission. However, there are two important exceptions to this rule: fair use and compulsory music licensing. Fair use is described later in this chapter. *Compulsory music licensing* is discussed in Chapter 6.

Infringement Suits

Producers who use copyrighted works illegally may find themselves the subjects of copyright infringement suits. Because copyright infringement violates federal law, infringement suits are filed in federal district courts. A copyright owner who has brought an infringement suit can seek some or all of the following remedies:

•an injunction or restraining order to stop further infringements;

•a court order to impound the materials that are the subject of the suit;

•if the suit is successful, a court order to destroy the infringing materials;

•a court order requiring the infringer to turn over all profits from the infringement;

•compensation for "actual damages"—monetary losses resulting from the infringement that the copyright owner can actually prove;

•compensation in the form of "statutory damages"—a sum that is set by the court when actual damages are small or difficult to prove; and

•reimbursement of court costs and attorney fees.

As mentioned earlier in this chapter, the last two remedies in this list—statutory damages and reimbursement of legal costs—are available only if the work in question was registered with the U.S. Copyright Office at the time the alleged infringement occurred.

To prove that an infringement occurred, the copyright owner must establish that the alleged infringer had access to the work in question and that the infringer used a substantial portion of the work without permission. Significantly, the copyright owner does not have to prove that the infringement was conscious, deliberate or malicious—only that it occurred.

Amount of Actual and Statutory Damages

The amount of actual damages awarded in infringement suits varies, depending on how much monetary damage the infringer actually inflicted on the copyright owner. Although actual damage awards can be substantial, the burden of proof rests with the copyright owner who has filed the suit.

The copyright owner must begin by providing evidence of the infringer's gross revenues from the use of the disputed material for the period in question. In determining the actual award, the court first allows the infringer to prove that part of that gross revenue was derived from sources other than the copyrighted work in question. The court then deducts these "other" revenues plus any documented expenses from the infringer's total revenues. This sum is then added to the copyright owner's losses to derive a final figure that becomes the basis for the actual damage award.

Because actual damages are often difficult to prove, many copyright owners opt to sue for statutory damages. With statutory damages, the amount of the award is set by the court. However, the Copyright Act of 1976 does require that the awards fall within some fairly specific boundaries. In most individual infringement cases, the law stipulates that the court must award statutory damages of "not less than $250 or more than $10,000." However, in cases where the infringement was deliberate and willful, the court can award up to $50,000.

Under certain circumstances, infringers many also be subject to criminal penalties. Those circumstances include cases in which:

• the infringer knowingly places a fraudulent copyright notice on a work;

•the infringer knowingly removes a copyright notice from a work; and

•the infringer willfully, and for purposes of commercial gain, violates the copyright of sound recording or motion picture.

For these criminal offenses, the law provides for a fine, imprisonment or both.

FAIR USE OF COPYRIGHT WORKS

Is it ever legal for producers to use copyrighted works without securing permission from, or making payment to, the copyright owners? Surprisingly, the answer to this question is yes, but only when the producer's actions fall within the fair use guidelines set down in section 107 of the 1976 copyright law. Four factors determine whether an unauthorized use is a fair use:

1. the purpose and character of the use, including whether such use is of a commercial nature or is for nonprofit educational purposes;

2. the nature of the copyrighted work;

3. the amount and substantiality of the portion used in relation to the copyrighted work as a whole; and

4. the effect of the use on the potential market for/or value of the copyrighted work.

Because these criteria leave much room for interpretation, there is no way to be certain in advance that a specific use of a copyrighted work constitutes a fair use. However, an unauthorized use stands the best chance of securing fair use protection if it is educational or informational in nature, if the work being copied is a reference or other non-fiction work, if the use involves copying a relatively small portion of the work and if the use has little or no effect on the potential market for the copyrighted work.

Unfortunately, very few cases are this clear-cut. As a result, the courts must often mix and match the section 107 criteria and other considerations to come up with fair use determinations. For example, a court might decide that, although an unauthorized use was commercial rather than educational in nature, the material used was small enough in relation to the entire copyrighted work to constitute fair use. Conversely, a court might rule that a purely educational use of copyrighted material fails the fair use test because it involves enough of the entire work to diminish the potential market for the work.

If this seems confusing, the copyright statute itself is partly to blame. In addressing the fair use question, Congress deliberately drafted guidelines that require the courts to review each case on its own merits. Even so, the situation is less confused now than it was before the Copyright Act of 1976, when fair use existed only as a common law concept. The 1976 law at least defines a single set of statutory guidelines that must be applied in *all* fair use determinations.

The Fair Use Checklist

How can you determine whether a particular use of copyrighted material falls within the federal fair use guidelines? Although there is no sure fire formula that will apply to all situations, the checklist shown in Figure 4.1 can help. The checklist includes a list of questions that will help you evaluate the risks involved in using copyrighted material without the copyright owner's permission. Keep in mind, though, that a court will weigh and balance these and all other relevant factors to come up with a fair use determination. As a result, you should evaluate all of the circumstances surrounding your production and your use of the copyrighted materials before assuming that your actions will constitute fair use. When in doubt, contact a competent copyright lawyer.

The nine items in the fair use checklist are presented in question form. Before going ahead with an unauthorized use of copyrighted materials, review the checklist and answer "yes" or "no" to each. If all of the responses are "yes," the unauthorized use probably constitutes fair use. One or more "no" responses indicates that the use is problematic and that a call to a copy-

Figure 4.1: Fair Use Checklist for Media Producers

1. Is your production a noncommercial (nonprofit) production?

An unauthorized use is more likely to be considered a fair use if the copyrighted material is being added to a noncommercial, educational production. Conversely, adding the copyrighted materials to a commercial production—a category that includes corporate video programs intended for internal distribution—is less likely to pass the fair use test.

2. Is your production informational in nature?

The courts tend to be more generous in conceding fair use when the copyrighted material is used in a production that serves some informational or educational purpose. Productions that fit this criterion include commercial or nonprofit documentaries, and public affairs and instructional programs.

3. If the material is being added to an informational production, will it serve informational goals?

When you are adding copyrighted material to an informational production, make sure that you are adding the material for informational rather than artistic or entertainment purposes. For example, using a brief clip from the movie *The Godfather* in a documentary on the public's perception of organized crime could probably constitute fair use, as long as you could show that the clip is directly tied to the informational content of the production. Using the clip simply for artistic purposes—as the background for a credits sequence, for example—would probably not constitute fair use.

4. Is the copyrighted material taken from a factual or reference work?

Generally, the courts are more likely to let you lift material from an encyclopedia or almanac than from a short story, novel or other work of fiction. The assumption here is that, as reference works, encyclopedias and other compilations of factual information are intended to be used as resources in the creation of other works. Even so, the courts will look closely at the amount and nature of the material taken from a factual

Figure 4.1: Fair Use Checklist for Media Producers (cont'd.)

work.

5. Are you using a small enough excerpt of a copyrighted work to have little or no effect on the market value of the whole work?

Under the federal fair use guidelines, the courts must consider "the effect of the use upon the potential market for or value of the copyrighted work." To determine this effect, a court will usually begin by looking at how much of the work you used. A production that incorporates a 30-second segment from a two hour film would probably pass this part of the fair use test, since the court would probably find that the use is small enough to leave the market for the work unaffected. Taking 30 seconds of material from a five-minute film would be a different matter, however, since the excerpt is a large enough portion of the entire work to undermine the potential market for the work.

6. Will the copyrighted material comprise only a small portion of your production?

The courts tend to frown on productions that use too much copyrighted material without authorization. Although the definition of "too much" can vary, the use would probably not be considered fair use of unauthorized copyrighted material comprises more than a small part of the total production.

7. Is the production intended for limited distribution?

If your production is intended for limited distribution to selected audiences, you stand a better chance of securing a fair use waiver than would the producer of a program that is scheduled for repeated showings to more general audiences.

8. Is this unauthorized use of copyrighted material a single, spontaneous occurrence?

A single, spontaneous use of copyrighted material is more likely to be considered fair use than an instance that is part of an ongoing pattern of copyright abuse.

Figure 4.1: Fair Use Checklist for Media Producers cont'd.

---

9. Will you credit the copyright owner?

When you use a copyrighted work without authorization, you should always credit the copyright owner in the production. Although this will not guarantee a favorable fair use ruling, crediting the copyright owner will at least show that you are acting in good faith. Without this show of good faith, most courts are reluctant to grant a fair use waiver.

---

right lawyer is in order. The more "no" responses, the less likely it is that the use would pass the fair use test in a court of law.

As the checklist shows, fair use is almost always problematic for media professionals who produce programs for profit. Significantly, this group includes video producers working in corporate settings, even when the programs that they create are limited to internal distribution. Although most corporate video programs are not sold for profit, lawyers for copyright owners can claim that the productions generate profits for companies by enhancing the performance of employees. Otherwise, why would companies put up the money to make them?

PUBLIC DOMAIN

When the copyright on a work expires, the work falls into the public domain. Once a work is in the public domain, you are free to use it without the copyright owner's permission. You can make and sell copies of public domain materials, and you can incorporate the materials into other works. But you cannot copyright public domain materials yourself, even when those materials are being used as part of another production. In that case, you could copyright the part of the production that you created, but your copyright would not give you any right to control the distribution or use of the public domain portion.

What Materials Are In the Public Domain?

Public domain works include materials that were never copyrighted, materials that cannot be copyrighted (a category that includes U.S. government publications) and copyrighted materials for which the copyright has expired (a category that now includes many of the early silent films). Because copyright is granted for only a limited period of time, all copyrighted materials eventually do fall into the public domain. But it is not always easy to determine whether and when that fall from copyright protection occurred. You can start by checking the copyright notice on the work. If the original copyright is more than 75 years old, the work is in the public domain. If there is more than one copyright notice on the work, as there might be on updated versions of an older work, the most recent copyright must be more than 75 years old.

What about works that do not carry a notice of copyright? In many cases, works without copyright notices are in the public domain. To make sure, ask yourself the following questions:

• Is the work truly a published work? Prerelease or prepublication versions of a work are not required to carry a copyright notice; most are eventually copyrighted upon publication.

• If the work is a published work, when was it published? Works published before January 1, 1978 with the copyright owner's consent, but without a copyright notice will be in the public domain. However, If the work was published after January 1, 1978, the copyright owner has five years to correct the error before the work falls forever into the public domain. Works published after the U.S. joined the Berne Convention in 1989 are even more problematic, since the Berne Treaty does not require the display of a proper notice to ensure continued copyright protection.

• Is this work based on another work? Although the work in question may not include a copyright notice, it may be based on or developed from a work that does.

• Is the copyright notice absent or just missing? In some cases, the copyright notice may have appeared on the original work, but it has since been accidentally or intentionally removed. When this happens, the work is still protected by copyright.

Once a work falls into the public domain, the author cannot reclaim it and reinstate copyright. It remains in the public domain forever.

As mentioned earlier, works created by U.S. government employees as part of their official duties cannot be copyrighted. This means that most print and media materials published by the federal government are in the public domain, and you are not required to seek permission to use them. However, you are required to identify the U.S. government as the source, particularly if your work contains a high percentage of U.S. government material.[2]

---

[2]These provisions apply only to U.S. government materials. Materials published by state and local governments may be copyrighted.

Determining Whether a Work Is in the Public Domain

To determine whether a work is in the public domain, you should first examine the work for a copyright notice. Once you find the notice, check the date of copyright. If the date indicates that the work was copyrighted:

•more than 75 years ago, the work is in the public domain—unless the work was modified and published with an updated copyright notice;

•less than 75 years ago but before 1950, the work is probably *not* in the public domain—unless the copyright expired before 1978 and was not renewed;

•in or after 1950, the work is almost definitely not in the public domain—unless the last copyright owner took the unusual step of abandoning the copyright.

In the last two cases, the only way to determine for certain if the work is in the public domain is to run a formal copyright search. Copyright investigations are discussed in detail later in this chapter.

If there is no copyright notice on the work, the public domain status is even more difficult to determine. For reasons described earlier, the absence of a copyright notice does not necessarily mean that the work is in the public domain. To make sure, you must determine whether the work is a published or prepublication version, whether the copyright notice was truly left off the published work or is simply missing from your copy, and whether the work might include other copyrighted material. You must also determine when the work was published. Once you have all of this information, check to see which of the following guidelines applies:

•If the copyright notice is truly absent from a work that was published before 1978, it is in the public domain.

•If the copyright notice is truly absent from a work that was published after 1978 but more than five years ago, it is *probably* in the public domain.

•If the copyright notice is truly absent from a work that was published after 1978 but less than five years ago, it may or may not be in the public domain, since the author still has a chance to claim copyright.

If you plan to use materials that fall into the last two categories, most copyright lawyers would recommend conducting a formal inquiry into the copyright status of the work. This is particularly true now that the U.S. adheres to the Berne Copyright Convention, since the Berne Treaty does not require the display of a copyright notice as a condition of copyright protection.

International Issues

The public domain question becomes even more complex when materials cross international boundaries. Here is how the U.S. Copyright Office describes the problem:

> **Even if you conclude that a work is in the public domain in the United States, this does not necessarily mean that you are free to use it in other countries. Every nation has its own laws governing the length and scope of copyright protection, and these are applicable to uses of the work within that nation's borders. Thus, the expiration or loss of copyright protection in the United States may still leave the work fully protected against unauthorized use in other countries.[3]**

As this statement warns, the laws governing the status and use of public domain materials often differ from one nation to the next. If you are planning to incorporate public domain materials in a production that will be sold or distributed internationally, be sure to consult a lawyer who is familiar with international copyright law. More information on international copyright appears later in this chapter

Purchasing Public Domain Materials

Rather than spending time searching for public domain materials, many producers prefer to purchase needed items from services that specialize in rights-free materials. There are two advantages to this approach. First, because most services stockpile and catalog large libraries of materials, they can usually help you find appropriate items quickly and efficiently. Second, because many agencies will warrant that the materials are indeed free from copyright claims, you need to worry less about infringement suits initiated by irate copyright owners. Considering how difficult it can be to determine whether a work is truly in the public domain, this last advantage is especially significant.

If you do plan to purchase public domain materials, make sure that your arrangement with the supplier is covered by a written agreement like the one shown in Figure 4.2. Your agreement should specify the items that you are purchasing, the rights that you have to use and modify those items, and how

---

[3]How to Investigate the Copyright Status of a Work. Circular R22, Copyright Office, Library of Congress.

long you will retain the rights to the items. Just as important, your contract should contain warranty and indemnity clauses that protect you from any legal action arising from copyright claims.

The sample contract in Figure 4.2 is a blanket agreement that defines the relationship between cable television network and a supplier of film and video footage. In this case, the cable network is producing a program about animals, and the supplier will provide footage from its inventory to use in the program. The contract stipulates that the network, The Family Channel, can license footage from the supplier's inventory at a flat rate of $350 per minute for material actually used in the production. The contract also stipulates that the rights granted to the network are non-exclusive (meaning that the supplier is free to sell the same footage to someone else), that the rights to the footage are limited to the program specified (meaning that the network is not free to use the materials in other programs); and that the network is allowed to edit or modify the footage in any way that it sees fit.

The license period for the footage runs from January 1, 1989 to December 31, 1994. If The Family Channel plans to exhibit the programs containing the footage after that date, it must negotiate a new agreement with the supplier. Other clauses in the contract define the territory where the programs containing the footage can be transmitted, how many times the programs can be transmitted, and how and when the supplier will be paid for the footage.

Although the contract shown in Figure 4.2 was written to cover the purchase of copyright-free material, a similar sort of agreement should be drawn up when you are negotiating for the right to use copyrighted materials. For more information, see the section on negotiating with copyright owners that appears later in this chapter.

CONDUCTING A COPYRIGHT INVESTIGATION

If you are unable to determine whether a work is copyrighted, or if you require more information about the current copyright status of a work, a copyright investigation may be in order. Although this may sound like something that only a lawyer could conduct, the process is quite simple. All it requires is a little time, a little information and a little money. Because a copyright investigation involves the services of a government agency, it also requires a little paperwork.

Initiating a Copyright Investigation

Most copyright investigations follow a straightforward, two-step process. You first examine the work in question for a copyright notice and any other information that may help to identify the author, publisher, and place and date of

Figure 4.2: Contract Covering the Licensing of Public Domain Footage

AGREEMENT dated November 6, 1988 by and between The Family Channel, Inc., 1108 Broadway, New York, New York 10017 ("TFC") and Hanczor Film Library, 217 West 62th St., New York, NY 10019 ("Grantor").

The parties hereby agree as follows:

1. Grant of Cable Television Rights

For each Picture, Grantor hereby grants to TFC the non-exclusive right and license to exhibit, distribute, transmit and perform each Picture or part thereof on Cable Television as part of the TFC program "Nature's Way" in the Territory an unlimited number of times on each Exhibition Day during the License Period, and in connection therewith to use and perform any and all music, lyrics and musical compositions contained in each Picture.

1.1. "Picture" means any film material selected from the Grantor's library.

1.2. "Cable Television" means the medium in which exhibitions of audiovisual works are delivered or transmitted by any technological means, now or hereafter known, through affiliates (such as affiliated systems or stations), to customers ("Subscribers") who are not all assembled in a single location and who are obligated to pay for the privilege of receiving such exhibitions on a particular channel or station, it being understood that the license to the subscribers shall not entitle them to receive possession of physical materials embodying such audiovisual works and that TFC will not authorize subscribers to charge an admission fee for the privilege of watching any such audiovisual work.

1.3. "Exhibition Day" means any 24-hour period beginning at such time as TFC shall determine in each instance, which may vary from day to day and from time zone to time zone. Under the terms of this Agreement, the number of Exhibition Days in the License Period will be unlimited.

1.4. "License Period" under the terms of this Agreement means the period from January 1, 1989 through December 31, 1994.

Figure 4.2: Contract Covering the Licensing of Public Domain Footage (cont'd.)

1.5. "Territory" means the United States, its territories and possessions (including Puerto Rico) and Canada.

2. Reserved Rights

All rights not specifically granted herein are reserved to Grantor.

3. Delivery of Materials

Copies of materials selected from the Grantor's library shall be delivered to TFC on 1-inch videotape within five working days of the Grantor's receipt of a written request for the materials from TFC. At the end of the License Period, TFC will return all materials received under this Agreement to TFC.

Upon Grantor's request, TFC shall deliver individual copies of programs in which Grantor's materials have been used to Grantor and Grantor shall store the copies throughout the License Period at Grantor's sole cost and expense. At the end of the License Period, Grantor shall return the copies to TFC.

4. Consideration and Payment

In full consideration of all rights granted herein and all services performed hereunder, TFC shall pay Grantor a License Fee of $350 per minute of material selected from the Grantor's library and used in the TFC program "Nature's Way."

Grantor will invoice TFC for materials used on a monthly basis. Payment will be due within 30 days following the receipt of each invoice by TFC.

5. Incidental Rights

TFC shall have editing rights with respect to each of the Pictures, including the right to cut and dub each Picture, to excerpt portions of each Picture and to combine the excerpts with material from other pictures and programs, and to replace or superimpose matter over the music and sound

Figure 4.2: Contract Covering the Licensing of Public Domain Footage (cont'd.)

effects track or over the full sound track of each picture.

6. Warranties

Grantor hereby represents and warrants that it is free to enter into and fully perform this Agreement. Grantor also represents that each Picture is in the public domain and that Grantor has the right to grant all rights granted herein with respect to the copies of the Pictures.

7. Indemnity

Grantor shall at all times indemnify and hold harmless TFC, its licensees, assignees, and affiliated companies, and the officers, directors, employees and agents of TFC against and from any and all claims, damages, liabilities, costs and expenses, including reasonable counsel fees, herein collectively called "claims," arising out of any breach by Grantor of any representation, warranty or other provision hereof. In the event of any claim or service of process upon TFC involving the indemnification set forth in this section of this Agreement, TFC shall notify Grantor of the claim. Grantor will promptly adjust, settle, defend or otherwise dispose of such claim at its sole cost. If Grantor has been so notified and is not diligently and continuously pursuing such matter, TFC may take such action on behalf of itself and/or as attorney-in-fact for Grantor, to adjust, settle, defend or otherwise dispose of such claim, in which case Grantor shall, upon being billed therefor, promptly reimburse TFC in the amount thereof.

TFC shall at all times indemnify and hold harmless Grantor, its licensees, assignees, and affiliated companies, and the officers, directors, employees and agents of Grantor against and from any and all claims, damages, liabilities, costs and expenses, including reasonable counsel fees, herein collectively called "claims,' arising out of any breach by Grantor of any representation, warranty or other provision thereof or any unauthorized use of the programs in which Grantor's materials are used. In the event of any claim or service of process upon Grantor involving the indemnification set forth in this section of this Agreement,

Figure 4.2: Contract Covering the Licensing of Public Domain Footage (cont'd.)

Grantor shall notify TFC of the claim. TFC shall promptly adjust, settle, defend, or otherwise dispose of such claim at its sole cost. If TFC has been so notified and is not diligently and continuously pursuing such matter, Grantor may take such action on behalf of itself and.or as attorney-in-fact for TFC, to adjust, settle, defend or otherwise dispose of such claim, in which case TFC shall, upon being billed therefor, promptly reimburse Grantor in the amount thereof.

8. Miscellaneous

This Agreement contains the entire understanding and supersedes all prior understandings between the parties hereto relating to the subject matter herein. This Agreement cannot be changed or terminated orally.

This Agreement and all matters or issues collateral thereto shall be governed by the laws of the State of New York applicable to contracts executed and performed entirely therein.

IN WITNESS WHEREOF, the parties hereto execute this Agreement as of the date first specified above.

THE FAMILY CHANNEL INC. ("TFC")

BY:_____

HANCZOR FILM LIBRARY

BY:_____

publication. Then you complete the search request form shown in Figure 4.3 and submit the form to the Copyright Office. For a fee of $10 per hour or each fraction of an hour, the Copyright Office will review its records and issue a search report.

The more information that you are able to supply with your request, the more successful the search is likely to be. The Copyright Office asks that you

Figure 4.3 Copyright Search Request Form

search request form

Copyright Office
Library of Congress
Washington, D.C. 20559

Reference & Bibliography
Section
(202) 707-6850
8:30 a.m.-5 p.m. Monday-Friday

Type of work:

☐ Book ☐ Music ☐ Motion Picture ☐ Drama ☐ Sound Recording
☐ Photograph/Artwork ☐ Map ☐ Periodical ☐ Contribution

Search information you require:

☐ Registration ☐ Renewal ☐ Assignment ☐ Address

Specifics of work to be searched:

TITLE: _____

AUTHOR: _____

COPYRIGHT CLAIMANT (if known): _____
(name in © notice)

APPROXIMATE YEAR DATE OF PUBLICATION/CREATION: _____

REGISTRATION NUMBER (if known): _____

OTHER IDENTIFYING INFORMATION: _____

If you need more space please attach additional pages.

Estimates are based on the Copyright Office fee of $10.00 an hour or fraction of an hour consumed. The more information you furnish as a basis for the search the better service we can provide.
Names, titles, and short phrases are not copyrightable.

Please read Circular 22 for more information on copyright searches.

YOUR NAME: _____

ADDRESS: _____

DAYTIME TELEPHONE NO. ( ) _____

Convey results of estimate/search by telephone   Fee enclosed? ☐ yes Amount $
☐ yes   ☐ no   ☐ no

C-768

provide as much of the following information as possible:

•the type of work involved (book, play, musical composition, sound recording, photograph and so on);

•the title of the work, with any possible variants;

•the name of the authors or creators, including possible pseudonyms;

•the approximate year when the work was created, published or registered with the Copyright Office; and

•the name of the probable copyright owners, which may be the publisher or, in the case of audiovisual works, the producer.

Many films, video productions and audiovisual works are based on copyrighted books, short stories or magazine articles. Many may also include music or video footage that exists under a separate copyright. If you want the Copyright Office to search for information about these underlying materials, you must indicate this in your search request. You must also provide as many details as possible about the underlying materials. Often, this information is available as part of the copyright notice or production credits on the work in question.

Once the Copyright Office receives your information, it will send you an estimate of how much your copyright search is likely to cost. If you prefer, the Copyright Office will convey the estimate and the results of the search by telephone. To receive the information by phone, you simply check the appropriate box on the search request form and provide your daytime phone number. Otherwise, the estimate and search report will be sent by mail.

The $10 per hour charge covers the cost of the Copyright Office employee who will perform your search. If you would rather not to pay this fee, or if you require the information immediately, you can conduct your own copyright search. Most records of the Copyright Office are open to public inspection weekdays from 8:30 a.m. to 5 p.m. Of course, unless you live in the Washington, D.C. area or near one of the libraries in the United States that maintains a copy of the Copyright Office's *Catalog of Copyright Entries*, a do-it-yourself search will cost you traveling expenses. It will also necessitate time away from the office, studio or editing room for you or a designated employee. For these reasons, most media producers let the Copyright Office do the searching for them. If you work in a corporate setting, your company's legal office may be willing to handle the search for you.

Limitations of Copyright Investigations

Although a copyright investigation can uncover key information about a work, the results of a copyright search are not always conclusive. Notably, you should not assume that a work is in the public domain simply because a search fails to turn up a record of the work. The reason for this is simple: the Copyright Office files contain records on all works registered through the office, but a work does not have to be registered to be copyrighted.

For reasons explained earlier in this chapter, the following types of materials are probably protected by copyright even though they are not registered with the Copyright Office:

•any work published after 1978 (although there are several advantages to registering);

•works published before 1978 with a copyright notice that are still in their first 28-year term of protection (although they must be registered by the end of the 28th year); and

•unpublished works created before 1978, which are entitled to copyright protection under provisions contained in common law.

A copyright search may also be inconclusive for any of these reasons:

•the work may have been registered recently, and the information has not yet been cataloged;

•the information in the search request may not have been complete or specific enough to identify the work; or

•the work may have been registered under a different title or as part of a larger work.

For all of these reasons, search reports are most useful for documenting the status of copyrighted works that are registered with the Copyright Office. They are much less useful for verifying that a work is free from copyright protection.

OBTAINING THE RIGHTS TO USE COPYRIGHTED MATERIALS

As the preceding sections have shown, media producers who use or "borrow" other people's material must consider the implications of their actions.

Producers who simply shrug off these concerns place themselves, their productions and their companies at considerable risk. This does not mean that producers should avoid using copyrighted material in their programs—only that they should follow proper permissions procedures.

When you are thinking of adding someone else's material to a production, follow these steps:

(1.) Determine whether the material is protected by copyright or in the public domain. To make this determination, use the guidelines provided earlier in this chapter on the use of public domain materials. If you determine that the work is in the public domain, you are free to use it without seeking permissions or clearances. If the work is *not* in the public domain, proceed to step 2.

(2.) Determine whether your use of the copyrighted material will qualify as fair use under the Copyright Act of 1976. To make this determination, review the fair use checklist and guidelines on fair use that appear on pages 86-90. If your use qualifies as fair use, you are free to use the materials without seeking permissions or clearances. If the use fails the fair use test, proceed to step 3.

(3.) If the materials fail the public domain or fair use test, you must contact the copyright owner and request permission to use the work.[4]

To receive permission to use a copyrighted work, you must first find the copyright owner. Then, once the copyright owner indicates a willingness to grant permission, you must negotiate the specific rights that you will have to the work. In most cases, you will also need to negotiate a fee for using the work.

Contacting the Copyright Owner

Reaching the current copyright owner is not always as simple as it sounds. Often the original copyright owner listed on the work is not the current copy-

---

[4]As mentioned earlier, the permissions process for music differs from the process described here. For more information about licensing music, see Chapter 6.

right owner. And even when the copyright notice does list the correct individual as the copyright owner, sometimes the work offers no clues to the individual's current whereabouts.

When information about the current owner is hard to come by, media producers must become copyright detectives. Start by searching the work for any clues that might help you locate the owner. For example, even though the copyright notice may not reveal the copyright owner's address, the address of the publisher or distributor is probably provided somewhere on the work. In many cases, the copyright owner has given the publishing or distribution company the rights to license the work. When this is the case, a call to the company's "rights and permissions" department may be all that is needed to get the permissions process started. If the copyright owner has retained these "sublicensing" rights, the publisher or distributor can usually provide the address or phone number of the current copyright owner.

Here are some suggested steps for producers who find themselves thrust into the role of copyright detectives:

(1.) Examine the work for a copyright notice. The notice will list the name of the company or individual who owned the work at the time that this version was published. Search the copyright notice and the area surrounding the notice, the title page (in the case of printed material) and the credits and outside packaging (in the case of videotapes and other audiovisual materials) for clues to where the copyright owner can be reached. If this search uncovers sufficient information, try to contact the copyright owner directly.

(2.) If you are unable to reach the copyright owner, search the work for information about the publisher or distributor. If this search is successful, contact the publisher or distributor and determine if the company has the rights to negotiate permissions for the copyright owner. If the company has these rights, begin the negotiations. If the company does not have the rights, have them put you in touch with the copyright owner.

(3.) If you are unable to determine the copyright owner or publisher, you may need to conduct a copyright investigation. As explained earlier in this chapter, a properly conducted copyright investigation will uncover any information about the work that is stored in the files of the Copyright Office. Assuming that the work was registered with the Copyright

Office, the files will contain information about the original
copyright owner and any transfers of ownership that have
been registered with the office.

Needless to say, this detective work can consume considerable time and
effort. Before beginning the process, determine how much you want the
work in question and exactly how much time you are willing to devote to
securing the proper permissions. You should also have some alternative
materials in mind. As you approach your time limit, evaluate the situation.
Are you close to reaching a deal with the copyright owner? If you are not
close, how much additional time and effort are the materials worth? Will
alternative materials suffice?

When the permissions process drags on, producers are sometimes tempted
to abandon the copyright quest and use the materials without permission. If
this temptation strikes, resist. If you do decide to give up the copyright quest,
be sure that you also decide, at the same time, to abandon any thought of
using the materials.

Negotiating with Copyright Owners

Once you contact the copyright owner, the negotiations for the right to use
the materials can begin. During the discussions, keep one key consideration
in mind: copyright is a property right. This means that copyright owners
truly do own and control their creative works, much in the way that you
might own and control the use of a home, automobile or some other piece of
personal property. In other words, if a copyright owner does not want to let
you use his/her creative property, he or she does not have to.

In actual practice, however, most copyright owners will be willing to grant
the permission that you are after—provided that they have something to gain.
Usually, this something is cash payment, promotional considerations or both.
For example, most movie studios willingly supply film clips to television
reviewers as part of their effort to promote their new films. For the same reason, many record companies have been willing to supply music videos to
MTV and other music-oriented television services. However, as production
costs have risen, some record companies have determined that the promotional value provided by the music TV programs is not sufficient consideration. As a result, a growing number of companies now require music TV programs to pay for the videos that they air.

Before you enter into serious negotiations with a copyright owner, take
time to assess your bargaining position. In many cases, you may discover
that *you* have the advantage in the negotiations, not the copyright owner.
After all, you will be offering many copyright owners what amounts to an

unexpected gift—the chance to collect a bit of revenue from a property that might otherwise simply sit on a shelf collecting dust. Of course, this is more likely to be the case if you are asking permission to use clips from a documentary production or corporate video program, rather than material from a hit TV show or feature film.

If possible, begin your negotiations with a phone call to the copyright owner. Explain what materials you would like to use, how you plan to use them and what you are willing to offer as consideration. Then, assuming you are able to agree on these fundamental terms, follow up with a written agreement that specifies:

•The material you are licensing. Include the running time of the segments, plus a brief description that identifies the material (e.g., "the five-minute, 45-second interview with Charlie Elliot, legendary jazz guitarist, from your film *The Guitar Slingers*);

•How you will use the material (e.g., "for use in a video documentary on the history of jazz music in the United States");

•How your production will be distributed (e.g., "for sale on videocassette to schools and libraries");

•How long you will have the rights to use the material (e.g., "for the 10-year period beginning January 1, 1990 and ending December 31, 1999");

•What rights you will have to modify and edit the material; and

•What "consideration" you will provide to the copyright owner for the right to use the material.

Like the agreement shown in Figure 4.2, your contract should also include a clause in which the copyright owner warrants that he truly does have the right to license the materials.

During your negotiations with copyright owners, much of the bargaining will focus on the consideration, or payment, that you are offering in return for the rights to use the material. As you negotiate the consideration, remember the guidelines offered earlier. Above all, know how badly you need the materials and exactly how much you are willing to pay. Do not expect the copyright owner to give materials away, but do not allow yourself to be held hostage to unreasonable demands. Instead, have some alternative materials in mind, and make it known that you are willing to use the alternatives if the price is not right.

Another potential snag in negotiations with copyright owners is the issue of artistic control. As the person who is paying for rights, you want complete control over how material will be used in your production. In particular, you want the right to edit and modify the materials so they fit with the purpose and "look" of your production.

That may be what you want, but that may not be what the copyright owner is willing to provide. As part of licensing agreements, some copyright owners insist on retaining some measure of control over how their materials are used. This is particularly true when the materials have historic or artistic significance. For example, the family of a deceased actor may be unwilling to license clips from the actor's classic films unless you certify that the clips will be used to portray the actor in a positive light.

As a rule, avoid agreements that place restrictions on the manner in which you can use the licensed materials. Even though these restrictions may seem innocent, they leave your production decision open to interpretation and, ultimately, legal action. If you must sign a licensing agreement that restricts your ability to edit or modify the materials, make sure that the restrictions are spelled out in detail. In particular, the agreement should specify how and when the copyright owner will be allowed to review the production, as well as how any dispute over the use of the materials will be resolved.

Moral Rights

Media producers should also be aware of the growing movement to grant artists the right to control how their work is modified even after they have sold the copyright. Proponents of "moral rights" or "droit moral" hold that artists in the United States should have the legal right to prevent the distortion or mutilation of their work. This right is well established in many European countries, particularly those countries that subscribe to the Berne Copyright Convention and its provision that authors should have the right to object to the distribution or modification of their works even after the works have been sold.

In the United States, federal law does not grant most creators of copyrighted works this type of protection. However, several states have enacted legislation in this area, and a 1990 amendment to the Copyright Act of 1976 did grant the creators of certain visual works (but not audiovisual productions) limited rights to protect the "integrity" of their works after sale.

What does all of this mean for media producers? First, producers in New York, California, Massachusetts and other states that have passed moral rights legislation should be aware of the restrictions that state laws place on their right to edit and modify licensed materials without the original copyright owner's consent. In these states, it is particularly important that your contract with the copyright owner spell out these rights in detail.

Second, producers who are licensing the rights to use works created in countries other than the United States should make sure that their use of the materials is governed by U.S. law, rather than by the laws of the nation in which the works were originally copyrighted. In most cases, this is simply a matter of making sure that the licensing agreement includes a clause to this effect.

Finally, producers should continue to monitor efforts at state and federal levels to broaden artists' moral rights to works that they sold or licensed. This will be especially important if, as has been proposed, Congress further amends the Copyright Act of 1976 to incorporate more of the moral rights granted in the Berne Copyright Treaty.

Errors and Omissions Insurance

Many licensing agreements include a clause that requires the licensor (the individual or company that is selling the materials) to certify that the transaction is covered by errors and omissions (E&O) insurance. Errors and omissions insurance protects both parties if the licensor's right to license the materials is ever called into question. A typical E&O clause might include the following legal language:

> **Upon execution of this agreement, and prior to the payment of any portion of the license fee described hereunder, the licensor shall secure a policy of Errors and Omissions liability insurance applicable to the program material described hereunder. Such policy shall name the licensee as additional insured and shall have limits of at least $1 million per occurrence with respect to each loss or claim involving the same offending act, failure to act, or matter whether made by one or more persons and regardless of frequency of repetition. Such policy shall be secured at the licensor's own cost and shall be maintained by the licensor until thirty (30) days after the expiration of the license period described hereunder. Promptly after execution, Licensor shall provide Licensee with a certificate of insurance outlining the foregoing terms and provisions.**

In simple terms, this language requires the licensor to certify that the materials are covered by an errors and omissions policy, that the licensee (the group that is purchasing the materials) is listed as an "additional insured" on the policy and that the policy provides for adequate levels of protection if disputes over ownership of the licensed materials result in judgments against the parties.

Errors and omissions clauses are most common in contracts that cover the licensing of entire films or videos from distributors and production companies. Because the distributor or production company is often not the original or sole copyright owner, the group that is licensing the work will usually seek some extra protection against the possibility of copyright suits over licensing rights. Errors and omissions insurance provides this protection. (For more information about production insurance, see Chapter 5.)

Additional Concerns for Licensing Photographs, Scripts, Works-Made-for-Hire and Other Special Materials

The guidelines offered so far should cover most situations in which a producer is licensing the rights to use copyrighted materials. However, some situations and materials warrant special caution. Here is a selected list:

•**The use of copyrighted photographs in media productions.** As intellectual properties go, an 8-by-10-inch photograph may seem too small to create much of a copyright fuss. However, as creative properties, photographs can be, and generally are, protected by copyright. As a result, you must secure permission from the copyright owner before using a photograph in a production. Significantly, since you will usually display the entire photograph, the use of a copyrighted photograph rarely qualifies as fair use.

•**The use of works created as works-made-for-hire.** In these cases, the copyright owner is not the creator of the work, but rather the company for which the creator worked. Make sure that you are negotiating with the correct party.

•**The licensing of scripts.** When you are licensing a finished script, take special care to define the rights that the writer will retain to the work. Is the deal a "buyout," or will the writer receive royalties from the revenues generated by the finished production?

•**The licensing of film or video rights to a literary work.** Is the deal a buyout, or will the author of the work receive royalties? Also, is the literary work based on underlying works that may raise additional copyright questions?

In the last two cases, the licensing agreement should take the form of a full-fledged contract that is prepared, or at least reviewed, by a competent copyright lawyer. For more information about contracts, see Chapters 2 and 3.

INTERNATIONAL COPYRIGHT

As you know, works created by the United States citizens are protected by the Copyright Act of 1976. But what about works created in foreign countries or works created in the United States by foreign citizens? These materials are also protected by the Copyright Act of 1976, provided they meet the following qualifications from Section 104 of the Act:

•They are unpublished works, which the Act protects "without regard to the nationality or domicility of the author."

•They are published works created by an author who, on the date of first publication, is a domiciliary of the United States or a "national, domiciliary, or sovereign authority of a foreign nation that is a party of a copyright treaty to which the United States is also a party."

•They are published works created by an author who, on the date of first publication, is a "stateless person, wherever that person may be domiciled."

•The work was first published in the United States or a foreign country that, on the date of first publication, was a party to the Universal Copyright Convention.

•The work was first published by United Nations or the Organization of American States.

•The work comes within the scope of copyright protection extended under a presidential decree issued when the president determines that a foreign nation is providing copyright protection to U.S. authors "on substantially the same basis" as that provided to its own citizens.

As Figure 4.4 shows, more than 80 nations are signatories to one or more international copyright treaties to which the U.S. subscribes. In most cases, this means that foreign authors from a signatory nation must receive the same copyright protection within the boundaries of another signatory nation as that nation extends to its own citizens.

Figure 4.4 lists countries that had established formal copyright relations with the United States as of June 30, 1987. However, you should not assume that a foreign work is free from copyright protection simply because it was created in a country that is absent from the list. The country in question may

Figure 4.4: Countries That Have Established Formal Copyright Relations With the United States as of June 30, 1987

The following lists countries have established some level of formal copyright relations with the United States. In most cases, this means that the country is a signatory to at least one international copyright treaty or agreement to which the United States is also a signatory.

Algeria	Germany	Nigeria
Andorra	Ghana	Norway
Argentina	Greece	Pakistan
Australia	Guatemala	Panama
Austria	Guinea	Paraguay
Bahamas, The	Haiti	Peru
Bangladesh	Honduras	Philippines
Barbados	Hungary	Poland
Belgium	Iceland	Portugal
Belize	India	Romania
Bolivia	Ireland	Saint Vincent and the
Brazil	Israel	Grenadines
Bulgaria	Italy	Senegal
Cambodia	Japan	Singapore
Cameroon	Kenya	South Africa
Canada	Laos	Soviet Union
Chile	Lebanon	Spain
China	Liberia	Sri Lanka
Columbia	Liechtenstein	Sweden
Costa Rica	Luxembourg	Switzerland
Cuba	Malawi	Thailand
Czechoslovakia	Malta	Tunisia
Denmark	Mauritius	United Kingdom
Dominican Republic	Mexico	Uruguay
Ecuador	Monaco	Vatican City
El Salvador	Morocco	Venezuela
Fiji	NetherlandsNew	Yugoslavia
Finland	Zealand	Zambia
France	Nicaragua	

be a recent signatory to a copyright treaty, it may have only recently clarified its copyright position or it may be covered by copyright protection extended under a presidential decree. To determine a country's current copyright status, contact the U.S. Copyright Office or a copyright lawyer.

For media producers, the message is clear—approach all works created by foreign citizens with the same care and caution that you direct toward American works. In fact, foreign materials often required extra caution and care. The exact copyright status of these works can be difficult to determine, and the copyright owner can often be difficult to contact. With this in mind, you may want to work with a lawyer who is familiar with international copyright law.

The Berne Convention

On March 1, 1989 the United States officially entered into the Berne Convention for the Protection of Literary and Artistic Work—the treaty more commonly known as the Berne Convention. As mentioned earlier in this chapter in the section on Moral Rights, one implication of the United States joining the Berne Union is that authors may eventually be given new rights to control the modification of their work. Another implication is that the display of a proper copyright notice is no longer required to ensure continued copyright protection. This last change was made when Congress passed the Berne Convention Implementation Act of 1988, a bill that made several, mostly small changes to the Copyright Act of 1976 to bring it more in line with the Berne treaty.

To media producers, one clear benefit of the United States joining the Berne Convention is broader international copyright protection of their work. All members of the Berne Convention must provide at least the minimum level of copyright protection specified in the treaty. In addition, members must agree to offer citizens of foreign countries the same level of copyright protection that they offer to their own citizens.

SUMMARY

What is copyright?

Copyright is a series of property rights granted to the creators of literary, artistic, musical, dramatic and audiovisual works. Copyright gives the creators of these works the exclusive right to reproduce and distribute copies of their works, to create derivative works, and to perform and display the work publicly. Copyright also gives creators and authors the right to determine whether their work will be used as part of another work, including films, video programs and other audiovisual productions.

What are the sources of copyright law?

In the United States, the primary source of copyright law is the Copyright Act of 1976. This comprehensive federal legislation supersedes all state copyright law and all previous federal copyright laws.

What can be copyrighted?

Almost any creative work that appears in a fixed form can be copyrighted. Works that can be copyrighted include: books and plays; films, TV programs and other audiovisual works; scripts for audiovisual works; photographs and paintings; music and sound recordings; and computer software.

What cannot be copyrighted?

Items that cannot be copyrighted include ideas, materials produced by federal government employees as part of their jobs, scientific and factual information, inventions and industrial processes, and titles of products or services. However, several of these items may be eligible for other types of protection, including patents and trademarks.

How is copyright established?

Under the current copyright law, copyright is automatically established as soon as a work is created in fixed form. To ensure maximum protection, the work should include a copyright notice and be registered with the U.S. Copyright Office.

How long does copyright last?

Works created after January 1, 1978 are protected for the life of the author plus 50 years. If the author is listed as a group or organization, as is often the case with media productions, the term of a copyright is 75 years from the date of publication. The term for works created before 1978 varies. The maximum term for these works is 75 years from the date that the copyright first became effective.

What is copyright infringement?

Copyright infringement occurs when someone uses a work in a manner that violates the copyright owner's exclusive rights in the work. The most common violations include duplicating copies of the work or creating derivative works without the copyright owner's express permission. Copyright infringement is a violation of federal law.

What is fair use?

Section 107 of the Copyright Act of 1976 defines several conditions under which it is legal to use a copyrighted work without the copyright owner's permission. When a use satisfies Section 107's criteria, it qualifies as a fair use. An unauthorized use is most likely to qualify as a fair use if it is educational or informational in nature, if the work being copied is a reference or other nonfiction work and if the use has little or no impact on the potential market for the work.

What are public domain materials?

Public domain materials are works that are free from copyright protection. This category includes works that were never copyrighted, works that cannot be copyrighted, works for which the copyright has expired or works for which the copyright has been abandoned. When a work is in the public domain, you are free to use it without seeking permission from the original creator or copyright owner.

How do you obtain the rights to use copyrighted materials?

To obtain the rights to use copyrighted materials, you must first contact the individual, group or company that controls the copyright. Then you must negotiate a licensing agreement that specifies the materials that are covered by the agreement, the rights that you will have to use and modify the materials, the duration of those rights and the consideration that you will offer the copyright owner.

5

PLAYING IT SAFE: PERMITS, RELEASES, LIBEL, AND PRODUCTION INSURANCE

As the preceding chapters have shown, part of a producer's job is to think defensively. Producers must anticipate the many legal matters that can come up during production, and they must work to protect their projects against the possibility of lawsuits and other legal challenges. Chapters 2 and 3 discussed ways that carefully written contracts can protect all parties in a media production, and Chapter 4 described steps that producers can take to prevent challenges over the use of copyrighted materials. This chapter introduces three more weapons that should be part of every producer's defensive arsenal: shooting permits, talent and location releases, and production insurance. You will also learn about privacy and libel law, two areas of media law that are of increasing concern for media producers.

SHOOTING OR LOCATION PERMITS

Many states and municipalities require producers to obtain permits for location work—particularly when that work will be performed on public thoroughfares or other government property. In many localities, these *shooting* or *location* permits are issued by state, county or city offices that serve as liaisons between producers and the police department, fire department and other public agencies that will provide services or supervision during the course of the shoot. For the names and addresses of these film and television offices, see Appendix A.

Types of Permits

The term *shooting permit* is actually a bit misleading, since keeping a location shoot legal can often involve obtaining an entire series of permits and licenses. If you were planning a location shoot in Los Angeles, for example, some of the federal, state, county and local forms required might include:

• If you will be shooting on property owned or controlled by the U.S. government, you may need to obtain a permit from the federal agency that administers the property.

113

Figure 5.1: Sample State Shooting Permit

```
                        STATE OF CALIFORNIA
                  PHOTOGRAPHY/MOTION PICTURE PERMIT


                                          Date_____

                                          Permit #_____
Company Name_____

Address_____

Telephone No._____Attachment_____

Production Title_____

Type of Production_____

Unit Mgr._____Assistant Dir._____

Location Mgr._____Other Personnel_____

Location (s)_____
_____
_____
_____

Activity_____
_____
_____

Exterior_____Interior_____

Date (s)            Between the Hours   Film  Construct  Strike

_____     _____     ( )    ( )       ( )
_____     _____     ( )    ( )       ( )
_____     _____     ( )    ( )       ( )
_____     _____     ( )    ( )       ( )
Total # of Days_____# of Personnel_____
Vehicles and Equipment_____

Pyrotechnics:_____License #_____Special FX #_____

Department Approval By _____

Estimated Department Operating/Personnel Cost _____

Permittee agrees to comply with all applicable laws and to maintain the premises in good
condition and to return said premises in the same condition as they were before said use.

Unless greater coverage is requested in writing by State, permittee agrees to furnish to
the State of California evidence of at least one million dollars comprehensive general
liability insurance in the form of a certificate, covering the entire period of this
permit, naming the State of California and its employees as additional insured.


_____    _____
    Name of Insurance Company           Expiration Date

                                                    CPO003
                                                    CALIF
```

Figure 5.1: Sample State Shooting Permit (cont'd.)

Permittee waives all claims against State, its officers, agents and employees, for loss or damage caused by, arising out of or in any way connected with the exercise of this permit and permittee agrees to save harmless, indemnify and defend State, its officers, agents and employees, from any and all loss, damage or liability which may be suffered or incurred by State, its officers, agents and employees caused by, arising out of or in any way connected with exercise by permittee of the rights hereby permitted, except those arising out of the sole negligence of State.

State shall have the privilege of inspecting the premises covered by this permit at any or all times.

This permit shall not be assigned.

State may terminate this permit at any time if permittee fails to perform any covenant herein contained at the time and in the manner herein provided. State agrees it will not unreasonably exercise this right of termination.

The parties hereto agree that the permittee, its officers, agents and employees, in the performance of this permit, shall act in an independent capacity and not as officers, employees or agents of State.

No alternation or variation of the terms of this permit shall be valid unless made in writing and signed by the parties hereto.

Permittee will not discriminate against any employee or applicant for employment because of race, color, religion, ancestry, sex, age, national origin or physical handicap. The permittee will take affirmative action to insure that applicants are employed and that employees are treated during employment, without regard to their race, color, religion, ancestry, sex, age, national origin or physical handicap.

Permittee agrees to comply with the terms and conditions contained in the attached Exhibit(s)_____, which terms and conditions are by this reference made a part thereof.

The permittee hereby agrees to comply with all the rules and regulations of the facility or institution subject to this permit.

_____   _____
Director,   Company Representative
California Film Office

I hereby further certify that all conditions for exemption have been complied with and this document is exempt from the Department of General Services' approval.

I hereby certify that all conditions for exemption set forth in State Administrative Manual Section 1209 have been complied with and this document is exempt from review or approval by the Department of Finance.

• If you will be shooting on any state owned or operated property, you will need to complete the State of California photography/motion picture permit (see Figure 5.1).

• If you will be employing actors who are minors, you will need an entertainment work permit from the California Division of Labor Standards Enforcement.

• Because the shoot will take place in Los Angeles, you will have to complete the Los Angeles filming permit (see Figure 5.2).

• If you will be shooting on roads or property controlled by the County of Los Angeles, you will also require a county filming permit.

• If your shoot will include any special effects that involve explosions, smoke, open flames or other pyrotechnics, you will need to obtain a special effects permit from the Los Angeles Fire Department.

• If you will be working with animals, you will need a motion picture, television and theatrical permit from the Los Angeles Department of Animal Regulation.

• Because Los Angeles has a motion picture production tax, you will need to complete forms supplied by the tax and permit division of the city clerk's office.

How can you determine which types of forms and permits apply to your production? Begin by contacting the film and television office operated by the state where you will be conducting your location work. Addresses and phone numbers for these agencies appear in Appendix A. The agency will be able to tell you what state permits you must complete and what, if any, county or local film bureau serves the area where you will conduct your location work.[1]

In your dealings with government film agencies, remember that they serve a dual role. Their first duty is to attract your media production business and the jobs and tax revenue that your business generates to the state or community that they serve. Then, once they have attracted your business, the agencies must make sure that you conduct your productions safely and with the

---

[1]In some localities, there is no film and video office at the state or local level. When this is the case, direct your initial inquiries to the mayor's office or police department in the community where you plan to conduct the shoot.

Figure 5.2: Sample Filming Permit

Distribution:
1—Permit Office (W)
2—Applicant (Pink)
3&4—Accounting (Blue)
5—Police (Goldenrod)
6—Fire (Green)
7—Servicing Dept. (Canary)
8—Council Dist. (W)

FILMING PERMIT

BOARD OF PUBLIC WORKS

CITY OF LOS ANGELES

DATE_____

COUNCIL DISTRICT_____

PERMIT Nº **22451**

MOTION PICTURE COORDINATION SECTION, CITY HALL
6640 SUNSET BLVD., SUITE 202, HOLLYWOOD, CALIFORNIA 90028 — PHONE 462-1805

This permit is issued to the applicant by the Board of Public Works, for the purpose of filming a commercial motion picture or still photograph in the City of Los Angeles in accordance with Ordinance No. 144,744 and 147,074.
This permit must be in the possession of the applicant at all times while on location.
Posted Parking Regulations and/or vehicle code violations will be vigorously enforced unless noted otherwise herein.
This permit does not constitute nor grants permission to use or occupy property not belonging to or under the control of the City.

APPLICATION —
TYPEWRITE ONLY — Complete Items 1 thru 12 — Signature is required on other side

1. Company | Address | City | State | Zip

2. Representative and Title | Phone | Ext. | 3. Name of Production and No. | Type

4. Locations (List additional on Schedule A) Public ☐; Private ☐; Restricted Area ☐; Consent Agreements Shown ☐ Yes No ☐
   Loc. 1

   Loc. 2

5. Dates of Filming | Approximate Times
   Loc. 1 | Loc. 2 | Loc. 1 | Loc. 2

6. Summarize Scene to be filmed: Street Closure ☐ YES ☐ NO; Traffic Control ☐ YES ☐ NO;
   Extraordinary Scenes (i.e. robbery, flight, use of fire arms, use of fire and/or explosives) ☐ YES ☐ NO EXPLAIN YES ANSWERS IN DETAIL

7. List Streets to be posted with Temporary Parking Regulation (List Additional on Schedule A)
   Loc. 1 | Date | Type | Log

   Loc. 2 | Date | Type | Log

8. Indicate Number of Vehicles
   Trucks | /Dressing Rms. | /Vans | /Buses | /Generator | /Prod. Cars | /Picture Cars

9. Number of Cast | Crew | WD | 10. Are Animals to be used? | 11. Business Tax Registration Cert. | 12. City services requested (other than Police & Fire) Personnel | Equipment

13. Police Dept. Approvals: | Off-duty Police Officers Required (to be paid by applicant) ☐ Foot Assigned by:
    By | Div. | Date | Number ☐ Motor ☐ City ☐ Applicant
    Special Conditions of Approval

14. Fire Dept. Approval — Issuance of this permit indicates compliance with Sec. 57.110.13 of the Los Angeles Municipal Code
    Fire Safety Officer Required? ☐ YES ☐ NO   Fire Patrol Truck Required? ☐ YES ☐ NO

    Chief's Written Special Permit issued | Permit No. _____ | **Special Effects Permit**
    and approval of this permit given by: | Date | **No.**
    Special Conditions Applicable to Fire Permit

    Approved CFSO _____

15. Fees and Charges — The applicant agrees to pay the following application fee and estimated charges upon request therefor and to pay any additional charges which may accrue incidental to any use or services provided to the applicant within 10 days after receipt of an invoice for said use or services.

SERVICING DEPARTMENT	USE AND/OR SERVICE APPROVED BY	Number days of use	Estimated Charges USE	SERVICE	Final Charges USE	SERVICE	FINAL CHARGES VERIFIED AS CORRECT — SEE ITEM 24 BY	DATE

16. Insurance Submitted CA No. | SUB-TOTALS
17. Filming Advisory Notice/Required | APPLICATION FEE | Still Photograph and/or S.P. Master No.
18. Jurisdictional Endorsements | Total Advance | ☐ CHECK | RECEIPT NO. | MCB NO.
    Applicable _____ | Payment | ☐ CASH

BPW-MPC-1 R. 9/81 | **7045 MOTION PICTURE COORDINATION FUND**

19. On or before the date of the expiration of this permit, the permittee shall remove from said properties all location sets, structures, rubbish and unsightly matter, placed on the property by the applicant; and in the event applicant fails so to do, the City may cause the same to be done and applicant agrees to pay the City its cost incurred therefor.

20. This permit shall not be assigned by the applicant without the written consent of the City.

21. This permit may be terminated at any time by either of the parties hereto, and, until so terminated the applicant agrees to abide by all the terms and conditions hereof, and to pay all fees and charges herein provided.

22. Applicant shall be subject to the City's control, and instructions of the City representative assigned for the purpose, in order to avoid any interference with the operations of the City's facilities or property.

23. Applicant acknowledges and represents that it has inspected City's properties, knows the conditions thereof, and assumes full responsibility for any injury to persons or damage to property by reason of the use of said properties under this permit, and undertakes and agrees to re-lease and hold harmless and indemnify the City and all its officers and employees from and against all actions, claims, loss, demands, expense, damage or liability of any nature whatsoever, for death or injury to any person or damage to any property in any manner arising by reason of or incident to the exercise or enoyment of the premises herein given wether or not caused solely or contributed to by any act or omission, active or passive, negligent or otherwise, of the City, or any officer, employee or agent

24. Other terms and conditions: _____

BOARD OF PUBLIC WORKS

By _____

Principal Coordinator or Authorized Deputy

Date _____

SERVICING DEPARTMENT REPRESENTATIVE — Upon completion of the filming activities, the final charge shall be computed, entered in the appropriate columns under Item 15 and mailed promptly to: Motion Picture Coordination Section.

proper permits. If you supply the agency staff with information about your production, they should be very willing to work with you to obtain and complete the necessary forms and permits. Some state film bureaus also provide one or more of the following services:

• listings and photographs of potential shooting locations,

• information about production insurance,

• assistance with highway and street closings, and/or

• help in resolving disputes with county and local agencies.

For a list of the government agencies that serve as liaisons with media producers, see Appendix A.

Typical Requirements

The sample permit forms shown in Figures 5.1 and 5.2 suggest the range of information and assurances that media producers must supply to secure location permits. Although the exact requirements will vary from one jurisdiction to the next, most applications for shooting permits ask producers to supply the following:

• the names and addresses of the production company and the principal contacts for the shoot,

• dates of the shoot and approximate times,

• a list of the locations and vehicles that will be used in the shoot,

• information about the nature of the production (TV movie or series, feature film, television commercial, etc.),

• brief summaries of the scenes to be shot,

• a list of traffic and crowd control requirements, and

• evidence of liability insurance.

Most applications also require producers to indemnify the issuing government authority against any claims for personal injuries or property damage that may arise from the production. In addition, the producer must assure the issuing authority that the production will comply with all local laws and regulations, and that all locations and public facilities used in the shoot will be left in their original condition. To help ensure that production crews comply with this last requirement, state and local governments sometimes ask production companies to post *faithful performance bonds*—deposits that are forfeited to the state or local government should the production company skip town without repairing any damage done to the location. For more information, contact the appropriate agency listed in Appendix A.

Fees and Penalties

The fees charged for location work will vary, depending on where you will be shooting and your need to involve the police department, fire department or other service agencies. You may be required to pay some or all of the following:

• an application fee for the shooting permit;

• application fees for any additional permits that you may need to obtain from the police department, fire department or other government agencies;

• fees to cover police, fire and custodial services required for the shoot, or a blanket payment that covers all government services provided during the course of the production; and

• any special rental fees required by the agency or authority that administers the shoot site.

If you are caught shooting without the proper permits, the penalties can be severe. At a minimum, you will be forced to suspend production until you obtain the necessary clearances—a delay that can prove extremely costly as talent, crews and rented equipment stand idle. You may also be subject to substantial fines. For some severe violations, particularly unauthorized use of pyrotechnics, the sanctions can include criminal penalties.

PRIVACY AND RELEASES

In the United States, privacy laws protect individuals from intrusions into their personal lives and the unauthorized use of their names or likenesses for commercial purposes. For media producers, this means that it is necessary to secure a written release from each person who appears in a production. In addition, if the production will include location footage shot on private property, it is necessary to obtain a written release from the property owner. Failure to do so can leave a production open to lawsuits for invasion of privacy.

Overview of Privacy Law

As legal concepts go, privacy is a relatively recent development. Most scholars trace the origins of privacy law in the United States to 1890, the year in which when Samuel D. Warren and future U.S. Supreme Court Justice Louis D. Brandeis, wrote an article that argued for statutory or common law recognition of an individual's right to lead a private life.[2] Samuel Warren's interest in privacy was to some degree a personal matter. His wife, a very proper Bostonian, had become the unwilling star of a local newspaper's gossip pages, and Warren was searching for some legal means to protect his family against this media intrusion.

Although the Warren and Brandeis article attracted attention to the issue of privacy, the statutory or common law recognition that the article recommended was slow in coming. After the turn of the century, however, a series of state and federal court decisions gradually began to shape a common law concept of the right to privacy, and some state legislatures passed statutes designed to protect individuals from certain types of intrusion. Unfortunately these state statutes and common law precedents often conflicted, and the privacy protection that emerged varied greatly from one state to the next.

Privacy law still continues to be a confusing mix of state and federal common law; state statutes directed at specific kinds of privacy violations, and a growing number of federal statutes aimed at preventing the misuse of government records and electronic surveillance. However, through all of the confusion and conflicting precedents, four fairly clear categories of privacy protection have emerged:

> **Appropriation:** Individuals have a right to protection against the unauthorized use of their name or likeness for commercial purposes (a right that is often referred to as the *right of publicity*).

> **Intrusion:** Individuals have a right to protection against unwarranted intrusion upon their solitude and private affairs.

> **False Light:** Individuals have a right to protection against publicity that places them in a false light.

> **Public Disclosure:** Individuals have a right to protection against the public disclosure of embarrassing facts about their private lives (although, as discussed later in this chapter, the law provides less protection for public officials than private citizens).

---

[2]Samuel D. Warren and Louis D. Brandeis, "The Right to Privacy," *Harvard Law Review 193 (1890)*.

Together, these four areas of privacy protection constitute the individual's "right to be left alone." Significantly, the right to be left alone includes the right to be left out of media productions.. When individuals consent to waive this, the waiver should take the form of a written, signed release that is retained by the producer.

Performer Releases

As the preceding paragraphs have suggested, releases play an important role in protecting productions from the possibility of privacy lawsuits. As a rule, producers should secure written releases from all performers who appear in a production. The only exceptions would be those individuals who show up as faceless forms in crowd scenes or remote shots. Just make sure that these individuals truly do appear in a form that would not be recognizable to family, friends or a judge and jury.

For performers who are professional actors, the release language is usually included in a complete contract that covers all aspects of their appearance in the production (see Chapter 3). For other performers, including employees depicted in corporate video productions, a release agreement similar to the model shown in Figure 5.3 should suffice. Although the exact wording will differ, all releases should share the following characteristics:

• Releases should be written, even though oral releases are valid in some states. By putting the release in writing, you create a record that documents the exact terms of the agreement.

• Releases should define the duration and extent of the producer's right to use the performer's name and likeness. Exactly what rights will the performer be waiving? How and where will the production in which the performer appears be distributed? How long will the producer retain the right to use the performer's appearance?

• Releases should require the performer to warrant that he or she is free to appear in the production and to sign the release. Is the performer under any other contract that would prevent his or her appearance in the production? Is the performer old enough to sign the release, or will a parent be required to sign?

• Releases should describe the consideration (compensation) that the performer will receive for appearing in the production. As discussed in Chapter 2, consideration is a critical component of all legally binding contracts. Because releases are a type of contract, they should spell out the consideration—even if the performer will receive only a nominal fee.

Figure 5.3. Sample Performer Release

I _____ (the Performer) hereby assign to
_____ (the Producer) the right to record my voice and like-
ness for use in a media production (the Production) that is tentatively titled
_____.

In assigning these rights, the Performer grants to the Producer and its successors, assigns, and licensees the full and irrevocable right to produce,
copy, distribute, exhibit and transmit the Performer's voice and likeness in
connection with the Production by means of broadcast or cablecast, videotape, film or any similar electronic or mechanical method.

The Performer acknowledges that any picture or recording taken of the
Performer under the terms of this license become the sole and exclusive
property of the Producer in perpetuity. The Performer and the Performer's
heirs and assigns shall have no right to bring legal action against the
Producer for any use of the pictures or recordings, regardless of whether
such use is claimed to be defamatory or censorable in nature.

The Performer further acknowledges that the Producer shall have the right
to use the Performer's name, portrait, picture, voice and biographical information to promote or publicize the Production and to authorize others to do
the same. However, nothing shall require the Producer to use the Performer's
name, voice or likeness in any of the manners described in this license or to
exercise any of the rights set forth herein.

The Performer warrants and represents that he or she is free to enter into
this license and that this agreement does not conflict with any existing contracts or agreements to which the Performer is a party. The Performer agrees
to hold the Producer and any third parties harmless from and against any and
all claims, liabilities, losses or damages that may arise from the use of the
Performer's voice or image in the Production.

In consideration for the foregoing grant of rights, the Producer agrees to
pay the Performer a fee of $_____.

- or -

It is agreed that the foregoing grant of rights is made for promotional consideration only, and the Producer's exercise of the grant of rights shall be
deemed full consideration for such grant.

Figure 5.3. Sample Performer Release (cont'd.)

AGREED AND ACCEPTED:

Signature_____
Printed Name_____
Address_____
City_____ State_____
Date_____

For the Producer
Signature: _____
Printed Name _____
Title: _____

In the event that the Performer is a minor:

I acknowledge that I am the legal guardian of the Performer described above.
Acting as the Performer's legal guardian, I consent to the terms of this
license and to the granting of the rights described herein. I also consent to
indemnify and to hold harmless the Producer and all third parties against any
claims that may arise from the use of the minor's name, image or likeness in
the Production.

Signature _____
Printed Name: _____
Relationship to Performer: _____

Some companies require employees to sign a blanket release as a part of their employment contract. If you are shooting in a corporate setting and using employees as talent, check with the company's legal department or personnel office to see if this is the case. Even when it is the case, however, the blanket release may only be valid as long as the employee continues to work for the company. As a result, it is still a good idea to obtain a written release from each employee depicted in a production.

Make sure that performers understand the terms of the release before they sign it. If a performer prefers not to sign, or if a performer demands extensive changes to the release before signing, find someone else to fill that role. Once all of the performer releases for a production are signed, store them in a secure, preferably fireproof location. You should also keep additional copies of the releases in a separate secure location.

Location Releases

Part of the right to privacy is the right to *zones of solitude* where individuals can reasonably expect to be left alone. Under most legal definitions of privacy, these zones include places that are generally recognized as private, particularly a person's home and property. However, under some common law interpretations, privacy zones can also include public places, such as offices, restaurants and parks where there is a reasonable expectation of privacy.

If you plan to conduct a shoot in a private area, be sure to obtain a location release. Otherwise, you leave yourself open to action for trespass—even though it may be only the person's property, and not their face or figure, that is pictured in the production. Along with protecting you from charges of illegal intrusion, location releases serve as contracts that define the terms under which you will be allowed to occupy the property and the rights you will have to use pictures and footage from the shoot.

Figure 5.4 is a model location release that you can modify to meet the needs of your production. Like performer releases, location releases should be written rather than oral. They should also specify the following:

• the dates that the production company will be allowed to occupy the property, with a provision for changing the dates if weather conditions or production delays require shifts in the schedule;

• the rights of the production company to bring equipment and sets onto the property;

• the responsibility of the production company to return the property to its original condition once the shoot is completed;

• the rights that the production company will have to use and distribute the video and sound material recorded at the location; and

• the consideration that the property owner will receive for allowing the location to be used for the shoot

To protect the property owner, most releases also stipulate that the owner will not be liable for injuries or property damage incurred by parties to the production, particularly when those injuries or damages result from negligence by the production company. Conversely, to protect producers who are paying substantial fees for the use of a location, many location releases require the property owner to guarantee that the premises will be safe and in good order.

Figure 5.4: Sample Location Release

The undersigned hereby grants to _____ (the Producer) the permission, right and license to photograph, film and videotape the premises located at _____ _____ (the Premises) for a media production (the Production) that is tentatively titled _____

Under the terms of this agreement, the Producer is permitted to occupy and use the Premises for the period beginning _____ (unless weather conditions or schedule delays result in a changed beginning date) and extending until _____. During this period, the Producer may place all necessary sets, equipment and facilities on the Premises.

The Producer agrees to exercise reasonable care to protect the Premises from damage and to leave the Premises used in the condition that they were found, with reasonable wear excepted. The Producer further agrees to reimburse the undersigned for any damage done to the Premises as a result of the actions of the Producer, his agents or employees.

The Producer warrants that it carries liability insurance that covers the presence of production employees and the operation of equipment on the Premises. The Producer further warrants that it will hold the undersigned harmless from, and indemnify the undersigned against, any injury to any persons that may occur on the Premises as a result of the Producer's activities during the production period, provided, however, that the Producer shall control the defense of any claim for which it provides such indemnity.

Any pictures or recordings taken of the Premises under the terms of this license become the sole and exclusive property of the Producer in perpetuity. The Producer will retain the full and irrevocable right to produce, copy, distribute, exhibit, and transmit the pictures and recordings by means of broadcast or cablecast, videotape, film or any similar electronic or mechanical method. The undersigned and the undersigned's heirs and assigns shall have no right to bring legal action against the Producer for any use of the pictures or recordings.

As full and complete consideration for the rights granted herein, the Producer agrees to pay the undersigned a fee of $_____ for each day or part thereof that the Premises are occupied by the Producer, with the total fee payable when the Producer has completed its use of the premises. No other fees or payments shall be due under the terms of this license.

Nothing in this agreement shall obligate the Producer to use the Premises

for filming or recording purposes or to include material shot on the premises in the Production. The Producer may at any time cancel this agreement by notifying the undersigned, in writing, of its intent not to use the Premises. If

Figure 5.4: Sample Location Release (cont'd.)

this cancellation occurs before the Producer has occupied the Premises, no payment is due to the undersigned. If cancellation occurs after the Producer has occupied the Premises, payment shall be due for each day or part thereof that the premises were occupied.

The undersigned represents that he or she has the right to enter into this agreement and the authority to grant the rights described herein. The undersigned further represents that the rights granted hereunder do not conflict with the terms of any existing contract, license or agreement.

AGREED AND ACCEPTED:

Signature_____
Printed Name_____
Address_____
City_____ State_____
Date_____

For the Producer:
Signature: _____
Printed Name: _____
Title: _____

Requiring Releases

As the preceding sections have shown, releases can help protect productions from charges of unlawful appropriation of a person's right of publicity—the area of privacy law that raises the most immediate concerns for most media producers. Of course, this sort of blanket protection requires one key ingredient—a subject or subjects who are willing to sign releases. When this ingredient is missing, producers should find another subject or shooting location.

Other Privacy Concerns

Obtaining the appropriate releases is a key step in protecting a production against invasion of privacy challenges. However, producers may also find themselves in situations that pose other, more complex privacy concerns. Several of those situations and concerns are discussed below.

Privacy Laws and News Programs

Privacy concerns present special challenges for producers of news programs. By their nature, news programs often disclose embarrassing facts about individuals. In addition, the individuals portrayed in news productions are often unwilling to sign releases authorizing either the disclosure of those facts or the use of their names or likenesses. This is particularly true when the program deals with matters that may be the subject of a criminal investigation.

Fortunately for news producers, the courts have acknowledged that, along with the special challenges that news programmers face, they also enjoy special privileges. Specifically, the courts have recognized "newsworthiness" as a legitimate defense in lawsuits that center on the public disclosure of private facts. If a producer can prove that the disclosure of private facts served a legitimate news purpose, the lawsuit challenging that disclosure will usually be dismissed. However, this common law defense does not necessarily protect news producers who have knowingly placed a person before the public in a false light, or who have obtained private facts by trespassing or intruding on an individual's right to solitude and seclusion. It also does not protect news producers who have deliberately and recklessly misrepresented the facts (see the section on libel that appears later in this chapter), or who have violated an individual's right to publicity by appropriating his or her name or likeness for commercial purposes. In the latter case, the only legitimate defense is the person's consent, preferably secured through a written release.

The newsworthy defense also does not protect media producers who appropriate news footage for non-news uses. In other words, a producer who takes news footage of a celebrity and uses it in a music video or television commercial would not be protected against a lawsuit for illegal appropriation simply because the original footage was newsworthy. In these instances, the producer's appropriation of the celebrity's image clearly would not have served a legitimate news purpose.

The Right of Publicity After Death

As discussed earlier, one component of privacy law is the *right of publicity,* the 'individuals' right to protection against the unauthorized use of his or her name or likeness for commercial purposes. Does the right of publicity die with an individual? In other words, is it safe to appropriate the image or name of individuals who are no longer living? Unlike privacy, which has been defined as a *personal* right in statutory and common law, the right of publicity is a much less defined *property* right that has evolved through case law. In one case decided by the California Supreme Court in 1979, the court ruled that the right to publicity could not be inherited or "descended," denying the heirs of actor Bela Lugosi the right to prevent Universal Pictures from marketing T-shirts and other items that depicted Lugosi in his famous Dracula role. In another, confirming ruling, the second circuit U.S. Court of Appeals reversed its earlier decision and ruled in 1981 that, under Tennessee law, Elvis Presley's right of publicity did not survive him, thus leaving anyone free to exploit Presley's name or likeness for commercial purposes. However, because the right to exploit a deceased person's name for commercial purposes is a matter of case law, subsequent court decisions may place restrictions and qualifications on this right. State legislatures have also been active in this area. California and several other states have already passed laws that grant the heirs of celebrities some level of control over the celebrity's image, and the New York legislature has considered a so-called "Dead Celebrities Bill" that would keep a celebrity's image under family control for 50 years after his or her death. Keeping all of this in mind, producers should consult with a lawyer who is familiar with the latest developments in privacy law at the state and federal levels before appropriating anyone's likeness for commercial purposes—regardless of whether the person is living or dead.

Celebrity Look-Alikes and Sound-Alikes

Some producers try to get around the right of publicity problem by using celebrity "look-alikes" or "sound-alikes" in their productions. Unfortunately, the courts have found that this too can often be considered a violation of the right to publicity, since it does involve an appropriation of the celebrity's image. Woody Allen and Jacqueline Onassis have both won celebrity look-alike challenges, and Bette Midler has won a sound-alike case. The Midler case is discussed in more detail in Chapter 6.

The Changed Name Defense

On another matter of privacy law, is it safe to disclose private facts about individuals, or even facts that place individuals in a false light, as long as you do not use their real names? This issue is particularly relevant, and particularly problematic, to producers of "docudramas" or other fictional works that are based on real events or real people. Until a 1980 California case, writers and producers could protect themselves by simply changing the names and descriptions of the real people, places and events on which the work as based. However, in the case of *Bindrim v. Mitchell*, a California appeals court ruled that a person's privacy could still be considered invaded if the individual can prove that he or she remained "reasonably recognizable" in the work— even if names and descriptions have been changed. This decision set a very troublesome precedent for writers and media producers, since it opened the courtroom doors to almost any individual who believes that he or she is the model for a character in a production. Although subsequent decisions in other states have helped to lessen the impact of *Bindrim v. Mitchell*, this remains a very difficult and complex area of privacy law. As a result, producers who are planning a "docudrama" or other work of "faction" should consult a lawyer who is familiar with the latest precedents and developments.[3]

The Privacy Checklist

If this discussion of privacy law has left you confused, you are not alone. With so few federal statutes in this area, much privacy law remains a bewildering blend of state statutes and case law that can leave even the most experienced lawyers perplexed.

Figure 5.5 is a privacy checklist that should help clarify some of the confusion surrounding the areas of privacy law that are most relevant to media producers. The privacy checklist works much like the fair use checklist from Chapter 4. To use it, simply answer yes or no to each question. If all of the responses come up "yes," you are probably protected from privacy challenges. One or more "no" responses indicate that there is a potential problem, and that a call to a lawyer who is experienced with privacy law is in order. The more no responses, the more vulnerable you are to successful privacy lawsuits.

LIBEL

In recent years, libel suits against the media have become big news. In one heavily publicized case, actress Carol Burnett sued a national "gossip" newspaper for several sensational stories that the paper ran about her personal life. In two other widely reported cases, General Ariel Sharon sued Time maga-

---

[3]To help head off this sort of privacy lawsuit, many productions include a disclaimer declaring that "the events and characters depicted in this program are fictitious. Any similarity to actual persons, living or dead, or to actual entities or events is purely coincidental." Although this disclaimer may help deter casual lawsuits, it is unlikely to dissuade serious plaintiffs from pressing their cases. Further, attaching a disclaimer to a production will not provide a blanket defense if the case reaches court. You will still need to defend yourself against the plaintiff's claim that, contrary to what the disclaimer states, the production does indeed depict a real person.

Figure 5.5 Privacy Checklist for Media Producers

1. Have you violated someone's "right of publicity" by appropriating his or her name or likeness for commercial purposes without his or her permission?

This is one of the most common privacy violations committed by media producers and, as far as the courts are concerned, one of the most clear-cut. If you plan to use someone's name, voice or likeness in a commercial production (a category that includes corporate video productions), be sure to get the person's permission in the form of a written release (see Figure 5.3) or a performer's contract. Failure to do so will leave your production open to claims of unlawful appropriation.

2. Have you conducted a location shoot on private property without the property owner's permission?

Whenever you shoot on private property, be sure to obtain a written location release like the sample shown in Figure 5.4.

3. Are you disclosing embarrassing or offensive facts about a private individual?

Private individuals have a reasonable right to protection against public disclosure of embarrassing facts about their behavior, attitudes, history and personal preferences. This right is not shared by elected officials and other public figures, who are fair game for even the most intimate disclosures—as long as you can show that the disclosures have at least a remote relationship to their status as public persons. If your production does disclose embarrassing facts about a private individual, you have two defenses against a legal challenge. You can try to prove that the individual consented to the disclosures (an unlikely circumstance, and one that is best substantiated through a written release), or you can try to prove that the disclosures were newsworthy. To substantiate the *newsworthy defense*, you will need to show that the primary purpose of the disclosures was to inform the public and that the disclosures

Figure 5.5: Privacy Checklist for Media Producers (cont'd.)

were of legitimate public interest. In addition, unless the disclosures detail recent actions or events, you will need to show that the passage of time has not dimmed the public's interest, turning these once public facts into private facts.

4. Might your production place someone in a false light?

Sometimes, when facts are used creatively or haphazardly, they can place individuals in a false light. For example, imagine a situation in which a producer creates a television documentary about illegal drugs that includes hidden camera shots of actual drug transactions. One of the scenes shows a prominent businessman talking to several people who had just participated in one of the transactions. Although it is never stated, the inclusion of the scene and the tone of the accompanying narration imply that the businessman is also involved with illegal drugs. As it turns out, however, the businessman was there as part of an anti-drug campaign started by a church group. The businessman sues, alleging that the video documentary violated his privacy by placing him before the public in a false light. To avoid this sort of *false light* lawsuit, make sure that your productions portray scenes and situations accurately—particularly when you are juxtaposing shots for creative effect in documentary-style productions.

5. Does your production include fictional material that is based on real people or events?

"Docudramas" and other forms of "faction" raise privacy concerns that require producers to exercise extra caution. If your production falls into this category, consult a lawyer who specializes in privacy matters.

zine over its portrayal of his involvement in the 1982 massacres of Palestinians in Lebanese refugee camps, and General William C. Westmoreland sued CBS for allegations made during a report about the deliberate distortion of enemy troop strength during the Vietnam War. More recently, singer Wayne Newton won a libel suit against NBC regarding a news segment that connected him to an organized crime figure.

Although many of the specific issues differ, these celebrated libel cases share one key characteristic. In each case, the plaintiff charged that the defendant deliberately distorted the truth. This characteristic distinguishes libel lawsuits from invasion of privacy cases, in which the plaintiff usually concedes the truth of the information disclosed but challenges the defendant's right to bring the facts before the public. In general, if you are telling the truth, you are protected against a libel judgment. However, if you have disclosed embarrassing facts about a private individual or violated someone's right of publicity, you might still be vulnerable to a lawsuit for invasion of privacy or unlawful appropriation.

Defamation Law, Libel and Slander

Libel is a tort—a civil (rather than a criminal) wrong for which the court provides remedy. Libel and its twin tort, slander, form the larger legal category called *defamation law*. Historically, libel has been applied to defamation that is written or portrayed pictorially, while slander has meant defamation that is spoken or conveyed orally. In recent years, however, the boundary between libel and slander has become blurred, particularly in cases involving the audiovisual media. In many states, libel is now used as a general term that encompasses slander, even though the two forms of defamation are still technically distinct.

Although the exact definition of libel varies from state to state, a statement about an individual is generally considered to be libelous if it is a statement of false fact, if it is knowingly and deliberately communicated to at least one other person, and if it injures the individual's reputation. When these conditions are present, the injured individual may seek damages through a libel lawsuit.

Sources of Libel Law

There is no comprehensive federal libel law. Instead, like privacy law, libel law is a mix of common law and state statutory law. Because many libel cases involve free press and free speech issues, two rights that are protected under the First Amendment to the U.S. Constitution, many of the major rulings

in this area have come from the federal courts. In particular, a number of key U.S. Supreme Court rulings have helped establish the boundary between speech that is protected by the First Amendment and speech that can be considered libelous. Several of these Supreme Court cases are discussed in the sections that follow.

Media producers should note that, although the federal courts have established a number of key precedents, individual states are free to enact their own libel legislation—as long as that legislation does not conflict with federal common law. As a result, libel law often differs from state to state. Along with reviewing the general libel guidelines discussed here, be sure to consult with a lawyer who is familiar with libel law in the state where your business is based and in any other states where you produce or distribute materials.

Elements of Libel

How can you tell if a specific statement or scene has left your production vulnerable to a successful libel lawsuit? In most cases, five elements must be present to support an allegation of libel: *falsity, injury, publication, identification* and *fault*. Each of these elements is described in more detail below.

Falsity

To be considered libelous, a statement must be a false allegation issued as a statement of fact. If the statement in question is true, a libel lawsuit will usually be dismissed out of hand. Generally, a libel suit will also be dismissed if you can show that the statement in question was clearly made in jest or as an obvious expression of personal opinion, with little chance that someone would interpret it as statement of fact.

Injury

To satisfy the legal definition of libel, a defamatory statement must injure an individual's reputation or result in some other personal or economic damage. Statements that tend to satisfy this criteria include those that falsely accuse a person of professional incompetence, unethical business dealings, promiscuity, drunkenness, criminal behavior or physical or psychological illnesses. If the defamatory material includes one or more of these accusations, and if the other preconditions for libel are present, the court will usually presume that a plaintiff's reputation was injured, even if the plaintiff cannot prove that the injury resulted in tangible economic loss.

Publication

Publication is a prerequisite for libel. Under the law, publication means dissemination or distribution of the offending material to one or more third parties. Privately, you can have all the libelous thoughts or make all of the defamatory statements that you want. You can even communicate your libelous thoughts to the person who is the subject of your ill will—as long as there is no third party present to witness the communication.

The logic behind the publication prerequisite is simple. Without publication, there is little risk that the offending material will injure the plaintiff's reputation. And without injury to reputation, there is no libel case.

Media producers should keep in mind that there are different degrees of publication, and that publication can mean different things in different circumstances. For example, a corporate video program that contains defamatory statements about an employee could trigger a successful libel suit, even if the program was shown only to the employee's supervisor. In this case, publication exists because the program was screened by at least one third party. Also, because the third party was the defamed employee's boss, the employee could probably prove that the program injured his reputation.

Identification

Along with proving that a production contains defamatory statements, the plaintiffs in libel cases must show that others will identify them as the targets of the statements. If the plaintiffs are actually named or shown in the production, identification exists as a matter of course. If they are not actually named or shown, plaintiffs can still establish identification if they can prove that the libelous statements clearly referred to them, or that reasonable people who knew the plaintiffs would recognize them as the subjects of the statements.

Identification becomes more problematic when a member of a group sues for defamatory statements directed at the group as a whole. When this is the case, the court must determine whether the statements made about the group are likely to damage the reputations of individual members. To make this determination, the court will usually focus on two key considerations: the size of the group and the degree to which the defamatory statements single out certain members. The larger the group is and the broader the libelous statements made about the group are, the less likely it is that the court will find sufficient identification to support a libel lawsuit.

Fault

To win a libel lawsuit in many states, the plaintiff must establish fault by showing that the defendant displayed negligence, or lack of care, in publishing the defamatory material. When the case concerns defamatory statements directed at a public official, the plaintiff must go even further and prove actual malice on the part of the defendant. The actual malice requirement is discussed in more detail in the section that follows.

Public People, Private People and Actual Malice

In 1964, the U.S. Supreme Court a issued a decision that has become a landmark in libel law. The case, *The New York Times Co. v. Sullivan*, involved the appeal of a libel suit brought against the *New York Times* by L.B. Sullivan, the Commissioner of Public Affairs in Montgomery, AL. Sullivan had sued the *Times* because of an ad that civil rights groups had placed in the paper in 1960. The ad accused police and public officials in several southern cities, including Montgomery, of taking improper and unlawful actions against students who were participating in civil right protests.

In filing his suit, Sullivan claimed that the accusations made in the ad were untrue and that, even though he was not actually named in the allegations, his reputation as a public official had been damaged. A jury in Alabama agreed, awarding Sullivan a large libel judgment that was affirmed, on appeal, by the Alabama Supreme Court.

Defeated at both the local and state level in Alabama the *Times* turned to the U.S. Supreme Court. Although it had traditionally left matters of civil libel law to the state courts, the Supreme Court recognized that the *Times v. Sullivan* judgment raised important free press considerations, and it agreed to review the case. After extensive deliberation, the court unanimously overturned the Alabama libel award, citing several reasons for its decision:

•If the original *Times* judgment stood, it would open the door for a new form of press censorship through civil libel suits. This would in turn make the press reluctant to cover controversial topics that might trigger libel challenges by public officials in local communities.

•Because public debate is important in a democracy, the press requires some "breathing space" in its coverage of critical issues. When the press pursues these issues vigorously, some factual errors must be both expected and tolerated.

•Once they decide to seek public positions, individuals such as L. B. Sullivan should expect less privacy and more scrutiny by the press and the general public. Also, once they secure government positions, public officials can usually command more access to the media to reply to libelous allegations than can private citizens. For these reasons, public officials should both expect and receive less libel protection than the protection that the law affords to private citizens.

Taking the last rationale one step further, the Supreme Court ruled that public officials who file libel suits against the media must prove that the statements in question were made with *actual malice*. In other words, to win a libel lawsuit, public officials must prove that the libelous statement was made "with knowledge that it was false or with reckless disregard of whether it was false or not."[4] Needless to say, because actual malice is difficult to prove, the *Times v. Sullivan* decision has made it much more difficult for public officials to win libel judgments.

Although the *New York Times* ruling resolved the issues raised in this particular case, the decision also created a troublesome new problem. Now that public officials must be treated as special cases under libel law, just how do judges determine who is a public official and who is not? Does the term public official refer only to elected officials, or does it include anyone who holds a government position? What about film stars, professional athletes, political activists, retired politicians and other prominent people? Do these public figures qualify as public officials under the *Times* ruling?

Gertz v. Welch

In the years since the *New York Times* decision, the Supreme Court has helped to answer these questions through a series of additional libel rulings. In *Gertz v. Welch*, a ruling handed down in 1974, the court decreed that private citizens who are public figures for a limited purpose (in Gertz's case, an attorney who had represented the family of a black man killed by the Chicago police) do not need to prove actual malice in libel suits against the media—as long as they have not deliberately sought public figure status in the context of the case at hand. However, the *Gertz* ruling did require private citizens to prove some level of fault on the part of the media. In other words, it is not enough to prove that the media simply published a false and libelous statement. Instead, a private citizen suing the media for libel must also prove some degree of negligence or intent on the part of the defendant.

It is significant that the *Gertz* ruling left it to state courts to determine just how much fault private persons are required to prove in libel suits. As a result, the required level of fault can vary greatly from state to state. In some

---

[4] *New York Times Co. v. Sullivan*, 376 U.S. 254 (1964).

states, private citizens must prove the same level of fault or malice as public officials. In others, private citizens must prove only simple negligence on the part of the media. An attorney who specializes in libel law will know which standard applies in the states where you produce and distribute programs.

Time, Inc. v. Firestone

In more recent libel decisions, the Supreme Court has continued its struggle to define the boundary between public figures and private citizens who have been involuntarily placed in the public eye. For example, the 1976 ruling in *Time, Inc. v. Firestone* established that people do not necessarily become public figures simply because they are involved in prominent court cases:

> **While participants in some litigation may be legitimate "public figures," either generally or for the limited purpose of that litigation, the majority will more likely resemble [the] respondent [Mrs. Firestone], drawn into a public forum largely against their will in order to attempt to obtain the only redress available to them or to defend themselves against actions brought by the state or by others. There appears to be little reason why these individuals should substantially forfeit that degree of protection which the law of defamation would otherwise afford them simply by virtue of their being drawn into a courtroom.[5]**

For media producers, the message conveyed by *Time, Inc. v. Firestone* and subsequent Supreme Court rulings is clear: do not assume that you enjoy special protection from libel suits simply because the target of your accusations is a celebrity or other prominent figure. In most states, only government officials or individuals who have voluntarily placed themselves at the forefront of specific public controversies must prove actual malice in libel lawsuits.

Libeling Corporations and Organizations

When corporation's reputations are defamed by false statements, they have the same right as individuals to sue for libel. However, when a corporate entity is libeled, the right to sue for libel is not tied to the life-spans of indi-

---

[5]*Time, Inc. v. Firestone*, 424 U.S. 448 (1976).

vidual officers or employees. As a result, corporations can, and sometimes do, pursue libel lawsuits for decades. Similar rules apply when clubs, non-government agencies and unincorporated organizations sue for libel.

Trade libel or *disparagement* is a special sort of libel that occurs when false and damaging statements are directed at a specific product or service sold by a company, rather than at the company itself. In filing a trade libel action, the company must prove that the defamatory statement, rather than the vagaries of the marketplace, resulted in reduced sales for the product or service. Because this can be difficult to prove, trade libel lawsuits can be very difficult to win.

Unlike corporations and private organizations, government agencies cannot sue for libel. However, individual employees of government agencies can, provided they can prove that the defamatory statements damaged their personal reputations.

Who Pays for Libel?

You have just been hired by a small video production company. One of your first assignments is to produce a program about toxic waste disposal violations. The program, which was written by a freelance scriptwriter and financed by a national foundation, alleges that the vice president of a waste hauling firm approved the illegal dumping of toxic substances near a public water supply. The program is transmitted over several cable television systems that are owned by a large media corporation.

After seeing the program, the vice president of the waste-hauling firm is furious. Alleging that the accusations made in the production are untrue, he decides to sue for libel. But who does he sue? You? Your company? The writer? The foundation that financed the production? The cable systems that transmitted it? The corporation that owns the systems?

In theory, the answer is "all of the above," since all of the parties involved in the production and distribution of libelous material can be held responsible. In actual practice, however, many plaintiffs will, in consultation with their lawyers, pick one or two targets for the suit. Depending on their purpose in filing the suit, the plaintiffs will pick either the party with the deepest pockets (the individual or group that can afford to pay the largest judgment) or the party that they would most like to "teach a lesson."

Libel Liability

If you are about to sign a contract to write, produce, distribute or display a media production, be sure to check the contract for libel liability language. To protect themselves from liability in libel suits, many companies include clauses in their contracts that require the second party to the agreement (the party that will produce or provide materials under the terms of the contract) to assume the responsibility for any libelous statements contained in the materials. Usually, the libel liability clause is part of the warranties, representations and indemnities section of the contract. Review this clause carefully and make sure you can buy into such a unilateral warranty before signing the contract. If you have any questions about what you are signing, or if you have questions about potentially libelous statements contained in your materials, contact a lawyer who is familiar with libel law.

Libel Insurance

As the threat of libel suits has increased, many media production and distribution groups have begun to carry libel insurance often as part of an "errors and omissions" policy. Although most libel policies require substantial deductibles, they do help protect media companies and their employees from the sting of large libel judgments (as well as from the often fatal sting of legal fees). In some cases, the policies can be extended to insure writers and producers who have contracted to provide materials for the company. If you are about to sign such a contract, check to see if the company carries a libel policy that could cover your work. If you can be covered, make sure that a clause to that effect is included in your contract.

Protecting and Defending Against a Charge of Libel: The Libel Checklist

The best protection against libel is to tell the truth. Start by checking the facts conveyed in your production, particularly those facts that form the basis of potentially libelous statements. As mentioned earlier, statements that bear special checking include those that accuse individuals or groups of professional incompetence, unprofessional behavior, unethical business dealings, promiscuity, drunkenness, laziness, criminal behavior or physical or psychological illnesses. If your production contains these sorts of accusations or implications, ask yourself if they are essential to the program. If they are not, cut them. If they are, and you decide to retain them, make sure that the statements are true. If you cannot prove that they are true, assume that the statements are false and edit them from the program (or, at a minimum, make it clear that they are offered as opinion, not fact).

What if you are not in a position to remove potentially libelous material from a program? For example, what if you are a distributor who has negotiated for a program that contains problematic statements, but the producer insists that you take it as is or forget the deal? Or, what if you are a producer who has already released a program, only to discover that the book on which the program is based is the subject of a libel suit? Under circumstances like these, how can you know just how vulnerable you are to a successful libel challenge particularly if you are not named as an additional insured on the producer's errors and omissions insurance?

Start by reviewing the libel checklist shown in Figure 5.6. If that review reveals that you are at risk, or if you have any doubts, consult a lawyer. With multimillion dollar libel judgments making headlines, it does not make sense to take chances.

Figure 5.6. The Libel Checklist

This checklist is designed to help you gauge the degree to which accusatory statements made in a media production carry the risk of a successful libel challenge. Before reviewing the checklist items, ask yourself one key question: Are the statements true? If the statements in question are true, and if you can prove that they are true, you will not lose a libel lawsuit. However, you may still face the hassle and cost of defending against a libel challenge in court. In addition, even if the statements are true, you may still be vulnerable to an invasion of privacy suit. The only sure way to avoid these unpleasantries is to remove the problematic material from the production.

If the statements may not be true, if they imply a condition or fact that may not be true, or if you cannot prove that they are true, the safest step is to edit the statements from the production. When this is not an option, review the questions listed below, answering yes or no to each one. If you answer no to all of the questions, you and your production are definitely at risk. If one or more of the answers is yes, you are protected, to some degree, from large libel judgments. To determine the exact degree of that protection, consult a lawyer who is familiar with libel law in the state or states where the program was produced and distributed.

1. Were the statements clearly offered as matters of opinion, rather than as declarations of fact?
   The First Amendment protects your right to offer statements of opinion, no matter how inaccurate or

Figure 5.6. The Libel Checklist (cont'd.)

injurious, as long as it is clear that you are offering an opinion. In other words, there is a big difference between saying "In my opinion, Mr. Smith has misled

the shareholders," and "Mr. Smith has misled the shareholders." In the first case, you are clearly offering the statement as a matter of opinion, so the First Amendment protects you from a libel judgment. In the second case, you are offering the statement as a matter of fact, so you had better be able to prove it. Do not assume, however, that you are shielded from a libel lawsuit simply because you preface a defamatory statement with "It is alleged. . ." or some similar qualifier. While qualifying a statement in this way may provide some protection, it is by no means a complete libel defense.

To a lesser degree, you are also protected if the remarks were clearly made in jest, with no danger that a listener or viewer would mistake them for statements of fact.

2. Were the statements made about the job performance of a public official?

Unlike private citizens, public officials must prove *actual malice* (defined as the "reckless disregard for the truth") on the part of the media to win libel judgments. Although this makes it much more difficult for public officials to win libel cases, it does not make them fair game for any accusations that you care to toss their way. If you must attack a public official, make sure that the attack focuses on the official's performance in office, rather than on his or her private or professional life outside of public service. Of course, to be fully protected from a libel judgment, you should also make sure that the accusations are based in fact and that you are not guilty of actual malice toward the official.

3. Were the statements the result of mistakes made during the production of a news program?

The courts tend to be somewhat more forgiving when the defamatory statements result from honest mistakes made

Figure 5.6. The Libel Checklist (cont'd.)

during the production of news programs—particularly
the production of regularly scheduled newscasts.
Recognizing the pressures involved in preparing
newscasts and acknowledging the important role that
newscasts play in keeping the public informed, the
courts tend to expect less
fact checking on the part of reporters and other
employees who prepare news under pressing deadlines.

4. Were the statements a fair reporting of direct
quotes taken from public proceedings, records or transcripts?

Under a common law concept called the *privilege*
defense, a news program is protected, to some measure, if libelous statements contained in the program
are direct quotations from public proceedings (trials,
government hearings, legislative sessions, etc.) or
public records (trial transcripts, government reports,
etc.). However, to be fully *privileged*, the statements
must have been made by a public official or someone
who is speaking at a public proceeding, and the statements must be reported accurately, fully and fairly.

5. Were the statements attributed to a normally reli-
able source?

Although attribution is not a complete defense, it
can provide some protection against a libel challenge,
particularly when it is used with one or more of the
other defenses described in this checklist.

6. Did the subject of the statements consent to publication?

Consent *is* a complete libel defense. If the subject
of the statements was generous enough to consent to
publication, and if you can prove that consent, you are
protected from a libel judgment if the subject subse-
quently changes his or her mind. As always, the best
proof of consent is a signed, written release.

7. If the production is a fictional work based on actual
events, have you changed the names and descrip-

Figure 5.6. The Libel Checklist (cont'd.)

tions of the people and places involved in the actual events?

As discussed in this chapter, changing the identities of people and places to protect the innocent—or even the guilty—no longer guarantees that a production is fully protected from libel challenges, but it can help. The more aspects that are changed (name, age, physical description, dates, and so on), the greater the protection.

PRODUCTION INSURANCE AND COMPLETION BONDS

With production costs rising rapidly, most major film and television producers are choosing to protect their investments through the purchase of production insurance. Typically, the premiums for a comprehensive policy run from 3% to 5% of the total production budget, with the exact cost determined by the risk factors (extensive location work, hazardous stunts, etc.) present in the project, the amount of the policy deductibles and the limits of the insurance company's liability.

A comprehensive production insurance policy usually includes the following types of coverage:

- Cast insurance, which protects the company against any extra production costs caused by the death, injury or illness of a performer or director. Bad weather insurance, which reimburses the production company for extra costs incurred if a shooting day must be cancelled due to inclement weather.

- Equipment insurance, which covers damages to equipment leased or owned by the production company.

- Wardrobe, props and sets insurance, which pays for fixing or replacing items damaged during production.

- Animal mortality insurance, which insures the company against the death of any animal that is listed on the policy.

- Videotape and negative film insurance, which reimburses the production company for damaged or lost videotape stock or negative film, recorded videotape or exposed film and recorded soundtracks.

- Aircraft and watercraft liability insurance, which protects the company against claims related to the use of planes, helicopters and boats in a production.

- Property damage liability insurance, which covers the cost of repairing or replacing property belonging to others that is damaged or destroyed during production.

- Comprehensive general liability and auto liability insurance, which shield the production company from claims for property damage and bodily injury as a result of accidents during production.

Comprehensive liability insurance is particularly important on productions that involve location work. When you are shooting on location, all sorts of accidents and mishaps can, and seemingly always do, happen. With the proper liability coverage, your production is protected from the many claims for personal injury and property damage that can result from even simple accidents. In addition (and as discussed earlier in the chapter), many states and municipalities require proof of liability insurance when you file for a shooting permit.

In some states, you may also be required to carry worker compensation insurance for production employees. In addition, many union and guild agreements specify that you must provide additional types of insurance for their members, including flight accident policies that cover travel to and from production locations. For more information, about union contracts, see Chapter 7. Many comprehensive production policies also provide for some level of errors and omissions coverage. For more information about errors and omissions insurance, see Chapter 4.

Along with the conventional categories of protection described above, large production projects (feature films, television miniseries, etc.) are often covered by a separate type of insurance called *completion bonds.* Sold by insurers known as *completion guarantors,* completion bonds shield the financial backers of a production from the effects of budget overruns, delays and other problems that can cripple the potential profitability of a film or television project. In return for providing this protection, the completion guarantor receives a substantial fee and the authority to exercise substantial control over key aspects of the production—including the right to approve casting selections. Most guarantors also reserve the right to take control of a faltering production, although this option is usually exercised only as a last resort after all other attempts at intervention have failed. For more information about completion bonds, contact a reputable completion guarantor. You will find the names of guarantors listed in the film and video producer's guides that are published in New York, Los Angeles and other major production centers.[6]

SUMMARY

What are shooting permits?

Shooting or location permits are temporary licenses that authorize production companies to conduct location shoots in public areas, including public parks, buildings, streets and highways. The permits are usually issued by state or municipal film liaison offices, often in conjunction with the government agencies that are responsible for the locations and facilities where the shoot will take place.

What other permits and licenses must media producers obtain?

Depending on the type of project and the area where the production will take place, producers may need to obtain a number of additional permits beyond the basic forms issued by state or municipal authorities. Those additional permits may include federal consent forms for shooting on property owned by the U.S. government; county permits for shooting on county-owned roads or facilities; work permits and releases for employing minors and other special categories of workers; pyrotechnic or fire department permits to cover any special effects that involve explosions, smoke or open flames; and authorizations from local animal regulation bureaus for any animals that will be used in the production.

What are the penalties for shooting without the proper permits?

If you are caught shooting without the proper permits, you will usually be forced to suspend production until you obtain the necessary clearances—a delay that can prove extremely costly as talent, crews and rented equipment stand idle. You may also be subject to substantial fines and, for some severe violations, criminal penalties.

What is privacy law?

Privacy law is the body of common and statutory law that protects an individual's right to be left alone. In the United States, the legal right to be left alone includes the right to protection against intrusion upon your solitude and private affairs, the appropriation of your name or likeness for commercial purposes (often called the "right of publicity"), disclosures that place you before the public in a false light and the public disclosure of embarrassing facts about your private life.

---

[6]See, for example, *The Producer's Masterguide* (New York: Billboard Publications, Inc.)

What are the sources of privacy law?

In the United States, privacy is a mix of state and common law, state statutes directed at specific kinds of privacy violations and a growing number of federal statutes aimed at preventing the misuse of government records and electronic surveillance. At this time, however, there is no comprehensive federal privacy law.

How can you protect a production against invasion of privacy lawsuits?

The best protection against invasion of privacy challenges is to secure a signed, written performer release from each person whose voice or likeness appears in the production. If the production will include location segments shot on private property, you should also secure written location releases from the property owners.

What is libel?

Libel occurs when a false and injurious statement is made about an individual, group or corporation. Although the exact guidelines vary from state to state, a statement about an individual is generally considered to be libelous if it is false, if it is knowingly and deliberately communicated to at least one other person, and if it injures the individual's reputation. When these conditions are present, the injured individual may seek damages through a libel lawsuit.

What is the difference between libel and slander?

Libel and slander form the larger legal category called *defamation law*. Historically, libel has been applied to defamation that is written or portrayed pictorially, while slander has meant defamation that is spoken or conveyed orally. In recent years, however, the boundary between libel and slander has become blurred, particularly in cases involving the audiovisual media.

What are the sources of libel law?

There is no comprehensive federal libel law. Instead, like privacy law, libel law is a mix of common law and state statutory law. Because many libel cases involve free press and free speech issues, many of the major common law rulings in this area have come from the federal courts, particularly the U.S. Supreme Court. Individual states are free to enact their own libel legislation—as long as that legislation does not conflict with federal common law.

How can you protect a production against libel lawsuits?

The best protection against libel is to tell the truth. Check all facts presented in your production, particularly those facts that form the basis of potential libelous statements, such as those that accuse individuals or groups of professional incompetence, unprofessional behavior, unethical business dealings, promiscuity, drunkenness, laziness, criminal behavior, or physical or psychological illnesses. Ask yourself if such statements are essential to the program. If they are not, eliminate them. If they are necessary, make sure that the statements are true.

If you have made libelous allegations as part of a news program, the courts recognize a number of additional defenses. In particular, the courts require public officials who are filing libel lawsuits to prove "actual malice" on the part of the news media.

What is production insurance?

Production insurance is a special type of insurance coverage that protects a company against many of the accidents, mishaps and acts of nature that can cause problems during a media production. A comprehensive policy provides protection against extra production costs caused by the death, injury or illness of a performer or director; the cancellation of shooting due to inclement weather; damages to equipment, wardrobes, props and sets leased or owned by the production company; the death of an animal featured in the production; damaged or lost videotape stock or negative film, recorded videotape or exposed film, and recorded soundtracks; and claims related to the use of planes, helicopters and boats used in the production. Production insurance policies should also include comprehensive general liability and auto liability coverage, which shield the production company from claims for property damage and bodily injury that result from accidents during production.

What is a completion bond?

Large production projects (feature films, television miniseries, etc.) are often covered by a separate type of insurance called *completion bonds*. Sold by insurers known as *completion guarantors*, completion bonds shield the financial backers of a production from the effects of budget overruns, delays and other production problems. In return for providing this protection, the completion guarantor receives a substantial fee and contingent authority to exercise substantial control over key aspects of the production.

6

Adding Music: Special Concerns Surrounding the Use of Music in Media Productions

The right music can bring a great deal of emotion and impact to a media production. That is why the Nike Corporation was willing to pay a great deal for the right to use the Beatles' song "Revolution" in its 1987 television ads introducing a "revolutionary" line of sport shoes. Unfortunately, music can also introduce a whole host of hidden legal concerns. That is why Nike and its ad agency soon found themselves caught up in a lawsuit contesting their right to use the Beatles' recording of "Revolution"—even though they thought that they had purchased all of the necessary rights to the song.

Nike was not naive. The company knew that it needed to secure the proper permissions to use "Revolution," and it assumed that it had done just that. Specifically, Nike paid for and received permission from Capitol Records, Inc., and EMI Records Ltd., the two companies that control the worldwide release of Beatles records. But Nike did not secure permission from Apple Records, Inc., the music company that continues to represent some of the Beatles' interests. Alleging that the Nike ad "wrongfully traded on the good will and popularity of the Beatles," Apple Records filed a civil suit in New York seeking $15 million in damages.

THE MUSIC PERMISSIONS PROCESS

Nike's problem points out just how complex music rights can be, particularly when you plan to use a popular song in a media production. At its most basic level, the permissions process for music is the same as the process for film clips, photographs and other non-music materials (discussed in Chapter 4.) You first contact the individual or group that controls the rights to the materials. Then you negotiate an agreement that specifies the rights that you will have to use the materials and the compensation that the copyright owner will receive for granting those rights.

With sound recordings, however, this fairly straightforward process can become complicated quickly. First, there are usually at least two parties that

149

control the rights to the recording: the music publisher or songwriter who owns the copyright to the song and the record company that distributes the sound recording. Second, as Nike discovered, there may be many more parties that claim some sort of ownership in the work: the independent production company that originally brought the song to the record company, the musicians who performed on the sound recording, etc. Finally, assuming that you can contact the correct parties and negotiate for the right to use the work, you should know that there are at least two distinct types of rights: synchronization rights and performance rights. To know which of these rights you need, you must know how you will use the song in your production and how the finished production will be displayed or distributed.

The sections that follow attempt to sort out these and many other issues and definitions related to the use of music in media production projects. Much of the discussion assumes that you are familiar with the fundamentals of copyright law introduced in Chapter 4.

MUSICAL WORKS AND THE COPYRIGHT LAW

In most respects, the copyright law treats musical works the same as any other *intellectual property* that is eligible for copyright protection. Like the media materials discussed in Chapter 4, musical works are protected by copyright as soon as they are created, and the term of copyright runs for the life of the copyright owner plus 50 years. In addition, the registration, infringement, work-made-for-hire and fair use provisions discussed in Chapter 4 all apply to musical works.

But music also receives some special treatment under U.S. copyright law. For example, the copyright law defines several distinct categories of musical rights: *mechanical* rights, *synchronization* rights and *performance* rights. The copyright law also provides for several types and categories of musical works: songs or compositions, sound recordings and phonorecords. In addition, music is the only category of intellectual property that falls under the *compulsory mechanical license* provision of U.S. copyright law. Each of these special terms, definitions and provisions is discussed in more detail in the sections that follow.

Musical Works

Under U.S. copyright law, a song is not a song, it is a *musical work*. As defined in the current copyright law, a musical work consists of the music—the particular combination of notes that defines the composition as an original work—and the lyrics if there are lyrics. A rock-and-roll song, a symphony, an opera any other musical composition that can be performed or recorded are all musical works. It is important to note that a musical work exists as a separate, copyrightable entity that is distinct from sound recordings, copies and phonorecords of the work. Think of a musical work as the notes and words that would appear on sheet music for the composition.

Sound Recordings

When musicians perform the notes and words of a musical work and the performance is recorded, the result is a *sound recording*. Like the musical work itself, each sound recording is a distinct, copyrightable property. In other words, each time that a musical work is recorded, a new, copyrighted sound recording is created. For example, Norman Whitfield and Barrett Strong wrote a song called "I Heard It Through the Grapevine" that has been recorded by a number of performers, most notably Marvin Gaye and Gladys Knight and the Pips. The song "I Heard It Through the Grapevine" exists as a distinct musical work that is copyrighted by Whitfield and Strong. In addition, each time that "Grapevine" is recorded, a new sound recording is created as a separate, copyrightable work that is distinct from all other recordings of the work (Marvin Gaye's recording of "Grapevine" is a distinct, copyrightable work; Gladys Knight's recording is distinct, and so on). Of course, because the song "Grapevine" is itself a copyrighted musical work, Marvin Gaye, Gladys Knight and anyone else who records the song are required to compensate Whitfield and Strong for their use of the work. The rules governing this compensation are discussed in the section of this chapter titled Compulsory Mechanical Licenses.

Copies and Phonorecords

Once you understand the distinction between musical works and sound recordings, you should learn two more terms that are important in the music rights game: *copy* and *phonorecord*. A *copy* is sheet music that shows the notes and words that comprise the composition, or some other physical manifestation of a musical work that allows it to be perceived visually.

A *phonorecord* is the physical object (phonograph record, audiotape, compact disc, computer disk, etc.) that contains the fixed sounds of a sound recording. To create phonorecords, you first create a sound recording of the musical work. Then you copy the sound recording to phonograph records, audiotapes, compact discs or some other distribution medium. Each physical copy that you create from the sound recording is a phonorecord. Note, however, that a phonorecord is not a *copy* of the musical work or sound recording in the copyright sense of the term, since you cannot actually see the notes and words that comprise the musical work or the audio signals that comprise the sound recording by simply looking at the phonorecord.

Role of Music Publishers and Record Companies

In the music industry, particularly the popular music industry, very few composers and performers act as independent agents. Instead, most are affiliated with one or more music publishers and record companies that own part or complete interest in their songs and sound recordings. Remember, under copyright law, a song and a sound recording are different, distinct works. As a result, the individual who wrote the song does not necessarily have an ownership stake in sound recordings of the song, and the performers and record companies who created the sound recordings do not necessarily have any ownership interest in the song itself.

Here is how the process typically works. Once a song is created, and before it is recorded, the composer or songwriting team will usually assign it to a music publisher. Under the standard publishing arrangement, the publisher receives the copyright to the song, and in return, the composer receives a guaranteed percentage of the income generated by the publisher's efforts to promote and sell the song. Usually, the composer will receive about 50% of the publisher's income from the song, after the publisher has deducted 10% to 20% of the gross revenue as an administration fee.

In years past, music publishers generated the bulk of their revenue by convincing popular performers to record or "cover" songs. Additional income came from licensing songs for use in movie and television soundtracks. However, like many aspects of the music industry, publishing practices have become more complex in recent years, particularly as more performers have written their own songs, and as more songwriters and record companies have formed their own music publishing ventures. Today, a typical a song might be published by the songwriter/performer's own music publishing company. The songwriter/performer then records the song as a work-made-for-hire for a record company, which pays the performer's publishing company for the rights to create a sound recording of the song.

Note that under this fairly standard setup, the songwriter/performer owns neither the song nor the sound recording of the song. The copyright for the song is owned by the music publishing company, which may, in fact, be partly or wholly owned by the songwriter/performer, and the copyright for the sound recording is owned by the record company. As mentioned before, the contract between the songwriter/performer and the publishing company requires the publisher to pay the songwriter a percentage of its income from licensing rights to the song. In addition, a separate contract with the record company requires the record label to pay the performer a percentage of its income from selling copies of the sound recording. The performer also receives a percentage of any income that the record company generates by licensing the sound recording for use in film or television soundtracks. Finally, both the publisher and songwriter share the performing rights royalties generated by public performance (primarily radio airplay) of the sound recording.

The contractual relationships among songwriters, performers, publishers and record labels can become very complicated, particularly when there are third and fourth parties involved. For example, a rock group might have a contract with an independent producer to record a song that one member of the group wrote several years earlier and sold to a music publisher. Once the independent producer has secured the rights to the song from the music publisher, and once the group has made a sound recording, the producer will try to sell distribution rights to the sound recording to a major record label.

It is usually not necessary for media producers to know the full copyright history of a song that they are interested in including in a production. In most cases, it is enough to know who currently controls the rights to the song and who controls the rights to the sound recording.

Implications for Media Producers

What difference do all of these definitions and distinctions make to producers who are simply interested in adding a little music to a production? Consider the fictional case of Paula Hernandez and Howard Allen, two producers who are developing a motivational video called *Together Today, Together Tomorrow* for a Fortune 500 corporation. As a musical theme for the production, Hernandez and Allen plan to use "Made for Each Other," a popular song written by Jerry Miles and published by Miles Ahead Music, Inc. The hit version of the song was recorded by a group called Sure Thing for Dynamic Records, Inc.

The producers, Hernandez and Allen, have two basic options: they can secure the rights to use the musical work (the song itself) and the Sure Thing sound recording of the work, or they can secure the rights to just the musical work and arrange for other musicians to perform the version that will be used in their production. In both cases, Hernandez and Allen must obtain the rights to the musical work from Miles Ahead Music, Inc. In the first case, they must also secure the rights to use the sound recording from Dynamic Records.

Which is the right choice for Hernandez and Allen? That depends on their priorities. If the production budget and schedule are their main concerns, they must determine which option will cost the least time and money: securing the rights to the Sure Thing recording of "Made for Each Other" from Dynamic Records, or buying the rights to the song from Miles Ahead Music and paying to have their own version recorded. Of course, Hernandez and

Allen must also consider how their choice will affect the quality and impact of their production. Is it critical to have the Sure Thing version of the song, or will a remake suffice?

In actual practice, it is usually easier and cheaper to secure permission from a music publisher to create your own version of a song than it is to receive permission from the record company to use the original recording. The reason for this is simple: music publishers make money by selling the sort of rights that you are requesting, while record companies make money by selling records. Unless you can convince the company that your use of the recording will boost record sales, the company will probably be reluctant to grant your request. Also, in some cases, the contract between the recording artist and the record company prohibits the company from licensing the sound recording for commercial applications.

If you plan to record your own version of a popular song, it may be possible to purchase a pre-recorded instrumental track, or "music bed," over which you add your own version of the vocal track. If you do this, you will still need to secure all of the rights and permissions previously described. In addition, you should obtain a written agreement with the company that provides the instrumental track. The agreement should spell out the terms under which the company will provide the instrumental track and the exact extent of your right to use it.

Record companies can be particularly tough on corporate video producers who are thinking of adding an original recording to an in-house production, since there is little chance that this type of nonbroadcast use will result in a significant increase in record sales. When record companies do grant permission for corporate use of a recording, the price is usually high—from $1000 or more for a license that permits one-time use of the song (in other words, permission to use the recording in a production that will be shown once) to $10,000 or more for a license that permits longer term use. Of course, you will also need to pay the music publisher for the right to use the song contained in the recording. Fortunately, these fees are usually a bit more reasonable, typically running from 25% to 35% of the charge that record companies would assess for granting rights to the recording.

In some circumstances, a producer may need to seek other types of permission from a music publisher or recording company, including the right to alter the lyrics to fit the needs of a particular production or to use an existing sound-alike recording of the work. This is often true in the production of television commercials and corporate sales presentations, where the producer wants to modify the lyrics or a popular song to promote a particular product. For a more complete discussion of these options, see the Music Rights Checklist that appears on page 168.

TYPES OF RIGHTS

Before you begin negotiating for the right to add a song or sound recording to a production, you need to know which type of rights you require. For media producers, the two most important kinds of rights are *synchronization* and *performance* rights. You should also be familiar with *compulsory mechanical* licenses and a few other terms that can come up during licensing discussions.

Synchronization Rights, Performance Rights and Master Recording Licenses

If you are licensing music materials for use in a production, you will usually require both *synchronization* and *performance* rights to the material. Synchronization rights allow you to link the song to the video track of your production. Performance rights allow you to show the completed production that contains the song to an audience.

Blanket Licensing Arrangements

If your production will be shown exclusively on broadcast television, you probably do not need to worry about performance rights. They have probably already been secured for you, courtesy of the blanket licensing arrangement that the major performance rights organizations (ASCAP and BMI) have negotiated with broadcasters. Although this blanket license has been challenged in the courts (it is an all-or-nothing arrangement that requires broadcasters to pay a fee to cover all music licensed by the organization or receive no rights at all), most U.S. television stations still hold such licenses. As a result, producers of broadcast television programs usually need only secure synchronization rights for the copyrighted songs that they use in their productions. Of course, if you plan to use an original sound recording of the song, you will also need permission from the record company that controls the rights to the recording.[1]

Securing Synchronization Rights

How do you go about securing synchronization and, if necessary, perfor-

---

[1] After their broadcast run, some television programs are shown on cable television or foreign television. When this is the case, producers may need to secure performance rights to cover these forms of distribution. Be aware, though, that many of the major cable networks have negotiated their own blanket licensing arrangements with the performing rights societies. You should consult with each licensee to determine whether you will need to secure performance rights.

mance rights to a musical work? As discussed in the preceding section, you must first determine whether you are seeking rights to the song alone or to both the song and a specific recording of it. If you are seeking rights to the song alone (in other words, if you plan to record your own version of the song), you will need to obtain permission from the music publisher. If you are seeking the rights to a specific recording of the song, you will need permission from both the music publisher and the record company. The permission from the record company should be in the form of a *master recording license* that grants you the right to use the recording in your production. The music publisher and record company should be listed on the jacket or label of the record, cassette or compact disc that contains the sound recording.

When you are ready to negotiate rights to a song, you may want to consider working with an agency that specializes in obtaining music rights and permissions for media producers. For more information, see the section titled Working with Rights and Permissions Agencies that appears on page 158.

Compulsory Mechanical Licenses

Imagine this scenario. Several years ago, you wrote and retained the copyright to a catchy pop song. Then you granted a popular recording group and its record label permission to create and distribute phonorecords of the song in return for a royalty on each copy sold. The recording was released, it became a big hit and everyone made money.

Now another performer wants to record and release phonorecords of the song. You have never liked the performer, and you are concerned that the resulting sound recording might damage your song's growing reputation as a pop music classic. Is there any legal way for you to stop the performer from recording the song and selling copies?

Surprisingly, the answer to that question is no, as long as the performer is willing to fulfill his responsibilities under the *compulsory mechanical license* provision of U.S. copyright law. Under that provision, anyone can obtain a license to create and distribute phonorecords of a published musical work. To secure the license, the performer or group must simply:

• notify the copyright owner of its intent to use the song;

• agree to pay the royalty rate specified in the Copyright Act; and

• agree not to change the fundamental character of the work.

The compulsory mechanical licensing provision does allow the performer some latitude in arranging and interpreting the song to create a distinct sound recording. However, any changes to the lyrics or basic melody must be approved by the copyright owner through a separate agreement.

The royalty rate for compulsory mechanical licenses is defined in the copyright law. The current rate is 5 cents per phonorecord sold or .95 cents per minute of playing time or fraction thereof, whichever is greater. However, many performers try to obtain lower rates through a voluntary license with the copyright owner. To facilitate this process, most owners of musical works arrange for the Harry Fox Agency, Inc.,[2] to serve as their representative in negotiating mechanical use royalties. The Harry Fox Agency also acts as a payment processing center for its clients, collecting and distributing fees for mechanical licenses.

Media producers should note that the compulsory mechanical licensing provision applies only to performers who will create and distribute phonorecords of a musical work. It does *not* apply to media producers who are planning to use a song as part of a production. As discussed earlier, producers who are planning to add a copyrighted song to a media production must secure synchronization and, in most cases, performance rights directly from the copyright owner or the appropriate performing rights society.

BMI, ASCAP AND OTHER PERFORMING RIGHTS SOCIETIES

No discussion of music rights would be complete without some mention of the performing rights societies that act as agents for composers, songwriters and music publishers. The three dominant performing rights organizations are Broadcast Music Incorporated (BMI), the American Society of Composers, Authors and Publishers (ASCAP), and the Society of European Songwriters, Authors, and Composers (SESAC). ASCAP has been around the longest, but BMI is currently the largest of the three groups.

The performing rights societies devote most of their efforts negotiating with television and radio broadcasters and cable networks over the blanket performing rights licensing agreements discussed earlier As a result, they are not set up to provide any rights other than public performance rights to musical compositions for productions that will be shown on broadcast and cable television. To secure these other sorts of rights, contact the music publisher directly.

It is important to note that the BMI, ASCAP and other performing rights societies represent composers and music publishers in their negotiations, not record companies. As a result, performing rights societies are able to license the rights to songs, but not to sound recordings. If you want to use a sound

---

[2]The Harry Fox Agency is located at 110 E. 59th Street, New York, NY 10022 (212-751-1930).

recording in a production,that will be exhibited publicly, you will need to secure permission from the songwriter or music publisher that owns the song (i.e., synchronization rights), its ASCAP or BMI representative (for broadcast and cable uses only), and the record company that owns the sound reacording. Otherwise, performing rights must be obtained directly from the publisher.

How do you know which performing rights society represents a particular author, composer or music publisher for a particular song? Check the sheet music or the jacket of the phonorecord. If the performing rights society is not listed there, try calling or writing ASCAP, BMI or SESAC. They will be able to tell you if they represent the songwriter or music publisher in question. Addresses and phone numbers for the major performing rights organizations are listed in Appendix B.

WORKING WITH RIGHTS AND PERMISSIONS AGENCIES

Rather than seeking and securing music permissions themselves, some producers prefer to use agencies that specialize in obtaining clearances for music and other copyrighted works. The producer provides the agency with the name of the song or sound recording and, for a fee, it will determine who owns the copyright and how much it will cost to obtain the rights you require. Most agencies will also counsel clients about the options available if the rights to the original song or sound recording are either unavailable or prohibitively expensive. For producers of nonbroadcast programs, those options include making your own original recording and buying the right to use a sound-alike recording.

Should you use an agency to secure music rights and permissions, or should you do it yourself? Because agencies specialize in this line of work and because they will do all of the legwork for you, going with an agency will usually save you considerable time and hassle. In addition, because they are experienced in this area of media law, an agency can help make sure that you obtain all of the music rights and permissions required for the type of project you are producing. A good agency can also provide you with a standard music agreement that clearly defines those rights in language that will stand up in a court of law.

Of course, all of these benefits must be weighed against the cost of doing business with an agency. In fact, for most media producers, the choice comes down to a simple cost/benefits equation. If the benefits that the agency will provide are worth the fee that it will charge, go with the agency. If not, do it yourself.

If you do decide to go with an agency, be sure to establish, up front and in writing, what services the agency will provide and how the final bill will be tabulated (flat rate or hourly fee). Be sure to check on the agency's reputation before agreeing to a business arrangement. Call colleagues in the industry

who might have used the agency in the past, and ask the agency for references. Appendix B lists several music rights agencies that will be willing to
provide you with references and descriptions of their services.

USING MUSIC LIBRARIES

Much of the discussion of music clearances has focused on the complex
permissions process necessary when you plan to feature a copyrighted song
or sound recording in a production. But what if you are simply interested in
adding a bit of background music or some sound effects to a production? To
fill this need, many producers subscribe to one or more music libraries.

Choosing a Music Library Service

Music libraries specialize in providing copyright-clear music and sound
effects to producers of radio, film, multimedia, broadcast and cable television, and corporate and educational video productions. Although most
libraries offer a wide range of recordings, some specialize in selected areas
(classical themes, advertising jingles, sound effects, rock-and-roll selections,
and so on). Most libraries also offer their material in a range of formats: LP
records, audiotapes and compact discs. A list of several major U.S. music
libraries appears in Appendix B.

How do you decide which of the many competing music library services is
right for you? Start by determining which libraries offer the music or sound
effects materials that match your needs. Call or write to several library services and request their catalogs. Many music libraries will also provide a
sample of their collections on record or tape.

Fee Options

Once you have discovered which libraries fit your musical needs, you are
ready to determine which library can best meet your financial needs. This is
where the process becomes a bit more complicated. As the sample rate card
in Figure 6.1 shows, most libraries offer at least three fee options:

- a *needle drop* fee that requires you to pay a specified amount each time that
you use a library selection in a production;

- a *bulk rate* that provides reduced fees for high-volume use of single or mul-
tiple selections ; and

- a yearly *blanket rate* or *license* that permits unlimited use of the library's

Figure 6.1: Sample Music Library Rate Card

MAJOR MUSIC
Total Music Library Service

ANNUAL LICENSES
An annual blanket license provides for unlimited use of the entire Major Music library for a period of one year.

NONBROADCAST LICENSE $ 800.00
(for corporate, educational and independent producers of non-broadcast video, film and audiovisual productions)

BROADCAST/CABLE LICENSE $ 995.00
(for TV stations, cable television companies, video and film production companies and other producers of programs that will be displayed on broadcast or cable television)

NEEDLE DROP (INDIVIDUAL USE) FEES
Individuals and organizations that choose not to purchase an annual license can pay for Major Music materials on a individual use, per-production basis.

Length of Production	Nonbroadcast Use	Broadcast Use
5 minutes or less	$ 80.00	$120.00
10 minutes or less	$140.00	$210.00
15 minutes or less	$180.00	$250.00

Add $60.00 for every additional 5 minutes in production time.

BULK RATE

Unlimited use of any one piece for one year. $300.00

RECORDS, TAPES AND COMPACT DISCS

The Major Music collections are available on record, tapes, and compact discs. Prices are as follows:

Records (each)	$ 10.00
Tapes (7.5 ips or 15 ips) (each)	$ 20.00
Compact Discs (each)	$ 25.00

material for a single annual fee.

A few music libraries also offer a buy-out option. Under this arrangement, you make one large payment up front, and the library is yours to use forever. There are no needle drop fees, and there is no annual license payment.

Many music libraries add an extra layer of complexity to their pricing structures by charging different fees for different uses of their material. For example, producers of broadcast projects are typically required to pay more for an annual license than producers of nonbroadcast programs. In addition, needle drop fees often vary with the length of the production. The longer your production, the higher the fee. Some music libraries also charge higher needle drop rates when their material is used in television and radio commercials.

Annual licenses and buy-out arrangements are most appropriate for large production houses with hefty appetites for the sort of stock material that music libraries provide. For smaller production companies with more limited needs, a needle drop fee arrangement usually makes more sense. If you do go with an annual license, make sure that the deal requires the music library to provide you with any new material that it adds to its catalogue during the term of the agreement. In all cases, be sure that the music library states, in writing, that its materials are free from any copyright constraints that could restrict your options to use the materials.

MUSIC MADE-FOR-HIRE (COMMISSIONING ORIGINAL MUSIC)

Are you unable to locate stock music material that meets your needs or the permission you need to use an existing sound recording? Do you need a unique theme or musical motif for an important production? If any of these situations sound familiar, you may be a candidate for commissioning original music.

Contrary to what some producers assume, you do not have to be working on a big budget television or feature film project to consider commissioning original music. In fact, many producers of corporate and other nonbroadcast projects regularly contract with outside sources to obtain original songs and background music. However, while the heads of big budget productions can usually afford to hire big name composers and performers, producers of more modest projects must usually draw on the services of lesser known talent.

Full-Service Music Scoring Facilities

If you can not afford big name talent, how do you go about creating original music for a production? One option is to use a full-service music scoring and production facility. A true full-service facility can take your assignment from first concept through final mixing and laying down the music track on your master tape, provide music composition, orchestration and production services along the way. For the names of music composing and production companies in your area, look under "Music Arrangers and Composers" in the Yellow Pages or "Music Scoring and Production" in the various directories and production guides published for the video industry. As always, be sure to ask for references and samples of the company's work.

Music Production Contracts

Whenever you commission original music, the deal should be covered by a contract similar to the sample shown in Figure 6.2. The contract should start by spelling out the exact services that the individual or company will provide. Will the company be responsible for both composing and producing the music? For performing the final mix and layback? The contract must also specify who will own the rights to the music created under the agreement. Whenever possible, music for video productions should be created as a work-made-for-hire with you or your company, as the producer, possessing full ownership of and reuse rights to the materials. Try to avoid alternative arrangements in which the composer or music production house retains rights to the materials, since this can restrict your options to distribute the production in which the materials are used.

The sample contract in Figure 6.2 also includes several other provisions and clauses that should be part of any music production agreement:

• a consideration clause that spells out how much you will pay for the materials produced under the agreement and when you will pay it;

• a schedule that describes key stages of the project and when deliverables are due; and

• warranty and indemnity clauses that require the contractor to state that it has the right to enter into the agreement and full title to the materials that it will deliver.

In addition, if the project will involve individuals who are members of the various music and technical unions, the contract may have to include a clause that provides for residual payments. For more information on unions and residual payments, see Chapter 7.

Figure 6.2. Sample Music Production Contract

January 16, 1990

Ms. Rachel Wright
Wright Sounds, Inc.
1775 Irving Boulevard
Suite 22-B
Dallas, TX 75212

Dear Rachel:

This letter, when signed by you in the space provided below, will constitute a contractual agreement between Wright Sounds, Inc. (hereafter "WSI"), a Texas corporation with offices at 1775 Irving Boulevard, Dallas, TX 75212 and Industrial Media, Inc. (the "Producer"), a Texas corporation with offices at 740 Cortland Ave., Fort Worth, TX 76109.

The Producer hereby engages you to provide sound effects and original music (the "Materials") for a fifteen minute industrial videotape production (the "Production") that the Producer is preparing on behalf of its client, International Semiconductors, Inc. (the "Client").

I. DESCRIPTION OF SERVICES AND MATERIALS

Under the terms of this Agreement, WSI agrees to provide the following materials and services:

A. <u>Original Theme Music</u>. WSI will write, arrange and produce original music to be used as an opening and closing theme in the production. The full length of the theme will be 60 seconds. In addition, 5- to 10-second clips from the theme will be used to accompany four scenes indicated in the script and storyboards for the Production. The script and storyboards will be provided to WSI upon execution of this Agreement.

Figure 6.2. Sample Music Production Contract (cont'd.)

B. Library Music and Sound Effects. The script and storyboards for the Production indicate approximately 10 locations that call for library music and/or sound effects (sfx). WSI will select the music and effects in consultation with the Producer.

C. Mixing and Layback. WSI will mix and layback the voice tracks that the Producer provides plus the music and sound effects that WSI creates or supplies. Producer will provide WSI with the 1-inch master and a 3/4-inch cassette of the conformed show with visible time code. WSI will supervise and pay for the stripping of the track(s) off the master, their layout and mixing, and the layback of the mixed tracks onto the master tape.

II. CONSIDERATION

As full and complete consideration for providing the services and materials described below, the Producer will pay WPI a flat sum of $10,500, with $3000 of this total to be paid within 15 days of the execution of this Agreement and $7500 to be paid upon delivery and acceptance of the master tape with completed audio.

III. SCHEDULE

The schedule below indicates key dates in the development and delivery of the Materials. WSI agrees to conform to these dates and to notify Producer promptly of any anticipated delays.

1. February 5, 1990 Producer will provide WSI with a rough cut of the Production.

2. February 16, 1990 WSI will meet with Producer and Client to present rough concepts for the original theme music. Once Producer and Client have selected and approved a concept, WSI should schedule and complete recording of the original theme music.

Figure 6.2. Sample Music Production Contract (cont'd.)

3. February 22, 1990 Producer will provide WSI with a 3/4-inch videocassette copy and 1-inch master for the conformed show. Upon receipt of these materials, WSI will begin to layout the music and sfx tracks.

4. March 1, 1990 WSI will meet with Producer and Client to present and preview the tracks and/or proposals of sfx that WSI has for sweetening. Upon approval of the tracks and/or proposals, WSI will schedule a mix session and subsequent layback of mixed master onto the 1-inch master tape. This work must be completed in time to permit final delivery of master tape on March 10, 1990.

5. March 1, 1990 WSI will deliver completed master tape to Producer.

IV. OWNERSHIP OF MATERIALS

WSI expressly agrees that the Materials will be created as work-made-for-hire as the term is defined in the U.S. Copyright Act of 1976. All rights, title (including copyright), ownership and interest in the Materials will reside with the Client. To the extent that the Materials are not deemed works-made-for-hire, then this Agreement shall serve as an assignment to the Client of all right, title and interest in and to the Materials. In addition, WSI agrees that the Materials are not to be reproduced or used by WSI in any fashion without the Producer's and the Client's express, written permission. If Client chooses to use all or part of the Materials in other productions, no reuse fees will be due to WSI.

V. WARRANTEES

WSI represents and warrants that it has the right to enter into and fully perform this agreement; that the Materials written, prepared, composed and submitted by WSI shall be wholly original and shall not be copied in whole or in part from any other work and shall not

Figure 6.2. Sample Music Production Contract (cont'd.)

infringe upon or violate the right of privacy or publicity of, constitute libel against or infringe upon the copyright, trademark, trade name, property right or any other right of any person, firm or other entity; that all original Materials prepared under this Agreement and any music or sound effects Materials purchased from other sources (including Libraries) and provided under this Agreement shall, when delivered, be free and clear of any lien or claim by any party including, without limitation, any claim by any union, guild or performing rights society for any payments hereunder including any reuse fees for the Materials; and that WSI will obtain all of the rights, permissions and licenses that may be required to enable Producer and Client to fully exploit the materials.

VI. INDEMNITY

WSI shall at all times indemnify and hold harmless the Producer and the Client, their officers, directors, employees and licensees from any and all claims, damages, liabilities, costs and expenses, including reasonable counsel fees, arising out of the use by Producer and Client of the Materials furnished by WSI hereunder, or the exercise by Producer and Client of any rights granted to them, or any breach by WSI of any representation, warranty or any other provision of this Agreement. Producer and/or Client shall promptly notify WSI of any such claims and WSI shall have the right at its sole cost and expense to participate in the defense of any such action.

VII. MISCELLANEOUS

This Agreement constitutes the entire understanding and supersedes all prior understandings between the parties relating to the subject matter herein. This Agreement cannot be changed, amended, or terminated by the parties except by an instrument in writing duly signed by all parties. This Agreement and all mat-

Figure 6.2. Sample Music Production Contract (cont'd.)

ters or issues collateral thereto shall be governed by the laws of the State of Texas applicable to contracts executed and performed entirely therein.

IN WITNESS THEREOF, the parties hereto hereby execute this Agreement as of the first date specified above.

INDUSTRIAL MEDIA INC.   WRIGHT SOUND, INC.

By: _____   By: _____
Michael Prellinger   Rachel Wright
President   President

USING SOUND-ALIKE PERFORMERS AND RECORDINGS

Imagine that you are producing a video program for a client, and the client insists that the sound track include a recent pop music hit titled "Ready for You." The record label reveals that "Ready for You" was written by Ginny Lewis and published by Too Loose Music, Inc. The hit version of the song was recorded by Janice Jones and released by Pacific Records, Inc.

After a few phone calls and some legal correspondence, you are able to purchase permission from the music publisher to use the song. However, your earnest pleadings notwithstanding, Janice Jones and Pacific Records are unwilling to give you permission to use their hit recording of "Ready for You." You explain the situation to your corporate client, but the client still insists that the Janice Jones sound is what he or she wants. What's a producer to do?

In the past, you could get around this sort of problem by creating your own *sound-alike* recording of the song. First you would secure permission to use the song from the songwriter or music publisher. Then you would bring in performers or contract with a music production house to create a new sound recording. Usually, the idea was to end up with a recording that was as close to the original as possible. In this way, you could derive much of the benefit from using the song without having to pay for permission to use the original sound recording— assuming that this permission was even available. Some recording artists, including Irving Berlin and Bruce Springsteen, have never granted permission for their recordings to be used commercially.

In 1988, however, a ruling by the U.S. Ninth Circuit Court of Appeals in San Francisco cast a legal shadow over the practice of using sound-alike recordings. The ruling was a reversal of a lower court decision in a $10 million lawsuit brought by pop singer Bette Midler against the Ford Motor Company and its ad agency, Young and Rubicam. Ford had purchased the rights to "Do You Wanna Dance," a 1958 song that it planned to use in a television commercial promoting the Mercury Sable line of cars. More specifically, Ford planned to use Bette Midler's 1973 recording of "Do You Wanna Dance" in the commercial. However, when Young and Rubicam approached Midler for permission, she refused. The agency responded by hiring one of her backup singers and creating a new recording that mirrored Midler's version.

The Mercury Sable commercial containing the sound-alike recording hit the air in 1985. Bette Midler responded by suing Young and Rubicam, claiming that she had a property right to the voice and vocal style that were imitated in the commercial. The trial court disagreed, ruling that Midler did not have the property right that she proposed, and declared that the suit should not be allowed to proceed. But the 1988 Federal Appeals Court decision reversed the lower court ruling, and the matter continued in litigation. The case was finally resolved in 1989, when a Los Angeles jury decided in Midler's favor and awarded her $400,000 in damages.

Even though the lawsuit is over, the full fallout of the Midler case has yet to be felt. In particular, it is not clear how widely a ruling in this suit, in which the sound-alike recording was made after a performer specifically denied permission to use the original recording, would be applied in cases that are less clear-cut. Even so, many producers have become much more cautious in their use of sound-alike recordings and unknown performers who imitate big-name talent. One example of this new caution is the disclaimers that now appear in many commercials or promotions that feature lesser known performers mimicking stars.

In any case, one outcome of all this legal wrangling is already clear: if you

Figure 6.3: Music Rights Checklist for Media Producers

This checklist describes six different options that producers have for using existing and original music materials in a production. Start by reading all of the options listed and checking those that apply to your current situation. Then go back and review the explanation under each of the options that you checked. The explanations describe the steps that you must take to make sure that a particular use of music is legal and trouble-free. In instances that involve the use of existing music, you will usually need

Figure 6.3: Music Rights Checklist for Media Producers (cont'd.)

to secure *synchronization* and, sometimes, *performance rights* and a *master recording license* to the materials, all of which were defined and discussed earlier in this chapter.

Be aware that most of the checklist items assume that you will be using the music materials in an in-house, industrial production that will never be shown to the general public, transmitted on broadcast or cable TV, or displayed to an audience that has been charged an admission fee. If this is not the case (for example, if you are producing a program for cable television or a feature film), additional restrictions may apply. Also, in all cases, keep in mind that nothing obligates copyright owners to grant the permission that you are seeking. For that reason, it is always good to have an alternate that you can turn to if your first choice is not available.

1. You plan to use all or part of an existing sound recording (for example, a recording by a big name rock group or jazz performer) in a production.

To use an original recording, you must secure permission from two sources: the music publisher or songwriter who owns the copyright to the song (the music and the lyrics) and the record company that controls the master recording license rights to the recording. The permissions should be in the form of written agreements that specify the fees that you will pay for the rights the materials and the nature and extent of your rights to modify, distribute and reuse the materials. In particular, you should make sure that you obtain all of the rights you need to distribute the production containing the recording in all applicable markets. The written agreement should also warrant that there are no hidden rights attached to the song that could work to restrict your ability to distribute the finished production.

2. You plan to record your own version of an existing song, using the music and lyrics exactly as written.

This option may make sense if the rights to a pop-

Figure 6.3: Music Rights Checklist for Media Producers (cont'd.)

ular sound recording of the song are not available, or if you prefer a version of the song that is more closely tailored to your production needs. To use the original music and/or lyrics, you will need to secure and pay for permission from the music publisher or songwriter who owns the copyright to the song. That permission should be in the form of a written agreement that specifies the fees that you will pay for the rights to the song and the nature and extent of your rights to use and reuse your recording of the song. In particular, you should make sure that you obtain all of the rights you need to distribute the production containing the song in all applicable markets. You will also need to secure written releases from the performers who are involved in the creation of your recording of the song.

3. You plan to record your own version of the song with changes to the lyrics or music.

This option is often exercised by producers of commercials or industrial productions who need to change the lyrics to accommodate references to a particular product or client. To do this, you will need all of the permissions described under Option 2. You will also need written permission to make the changes that you are planning. As you may discover, this permission is not always easy to obtain, since some songwriters refuse to allow their work to be altered for commercial purposes. If they do allow you to make changes, some songwriters and music publishers reserve the right to review and approve your recording of the modified song.

4. You plan to use an existing sound-alike recording of an original song.

A sound-alike recording is a remake of a popular tune in which unknown performers strive to create a recording that sounds very close to the original hit version. Because you are not using the original recording, you will not need the permission of the record company that distributed the original version. However, you will still need to secure and pay for permission from the songwriter or

Figure 6.3: Music Rights Checklist for Media Producers (cont'd.)

music publisher that owns the copyright to the song (the music and lyrics). As always, that permission should be in the form of a written agreement that specifies the fees that you will pay for the rights to the song and the nature and extent of your use and reuse rights. You will also need a written agreement with the company that distributes the sound-alike recording. That agreement should spell out the terms under which the company will provide the sound-alike recording and the exact extent of your rights to use the recording. The agreement should also warrant that the work is free and clear of any hidden restrictions, (including the right of performers to receive residuals) that could restrict your ability to distribute the finished production that contains the sound-alike recording.

As discussed earlier in this chapter, recent court decisions have raised concerns about the legality of creating and using sound alike recordings. Before adding a sound alike recording to a production, you should consult with a lawyer who is familiar with the current status of litigation and legislation in this area.

5. You plan to commission original music for a production.

If you plan to create original music for a production, you will need to commission the services of some or all of the following: a songwriter/composer, an arranger, a producer, performers (singers and musicians), a recording engineer, sound technicians and a sound recording facility. Or, like many media producers, you may prefer to contract with a music production house that can provide the complete package of staff and services and manage the entire process for you. In any case, your relationship with each individual or group should be covered by a contract like the one shown in Figure 6.2. The agreement should define the exact services and materials to be provided, delivery dates for the services and materials, and the compensation that the contractor will receive for providing the services and materials by the dates specified. The agreement should also define who will own the materials produced under the contract and whether any royalties or residuals will be

Figure 6.3: Music Rights Checklist for Media Producers (cont'd.)

payable to the songwriter, performers and others who worked on the project. With rare exceptions, music created for your productions should be created as a work-made-for-hire, with you, as the producer who is paying for all of this, retaining full ownership of and reuse rights to the material. Be aware, however, that agreements with musician, composer and technician unions may require you to pay residuals, particularly if the production is intended for broadcast, cable, home video or theatrical distribution. For more information, see Chapter 7.

6. You plan to use music or sound effects purchased from a music library.

Music libraries specialize in providing copyright-clear music and sound effects to media producers. When you purchase materials from a music library, be sure to let the library know exactly how you intend to use the materials and make sure that the library warrants, in writing, that the materials are free from any copyright constraints that could restrict your right to use them in the manner you intend. Your written agreement with the music library should also specify the terms under which the library will provide the materials, your rights to use the materials, and the fees that you will be assessed for using and, if applicable, reusing the materials.

plan to use a sound-alike recording in a production, or if you plan to use a performer who will impersonate a star, be sure to consult with a lawyer who is familiar with the current status of litigation and case law in this area. Otherwise, you may become caught up in a test case yourself.

THE MUSIC RIGHTS CHECKLIST

If you are still not sure about how the rules governing music rights and permissions apply to a particular production, check out the music rights checklist in Figure 6.3. By following the instructions at the top of the checklist, you can help make sure that a particular use of music is legal and trouble-free.

SUMMARY

Why does music present special concerns for media producers?

With music materials, particularly sound recordings, it can be difficult for producers to determine what rights they need to the materials and who controls those rights. First, to use an existing sound recording in a production, there are usually at least three distinct rights that come into play: *synchronization rights* and *performance rights* and *master recording rights*. Second, there are usually at least two parties that control the rights to the recording: the music publisher or songwriter who owns the copyright to the song, and the record company that distributes the sound recording. In addition, there may be many more parties that claim some sort of ownership in the work.

What are the sources of the laws and regulations governing music rights?

Like all intellectual properties, musical works are protected by the U.S. Copyright Act of 1976 and international copyright law. United States copyright law defines several special categories of rights that apply only to musical works: *mechanical rights, synchronization rights* and *performance rights*. The copyright law also provides for several types and categories of musical works: songs or *compositions, sound recordings* and *phonorecords*.

What are the key types of music rights?

For media producers, the most important types of music rights are *synchronization* and *performance rights*. Synchronization rights allow you to link a song to the video track of your production. Performance rights allow you to show the production that contains the song to an audience. In addition, *master recording rights* allow you to use a pre-recorded sound recordingas part of your production. You must also make sure that you secure all appropriate *reuse rights* to the song.

What are performing rights societies, and what role do they play in the music permissions process?

Performing rights societies, such as BMI and ASCAP, are organizations that act as licensing agents for composers, songwriters and music publishers. The performing rights societies spend most of their time negotiating blanket licensing agreements with television and radio stations, theaters, restaurants, night clubs and schools. However, in rare circumstances, the societies may also negotiate individual licenses for songs that will be used in nonbroadcast productions.

What are music libraries?

Music libraries are services that specialize in providing copyright-clear music and sound effects to media producers. As their name suggests, music libraries maintain collections, or libraries, of music and effects that they license for use in media productions. Most music libraries offer both *blanket license* (unlimited use) and *needle drop* (single use) fee arrangements.

What are the special concerns surrounding the use of originally commissioned music in a production?

In commissioning original music, producers must make sure that the relationship with the composer or music production facility is covered by a written contract. The contract should define the exact services that the individual or company will provide. The contract must also specify who will own the rights to the music created under the agreement. With rare exceptions, music for video productions should be created as a work-made-for-hire with the producer possessing full ownership of and reuse rights to the materials.

7
Working With Unions

For media producers, working with unions often means having to work through a thick tangle of rules, restrictions and requirements. First, you must be willing to guarantee that performers receive wages that are at or above union scale, and you must also agree to contribute an additional percentage of the performers' wages to the union's pension and health plans. Second, you must also make sure that working conditions on the production (total working time, meal and rest breaks, etc.) satisfy the stringent specifications laid out in union contracts. Just as important, you must be willing to buy into the strict residual and reuse provisions that are part of most union agreements.

With all of this in mind, why don't producers simply choose to conduct all of their projects as nonunion productions? Many producers, particularly those in charge of corporate and other nonbroadcast programs, do just that. However, many other producers find that they have no choice but to work with union performers and technicians, particularly if one or more of the following conditions apply:

• the project requires the services of experienced, professional actors or musicians (since most professional performers are union members, especially if they work in or near one of the major production centers);

• the production is a feature film, broadcast television, or cable television project being produced in the United States (since this level of production almost always requires the use of professional performers and technicians—most of whom are union members);

• the production will involve facilities that are union shops; or

• the program is a corporate production, and the corporation's agreements with other unions require in-house producers to use union personnel.

Of course, there are also some producers who simply prefer to work with unions. In particular, some producers like the security of knowing that, as signatories to union agreements, they are protected from strikes and other work actions during production—as long as they live up to the terms of the agreements. Some producers also like the fact that, on union projects, all of the ground rules are laid out before production actually begins, courtesy of the very detailed specifications contained in union agreements. On nonunion projects, these details must be worked out through individual contracts with each performer or crew member. Although this can work to the advantage of producers, negotiating individual contracts can also create headaches and hassles at a time when most producers prefer to be focusing all of their energies on the creative task at hand.

This chapter discusses many of the major issues involved in working with unions on media production projects. Keep in mind, though, that a production does not necessarily have to be either "union" or "nonunion." Instead, it is possible to run a production as a hybrid project that employs both union and nonunion personnel.

WHAT ARE THE SOURCES OF LABOR LAW?

In the United States, the relationships between unions and employers are governed by two major federal statutes: the National Labor Relations Act (the Wagner Act) and the Labor Management Relations Act (the Taft-Hartley Act). The National Labor Relations Board (NLRB) is responsible for administering both statutes and ensuring fair practices on the parts of both employers and unions.

One important provision of federal labor law is that all employees have a right to join unions. In addition, employers are prevented from taking any action that could be perceived as a threat to legitimate union organizing activity. Like all employers, media producers generally have the legal right to choose not to work with unions, but they can never legally prevent their employees from exercising their right to join unions and to participate in union activities.

Federal labor law also protects the right of unions to negotiate collective bargaining agreements that define wages and working conditions for their members. These agreements can be negotiated with individual employers or, as is often the case, with groups of employers in the same industry. In some cases, two or more unions might band together to negotiate a comprehensive collective bargaining agreement with groups of employers. This is true in the television and film industry, where the Screen Actors Guild (SAG) and the American Federation of Television and Radio Artists (AFTRA), two unions that represent performers, often work together to negotiate agreements with the Alliance of Motion Picture and Television Producers (AMPTP), the group that represents the employers who produce movies and TV shows. (Addresses and phone numbers for the major unions appear in Appendix C.)

Producers should be aware that, because collective bargaining agreements can take a long time to negotiate, interim and amended agreements are often in effect. When in doubt, contact the appropriate unions to determine which versions of which contracts are most current.

THE MAJOR PERFORMER AND TECHNICIAN UNIONS

Most professional film television and radio performers are members of SAG, AFTRA or both. SAG and AFTRA represent actors, actresses, announcers, and other on-screen and on-air talent.[1] The Writers Guild of America (WGA) represents the scriptwriters who create the lines that are spoken by SAG and AFTRA members, and the Directors Guild of America (DGA) represents the directors who tell the SAG and AFTRA members when and how to say those lines. (For addresses and phone numbers, see Appendix C.)

There are also a number of specialty guilds and unions that serve specific groups of performers. These include the Screen Extra's Guild and various stuntmen's associations.

The major technical unions are the International Alliance of Theatrical Stage Employees (IATSE) and the National Association of Broadcast Employees and Technicians (NABET).[2] These two unions represent a wide range of technical and other off-camera production professionals, including sound technicians, editors, publicists, script supervisors, makeup and hair stylists, wardrobe coordinators, costume designers and wardrobe attendants, cartoonists, propmasters and photographers.

Some productions may also require the services of technicians and crew members from other unions: electricians from the International Brotherhood of Electrical Workers, drivers from the International Brotherhood of Teamsters, and so on. (See Appendix C for phone numbers and addresses.)

UNION CONTRACTS

As already mentioned, most relationships between unions and producers are governed by carefully crafted collective bargaining agreements. These agreements are usually preceded by many months of hard negotiations between the performer and technician unions and the Alliance of Motion

---

[1]In many areas, SAG and AFTRA have negotiated "twin" agreements with the Alliance of Motion Picture and Television Producers. For example, the AFTRA "National Code of Fair Practice for Non-Broadcast/Industrial/Educational Recorded Material" and the SAG "Industrial/Educational Contract" are essentially the same agreement. The main difference is that the SAG contract does not cover audiotape recordings or slide/tape shows.

[2]As a result of a 1990 merger, many NABET members involved in remote and non-broadcast production have joined IATSE.

Picture and Television Producers, the organization that represents employers in the film and TV industries. When the negotiations break down, or when the groups are unable to agree on the renewal of an existing contract, a strike sometimes results. This happened in 1980, when an actors' strike shut down television production for 10 weeks. It happened again in 1988, when a strike by writers sent producers scrambling for 22 weeks.

When the negotiations succeed (as they eventually seem to do), the result is a comprehensive contract that defines and delimits almost every aspect of the relationship between the union members and producers. For example, the current "industrial/education" contract between SAG and AFTRA and the producers of industrial and educational programs spells out the following terms:

• minimum rates for various types and terms of work, as shown in the sample rate card in Figure 7.1;

• supplemental wages for overtime or work on nights, weekends or holidays;

• required pension and health contributions;

• additional payments required for supplemental distribution of the production (distribution beyond the industrial and education markets, as defined in the agreement);

• payment periods, late payment surcharges and tax withholding obligations;

• assorted rules specifying payments for and performers' rights and obligations during auditions, rehearsals and casting, makeup, wardrobe and fitting calls;

• wardrobe allowances (assuming that the performer is required to provide a personal wardrobe);

• numerous provisions governing travel and transportation (payment for travel time, flight insurance requirements, type and class of transportation, overnight location expenses, etc.);

• requirements for personal injury and property damage insurance to protect performers during the employment period;

• specifications for meal breaks and daily and weekly rest periods; and

• job category restrictions that prevent performers from being used as stuntmen, extra players from being used as performers who speak scripted lines, members of the casting or production staff from being used as performers, etc.

Figure 7.1 Sample Performer Rate Card

The rates listed below are from the SAG agreement covering Industrial/ Educational productions that remains in effect until April 30, 1990. These are minimum scale wages. Performers are free to negotiate for higher fees. Separate rate cards exist for feature film, broadcast television and other types of commercial production.

	Category I*	Category II*
ON-CAMERA PERFORMERS		
Day Performer	$ 319	$ 396
Stunt Day Performer	319	396
3-Day Performer	801	988
Weekly Performer (5 Days)	1118	1385
Weekly Performer (6-Day Overnight Location)	1230	1521
Singer, per day		
Solo/Duo	319	396
Group	192	237
Step Out	240	297
On Camera Narrator/Spokesperson		
First Day	580	686
Each additional day	319	396
OFF-CAMERA PERFORMERS		
Day Performer (Voice Over)		
First Hour	261	290
Each additional half hour	76	76
Retakes		
Entire Script, first hour	261	290
Entire Script, each additional half hour	76	76
Partial Script, within 30 days		
30 minute session	142	142
Singer, per hour		
Solo/Duo	171	192
Group	114	128
Step Out	143	161

Figure 7.1 Sample Performer Rate Card (cont'd.)

EXTRA PLAYERS, DAILY RATES	Category I or II
General Extra	106
Special Ability (including stand-in, photo double)	117
Silent Bit Extra	169
Choreographed Dancer, Swimmer, Skater, etc.	284

Extra players receive $8.50 for first change of clothing brought to the set and $6.00 for each additional change of clothing brought to the set at the producer's request.

PENSION AND HEALTH CONTRIBUTION RATE: 11.5%

*Category I productions are programs developed "to train, inform, promote a product or perform a public relations function" and that are exhibited to select groups that are not charged an admission fee. Category II productions include point of purchase displays and other programs designed to "sell specific products or services" and that are shown at public places such as coliseums, railroad stations, air/bus terminals or shopping centers."

Of course, this partial listing does not even hint at the degree of detail present in the full text of union codes and contracts. For example, the complete AFTRA "National Code of Fair Practice for Nonbroadcast Industrial/Educational Material" exceeds 100 single-spaced pages and includes such specifics as the need for clothes racks, locker rooms and a suitable number of seats and cots for use by union members on the set.

Keep in mind, also, that these contracts set out minimum wages and conditions that producers must meet in hiring union members. The more talented and experienced a union performer, the more likely it is that the performer (or, more probably, the performer's agent) will require you to go above and beyond the minimums to secure his or her services on a production. In the case of big-name talent appearing in feature film or broadcast television productions, going above and beyond the minimal requirements may mean having to pay the performer a seven-figure salary plus a percentage of the production's profits. It may also mean having to provide the performer with a very plush dressing room, limousine service and all sorts of other amenities on and off the set.

Finally, note that the contract terms listed above were taken from the agreement that governs guild participation in industrial and educational productions. Union involvement in other types of productions is covered by other types of agreements, and those agreements can differ substantially from the industrial/educational contract. For example, the SAG agreement governing feature film production includes detailed specifications for the payment of residuals from revenues generated through theatrical distribution of the film and from the sale of rights to cable TV, home video and other supplemental markets. These specifications are much less central to the industrial/education agreement, since no residuals or additional payments are required unless the production is distributed to the general public.

MISCONCEPTIONS ABOUT UNION AGREEMENTS

As the preceding sections have suggested, the relationships between producers and unions are far from simple. Contract negotiations among the various groups can run for months or even years, and the agreements that result from those negotiations can contain more than 100 pages of very detailed rules and regulations. To make matters even more complex, the relationship between the parties is often complicated by misconceptions on the part of the producers who are not fully familiar with the union agreements. For instance, many producers assume that hiring SAG or AFTRA performers means that they must also use a union crew. In fact, nothing in the SAG and AFTRA agreements requires you to hire a union crew if you hire union performers. In particular, it is perfectly permissible for a corporate video department that uses its own in-house, nonunion staff as crew to hire SAG or AFTRA performers for a production. Although the SAG and AFTRA agreements do include language referring to other labor organizations, this language is limited to provisions that prevent producers from penalizing their members for refusing to cross picket lines set up by other unions that are conducting lawful, sanctioned strikes against the production company.

Many producers also mistakenly assume that, by signing an agreement with SAG or AFTRA, they will be required to use only SAG and AFTRA performers in their productions. As a matter of fact, nothing in the SAG and AFTRA agreements requires you to use any union performers. However, the agreements do require you to give "preference of employment" to "qualified professional performers." In both the SAG and AFTRA contracts, a qualified professional performer is defined as an individual who has been employed in the industry at least once in the previous three years. Of course, most performers who fit this definition will probably be members of SAG, AFTRA or both. But the agreements do permit you to hire qualified individuals who are not union members—as long as these individuals are paid on the union scale. The SAG and AFTRA contracts also make exceptions for individuals who are portraying themselves (such as company executives appearing in corporate productions), performers possessing unique skills or abilities and other special cases.

Producers should never enter into union agreements blindly. At the same time, producers should not be misled by the many myths and misconceptions that tend to exaggerate the dangers inherent in union agreements. When you are in doubt about what is actually contained in a union agreement, or when you need answers to any questions about specific provisions, call the union for a copy of the agreement. When in doubt about what those provisions, may mean for you or your company, contact a lawyer who is familiar with the current agreements.

SIGNING UP: BECOMING A UNION SIGNATORY

To become a SAG or AFTRA signatory, you simply request a copy of the appropriate agreement and return a signed copy to the guild or federation office. If you produce corporate or educational programs, you should sign the industrial/educational agreement. Separate agreements cover other categories of programming, including feature film and broadcast television production.

Most union agreements run for several years. By becoming a signatory, you will be required to abide by the terms of the agreement until it expires. At that point, you can choose to sign the newly negotiated agreement (assuming that SAG and AFTRA have come to terms with the AMPTP), or you can decline to sign and return to non-signatory status.[2]

All union contracts contain very detailed requirements governing the hiring and employment of union members. Some of the more significant requirements are summarized in the sections that follow.

Hiring

As mentioned earlier in this chapter, the SAG and AFTRA agreements do not require you to hire union actors, but they do require you to give preference in hiring to qualified professional performers—most of whom will be union members. Further, the agreements require you to give preference to performers who live within a "preference zone" of 50 to 300 miles from the production location.

The SAG and AFTRA agreements also lay down ground rules for auditions and the hiring process. Performers must be properly notified of the time

---

[2]You do not need to be a union signatory to employ union actors. For more information, see the section titled "Working with Union Members When You Are Not a Union Signatory" that appears later in this chapter.

and place of the audition, and the audition must be conducted under the proper conditions (the performer must be provided with complete information about the role, scripts must be readily available at the the time of the audition, etc.). Finally, the agreements specify what constitutes a firm engagement—or commitment of employment—from a producer.

Work Conditions

In the major union agreements, much space is devoted to describing the rules that govern the conditions under which union members may work. If the work condition requirements of the contract are not met, performers have the right to refuse to perform.

Some of the work rules are generic regulations that apply to all union members, while others are specific to certain types of performers. For example, while the AFTRA "National Code of Fair Practice for Nonbroadcast Industrial/ Educational Recorded Material" includes many provisions requiring producers to provide the proper work conditions for all cast members, it also features specific requirements for dancers, singers and other special categories of performers. Included in the rules for dancers are stipulations that the "floors for choreographed dancers must be resilient, flexible and level" and that the dance surface" must be swept and mopped at least once a day with a germ-killing solution."

If you are bound by a union agreement, it pays to determine which of the work condition requirements contained in the agreement—particularly those requirements related to health and safety concerns—apply to your production before rehearsal and shooting begins. Otherwise, you may find that your production is held up as performers file a protest with their union.

Wages and Contracts

All union agreements include a scale of minimum wages for performers (see Figure 7.1). This scale applies to performers who are union members and to nonunion performers who are hired on a production that is employing union members. In other words, if the union scale applies to at least one performer on a production, it must apply to all professional performers on a production.

As mentioned earlier in the chapter, the minimum scale is just that—a listing of the minimum wages that must be paid to performers. Individuals can, and often do, negotiate a wage that is above minimum scale. If a producer decides that a performer's talent and experience justify a salary that is above scale, that salary should be specified in the contract between the performer and producer.

The unions provide a standard contract that is used to engage scale performers and that can be modified to include over-scale salaries. Modifications to the standard contract are permitted only when those changes work to the benefit of the performer (an actor cannot accept an under-scale wage, for example) and only when the producer and performer indicate, in writing, that they have approved the modifications. If the producer engages the performer through a separate, nonstandard contract, the union may require that the contract contains language confirming that the producer and performer are bound by the terms of the current union agreement. Producers must file copies of all employment contracts with the appropriate union office.

Payment and Reporting

Under most union agreements, producers do not pay performers directly. Instead, the producer submits checks made out to the individual performers, along with the required reporting forms, to the nearest SAG or AFTRA office. The union then takes care of delivering the checks to their individual members. This helps the union keep closer tabs on who is working where and whether all of the requirements of the union agreement are being met.

In addition to submitting copies of employment contracts, producers are required to file various forms and reports with union offices. First, there is the production report that is submitted with or in advance of the checks for the performers' services. This form must specify the name of the principal production company and the name of the "sponsor," if any, that is paying for the project; the names of the performers employed on the production; the type of program that was actually produced (industrial videotape, feature film, a television commercial, etc.); the total rehearsal and recording time; and various other pieces of information that allow the union to track the project.

Some unions also require a separate report for recording payments to their health and retirement funds. Under the current union contracts, health and retirement payments usually run around 11% or 12% of the performer's total earnings on the production, exclusive of certain expenses and allowances.

Individual performers may also be required to file their own reports with their union offices. These reports include information similar to that contained in the production report submitted by the producer. Responsibility for filing this report resides solely with the performer, with the producer obligated only to initial the completed form.

Filing production reports and forms on time is more than simply a matter of keeping on top of your paperwork. Under the various union agreements agreements, failure to file the required reports within the specified deadlines can be considered a breach of contract that triggers work stoppages, fines or both. In most cases, the union supplies standard forms for any required reports.

REUSE AND RESIDUALS

Reuse fees are supplementary, usually one-time payments made to performers or technicians when the work that they contributed to a production is used again in a different production, or when a program produced for one market is released to another market. Residuals are supplemental payments made to performers or technicians each time that a production is sold, broadcast or displayed to the public. For example, the contracts between actors and the producers of television commercials often call for the actors to be paid a residual each time that a commercial is aired.

Depending on the type of production, this can be very tricky territory. Reuse and residual issues have become much more complex in recent years, particularly as new technologies have opened up new avenues for distributing programming. In fact, the debate over residual payments on programs sold through secondary channels such as home video has been at the core of several of the more serious disputes between SAG and AFTRA and film and television producers.

Category I and Category II Productions

Reuse and residual issues are most straightforward on industrial and educational programs produced for nonbroadcast distribution. Under the current SAG Industrial/Educational Contract, industrial and educational program are divided into Category I and Category II productions. Category I productions are programs developed "to train, inform, promote a product or perform a public relations function" and that are exhibited to select groups in "classrooms, museums, libraries or other places where no admission is charged." Category II productions include point-of-purchase displays and other programs designed to "sell specific products or services to the consuming public" and that are shown at sites "where the products or services are sold. . .or at public places such as coliseums, railroad stations, air/bus terminals or shopping centers." Because Category II programs are designed to be displayed to the general public, the minimum wage scale for performers appearing in these productions is higher than the scale for Category I performers. For single-day performers, for example, the current SAG scale is $319 per day for Category I performers, compared to $396 for Category II.

Changing Categories

What happens if the production is a hit and you have an opportunity to distribute it beyond the original category? Let's assume, for example, that you are hiring a SAG actor to appear in a training program that will be used to introduce a new product at your company's annual sales meeting—a clear Category I production. You hire the actor as a day performer for a single day, and you pay him the Category I scale wage of $319. But the production goes over so well at the meeting that the marketing division decides to use it as a point-of-purchase display—a Category II application. Under the terms of the SAG contract, obtaining Category II rights to the actor's performance will cost you an additional 50% of his original salary (if you are within 90 days of the date that principal photography for the production was completed) or an additional 100% (if you are beyond the 90-day grace period).

Cable Television Rights

What if, by some odd chance, you need basic cable television rights too? The right to run the production on basic cable for three years will cost you an additional reuse fee of 15% (within 90 days) or 65% (beyond 90 days) of the performer's salary. The SAG contract also lists fee structures for theatrical exhibition; non-network broadcast television use in the United States and Canada; foreign television display; sale or rental to industry; and various other forms of supplemental distribution. The contract does not, however, list fees for network television use or for the sale or rental of videotapes to the general public. These forms of distribution are covered by separate SAG agreements, and they require prior negotiation with and approval of the guild. Most probably, the agreement negotiated with SAG for network television broadcast or videotape sale of the program would require you to pay an additional fee plus residuals to the performer.

Broadcast Television Rights

If you produce broadcast feature films, broadcast television programs or television commercials, residuals are a prominent part of the production landscape. However, as already mentioned, this portion of the landscape has been radically reshaped by the growth of new distribution channels for films and television programs. As a result of these developments, residual requirements have become very complex in recent years—too complex to be covered adequately in the space available here. For example, the contract between a popular performer and the producer of a feature film might call for the performer to receive a certain percentage of the film's revenue from theatrical release, a different percentage of the revenue from home video sales and still another percentage of the money made from the network television release of the film. The contract might also call for residuals on cable television sales, sales to the broadcast syndication market, revenue from international distribution and so on.

The current SAG and AFTRA agreements specify the minimal residual requirements for performers appearing in theatrical films, broadcast television programs and other relevant types of productions. Usually, residual fees are figured into the cost of distributing and exhibiting a program, rather than into the cost of production. However, any producer who is involved in commercial film or television projects should make it a point to keep current on the residual requirements contained in the latest union agreements—particularly if the producer has an equity position in the project. The best way to keep current is to request and read copies of the relevant agreements.

WORKING WITH UNION MEMBERS WHEN YOU ARE NOT A UNION SIGNATORY

Imagine yourself in the following scenario. You are an independent producer who is creating an industrial video program that will be distributed to the managers of a major corporation. Your company is not a signatory to a union agreement. However, the actress you have in mind for the key role is a member of the Screen Actors Guild. You really want this actress for the role. How do you go about hiring her?

Of course, one option is to have your company become a full SAG signatory. You rule that option out, though, since it would obligate you to conduct this and all subsequent productions as union projects for the term of the current collective bargaining agreement.

A second option would be to pay the actress on the sly with the understanding that she would not report the job to SAG. But this would put the actress in an awkward position, and she could be fined by her union if this is discovered. Besides, the actress might not agree to the arrangement, and you prefer doing everything aboveboard, anyway. This combination of concerns rules out option number two.

This leaves you with two choices. You can arrange for a guild payroll services contract with a third party or you can sign a one-production letter of agreement with SAG. (The payroll services contract and single production agreement options, however, are available only to producers of industrial and educational programs. These options are not part of the agreements covering broadcast television, feature film and other types of commercial productions.)

Guild Payroll Services Contracts

The first option, arranging for a guild payroll services contract, is most appropriate for small companies that are unable or unwilling to take on the accounting and paperwork involved in hiring and paying union performers. Here is how it works. As a producer who is not a SAG signatory, you contract with a payroll services company that is a signatory to serve as the intermediary between you and SAG. For a fee, the payroll services company becomes the employer of record for the SAG performers who will work on the production. The payroll services company pays the performers and takes care of all the record-keeping and reporting required by SAG.

One-Production Letter of Agreement

The second option, signing a one-production letter of agreement, is usually preferred by bigger companies that have the resources to handle the union accounting and reporting requirements. This group includes large production houses that are not union signatories and corporate video departments whose parent companies can provide the necessary payroll and bookkeeping functions. By entering into a one-production letter of agreement, you become, in essence, a union signatory for the term of this production. However, your obligations as a signatory apply only to this production and not to other projects that you may be producing at the same time. Once you have fulfilled your obligations under the agreement, your status as a guild signatory ends. To arrange for a one-production letter of agreement, call the nearest SAG office and request a copy of the contract. There is no fee.

Union Guidelines

It is important to realize that, under both the the payroll services and single production agreement options, you will be required to conduct the production as a union project. This means that you must provide "preference of employment" to professional performers, and that you must follow other union guidelines in the hiring and employment of talent. In other words, you will be taking on all of the obligations of a union signatory—but only for this particular production.

BEYOND SAG AND AFTRA

Much of this chapter has focused on the ins and outs of working with SAG and AFTRA, the two major performers' unions. As a producer, you may also have occasion to work with other unions, particularly those that cover technicians, directors and writers. In many respects, the agreements that define the rules for working with these unions follow the same structure as the SAG and AFTRA agreements. They all specify scale wages and working conditions for union members, and they all provide for penalties in the event that the producer fails to comply with the terms of agreement.

Agreement Specifics: The Writers Guild of America (WGA) and the Director's Guild of America (DGA)

Of course, along with the standard language, each of the union agreements also contains provisions that are specific to that union. For example, the agreement with the WGA details minimum fees for the various types of writing that its members might be asked to take on: treatments, plot outlines, stories, screenplays and teleplays, rewrites, etc. The agreement with the DGA is just as detailed in defining the different jobs covered by the contract: director, unit production manager, first assistant director, key second assistant director, second assistant director, additional second assistant director, etc.

The International Alliance of Theatrical Stage Employees (IATSE)

Of all the union agreements, those with IATSE can be the most complex—if only because there are so many of them. Dealing with IATSE means dealing with one or more local shops, each of which represents a different category of technical employee, and each of which is usually covered by its own agreement. Although there are basic "East Coast" and "West Coast" contracts that provide some standards, each local agreement may specify distinct working hours, wage scales and certain other conditions of employment.

One provision that is part of many IATSE agreements is the "minimum crew" clause that specifies how many union members must be hired under given production circumstances. For example, the agreement with IATSE Local 644, the cinematographers local for the eastern United States, specifies that the minimum camera crew on a production that is part of a television series must consist of a first cameraman, an operative cameraman, first and second assistant cameramen and a still cameraman.

When in Doubt, Call

Although all of the different contracts and agreements can make for considerable confusion, a few phone calls to the unions can usually get you most of the answers you need to determine what your options are—and whether working with or without unions is in your best interest. Phone numbers for the major unions appear in Appendix C. If talking to the unions does not help, talk to a lawyer who is familiar with the current agreements and who has your best interest at heart.

SUMMARY

What are the major advantages and disadvantages of working with unions?

The major advantages of unions include being able to choose from a pool of professional performers and technicians (since most professionals are union members, particularly those who work near major production centers) and being protected from strikes or other work stoppages as long as you live up to the terms of the union agreements. Some producers also like the fact that, on union projects, all of the ground rules are laid out before production actually begins, courtesy of the very detailed specifications contained in union agreements.

The major disadvantages of working with unions include having to pay performers and technicians at or above union scale and having to make sure that work conditions on the production satisfy the very stringent union specifications. In some cases, those specifications may require you to pay residuals to performers and to hire extra technicians to meet minimum crew requirements.

What are the sources of labor law?

In the United States, there are two major federal labor statutes: the National Labor Relations Act (the Wagner Act) and the Labor Management Relations Act (the Taft-Hartley Act). The National Labor Relations Board (NLRB) is responsible for administering both statutes.

One important provision of federal labor law is that all employees have a right to join unions. Federal law also protects the right of unions to negotiate collective bargaining agreements with employers. In addition, employers are prevented from taking any action that could be perceived as a threat to legitimate union organizing activity.

What are the major performer and technician unions?

In the United States, the major performer unions are the Screen Actors Guild (SAG) and the American Federation of Television and Radio Actors (AFTRA). Other unions that represent creative production personnel include the Directors Guild of America (DGA), the Writer's Guild of America (WGA), the American Federation of Musicians (AFM) and the Screen Extras Guild (SEG).

The major technical unions are the International Alliance of Theatrical

Stage Employees (IATSE) and the National Association of Broadcast Employees and Technicians (NABET). Other technical unions include the International Brotherhood of Electrical Workers (IBEW), the International Brotherhood of Painters and Allied Trades (IBPAT) and the International Brotherhood of Teamsters (IBT).

If you conduct a production as a union project, must all the performers on the production be union members?

The SAG and AFTRA agreements do not require you to use union performers. However, the agreements do require you to give "preference of employment" to qualified professional performers—individuals who have been employed in the industry at least once in the previous three years. Although most performers who fit this definition will probably be members of SAG, AFTRA or both, you are allowed to hire qualified individuals who are not union members—as long as these individuals are paid on the union scale and provided with the applicable union health and pension payments.

If you hire union performers, will you be required to hire a union crew?

Nothing in the SAG and AFTRA agreements requires you to hire a union crew if you hire union performers. In particular, it is permissible for a corporate video department that uses its own in-house, nonunion staff as crew to hire SAG or AFTRA performers.

Can a producer who is not a union signatory hire SAG and AFTRA performers for a production?

Yes, producers of industrial or educational programs can hire SAG and AFTRA performers by signing a one-production letter of agreement with the union or by entering into a payroll services contract with a group that is a guild signatory. In either case, the producer will be required to conduct the production as a union project. In other words, the producer will be taking on all of the obligations of a union signatory—but only for this particular production.

What happens if you violate the terms of an applicable union agreement on a union production?

If you violate the terms of a union agreement, your production may be subject to fines, work stoppages or both. Work stoppages usually occur only when the violation constitutes a clear health or safety hazard to union members working at the production site.

8

WRAPPING IT UP: PROTECTING YOUR FINISHED PRODUCTION

All of the creative work is complete, and you are in the process of wrapping up your production. Along with making sure that the program is really ready to display or distribute, you should do a final check to make sure that you have left no administrative or financial loose ends. As part of the wrap-up process, you should also take the time to give the production one last legal review.

At this point, if you have been following the guidelines presented in the preceding chapters, your production should be in solid shape. First, as discussed in Chapters 2 and 3, you should have obtained signed contracts covering your relationships with performers, writers, technicians and other production personnel. In addition, your production's legal portfolio should include the following:

• records of any footage acquired from outside sources, and signed agreements detailing your rights to use the footage (Chapter 4);

• all city, county, state and federal permits and licenses issued during the production (Chapter 5);

• signed releases from all persons depicted in the program (Chapter 5);

• all location releases obtained from private property owners (Chapter 5);

• any insurance policies purchased for the production (Chapter 5);

• all necessary agreements and records covering your use of copyrighted music materials (Chapter 6);

• copies of any forms or records related to your use of union performers or technicians (Chapter 7).

As discussed in Chapter 5, you should also check your production for any potentially libelous statements and for any scenes that might violate some-

193

one's right of privacy or publicity. If you spot any questionable material, consult a lawyer who is familiar with these areas of media law.

As you are wrapping up a production, it is also time to think about registering your newly created property with the U.S. Copyright Office. In addition, for certain types of productions, you may want to look into trademarking the title of the program with the U.S. Patent and Trademark Office. If you will be making arrangements with a third party to distribute copies of the program, you will also need to consider how to protect your rights through a publishing or distribution contract. Finally, if your production will be broadcast, you should also be aware of several federal regulations affecting the content of programs broadcast on U.S. television stations.

Copyright registration, trademarks and patents, broadcast regulations and publishing contracts are discussed in detail later in this chapter. First, though, you should think about how to store and protect all of those production records and legal documents that you have been collecting.

KEEPING YOUR RECORDS STRAIGHT

Now that you have carefully collected all necessary production records and legal documents, what should you do with them? Like all important papers, your production records and documents should be stored in a secure location. It also makes sense to make a duplicate set of your records and to store them in a separate location. In addition, if an attorney was involved in preparing any contracts or other legal documents, the law office should retain copies. Your attorney should do this as a matter of course, but it never hurts to confirm that the law office has kept copies.

The best place to store your copies of records and legal documents is in a fireproof safe or file cabinet. Store the documents from individual productions in separate folders. In other words, do not mix the records from more than one production in one folder. Since questions usually come up on a production-by-production basis (e.g., "What was our arrangement with the scriptwriter on that United Foods project?"), storing the records from each production separately makes it much easier to find the documents that you need to answer questions when they do come up. Also, try to keep legal records and documents separate from other production paperwork (treatments, scripts, lighting designs, etc.). This will help to limit the number of times people must rummage through the legal file—and reduce the risk that key legal documents will be misplaced in the process. As a general rule, try to limit access to production files to as few people as possible.

If you are one of the growing number of producers who uses a personal computer to create contracts and other production documents, a few additional precautions apply. First, if you store your document files on a hard disk drive, be sure to backup all of your files on floppy disks. As anyone who has experienced a hard disk failure can attest, backing up your files on floppy disks is one safety step that is definitely worth the time and effort. Second, be sure to store all of the document files for a particular production on a floppy disk that is labeled with the name of the production. Then place this disk in the folder that contains the printed versions of the documents. If you will be storing a second document folder at a separate location, make a backup copy of the floppy disk for that folder, too.

COPYRIGHT REGISTRATION

Chapter 4 explained how copyright laws prevent you from using other people's creative properties without their permission. Now that you have completed a creative property of your own, you will want to make sure that it is fully protected too. In most cases, this means that you will want to look into registering your production with the U.S. Copyright Office, an office of the Library of Congress.

As discussed in Chapter 4, registration with the Copyright Office is not required for copyright protection. Under U.S. and international law, a work is considered copyrighted as soon as it is created, and failure to register the copyright does not diminish your right of ownership in the work. However, registration with the Copyright Office does confer a number of important benefits, including the right to sue infringers for statutory damages in addition to actual damages. Even more important, registration establishes an official record for the work—a record that the courts will accept as evidence supporting the validity of your copyright.

To Register or Not to Register

Before proceeding with the copyright registration process, you should determine whether registration is really necessary for the work in question. Although registration can never hurt, it may not be worth the effort for certain productions, particularly those with very limited lifespans. For example, registration may not be worthwhile for a corporate video production that was developed for one-time-only display at a national sales conference, or for a corporate production that is so specific to your company that it would be of limited interest or usefulness to potential infringers. As a general rule, the longer the potential lifespan of the production, the broader the planned distribution and display of copies, and the higher the reuse value of the footage, the more important it becomes to register the production with the U.S. Copyright Office.

Even if you decide not to register a production, be sure to retain records that show when the production was created, and always make sure that a full copyright notice, including the date of publication, appears on each copy of the program that you distribute. Even though a copyright notice is no longer required as a condition of continued protection, including it will help prove precedence and originality if, down the line, you are challenged by someone who claims that your program violates the copyright of material that was actually created at a later date. A copyright notice also reminds potential infringers that they are not free to distribute copies of or "borrow" footage from the production without your permission. For a more detailed discussion of copyright notices, see Chapter 4.[1]

Before You Register: Determining Ownership

You have decided that you do want to register your production with the Copyright Office. Before proceeding with the registration process (and before placing a copyright notice on the work), you must determine who actually owns the production. The registration application must be filed by the individual or group that owns the copyright or the owner's authorized agent.

Typically, the copyright on a media production is not owned by an individual, but rather by the company that created it or the client who commissioned it. If the production was created by a video or audiovisual department within a corporation, the copyright is almost always owned by the corporation. If the production was created by an independent production house under contract with a client, the client will usually hold the copyright. In other words, most media productions are created as works-made-for-hire with someone other than the production group owning the copyright. This is especially true for corporate and other nonbroadcast productions. The copyright ownership question becomes much more complex when you move into the world of broadcast television and feature film production, in which a number of individuals and groups (for example, the production company, the studio or distributor, the novelist on whose work the production is based, or big-name performers) sometimes share ownership in the work. As discussed in Chapters 2 and 3, the ownership question should always be addressed in the contracts that define the relationships among the various groups involved in the creation of a media production.

---

[1]If you place a copyright notice on your production and you publish (distribute) one or more copies to the public, you are required by law to deposit a copy with the Copyright Office. This is true regardless of whether you plan to register the copyright. More information about the deposit requirements is included later in the section titled "Filing for Registration."

In many cases, a production also incorporates material owned by others (stock footage, music, and so on). Unless the production is purely or primarily a compilation of preexisting material, or unless it is based on another work (as would be the case with a film based on a novel or play), you do not need to list all of these works and materials separately on the copyright registration form. However, you should indicate in section 6 of the registration form (see Figure 8.1) that the production does include some preexisting materials, and you should retain the written agreements with the copyright owners that define your rights to use the materials or underlying work.

Completing Form PA

Figure 8.1 shows Form PA from the U. S. Copyright Office, the form used for registering works of the performing arts. As defined by the copyright law, the performing arts category includes motion pictures, videotapes, (which the registration rules treat the same as motion pictures) and other audiovisual works. You can also use Form PA to register, as distinct works, treatments, scripts, musical and other component pieces that underlie a production. Registering these pieces as separate works usually makes sense only when the copyright for the components is held by someone other than the owner that will be listed for the entire work. Otherwise, a single registration will cover the work as a whole and all of its component parts.

When you apply to register a media production with the U.S. Copyright Office, you must always complete and file Form PA. Other forms used in applying for copyright registration include Form SR (for registering sound recordings) and form TX (for registering books, manuals and computer programs). If the production is a multimedia package that includes some combination of film, video, slide, sound and print materials, it is not necessary to use separate forms to register each type of component as a distinct work. Instead, the entire multimedia kit can be registered as a single, integral work using Form PA. This registration will cover all of the component parts.

In Section 1 of Form PA, you must specify the title of the work, any previous or alternative titles, and the nature of the work. For "nature of the work," indicate the type of production that you are registering: motion picture, television program, video program (intended for distribution on videocassette), slide/tape show, etc.[2] It is not necessary to get too descriptive here. If the work is part of a series, you must register each episode or segment separate-

---

[2] If the sound track from the production will be issued as a separate sound recording, it may also be necessary to file Form SR with the Copyright Office to register the recording as a distinct work. For more information, contact the U.S. Copyright Office.

Figure 8.1

FORM PA
UNITED STATES COPYRIGHT OFFICE

REGISTRATION NUMBER

PA   PAU

EFFECTIVE DATE OF REGISTRATION

Month   Day   Year

DO NOT WRITE ABOVE THIS LINE. IF YOU NEED MORE SPACE, USE A SEPARATE CONTINUATION SHEET.

1

TITLE OF THIS WORK ▼

PREVIOUS OR ALTERNATIVE TITLES ▼

NATURE OF THIS WORK ▼ See instructions

2 a

NAME OF AUTHOR ▼

DATES OF BIRTH AND DEATH
Year Born ▼   Year Died ▼

Was this contribution to the work a "work made for hire"? □ Yes □ No

AUTHOR'S NATIONALITY OR DOMICILE
Name of Country
OR { Citizen of ▶ _____
Domiciled in ▶ _____

WAS THIS AUTHOR'S CONTRIBUTION TO THE WORK
Anonymous? □ Yes □ No
Pseudonymous? □ Yes □ No
If the answer to either of these questions is "Yes," see detailed instructions.

NOTE
Under the law, the "author" of a "work made for hire" is generally the employer, not the employee (see instructions). For any part of this work that was "made for hire" check "Yes" in the space provided, give the employer (or other person for whom the work was prepared) as "Author" of that part, and leave the space for dates of birth and death blank.

NATURE OF AUTHORSHIP Briefly describe nature of the material created by this author in which copyright is claimed. ▼

b

NAME OF AUTHOR ▼

DATES OF BIRTH AND DEATH
Year Born ▼   Year Died ▼

Was this contribution to the work a "work made for hire"? □ Yes □ No

AUTHOR'S NATIONALITY OR DOMICILE
Name of country
OR { Citizen of ▶ _____
Domiciled in ▶ _____

WAS THIS AUTHOR'S CONTRIBUTION TO THE WORK
Anonymous? □ Yes □ No
Pseudonymous? □ Yes □ No
If the answer to either of these questions is "Yes," see detailed instructions.

NATURE OF AUTHORSHIP Briefly describe nature of the material created by this author in which copyright is claimed. ▼

c

NAME OF AUTHOR ▼

DATES OF BIRTH AND DEATH
Year Born ▼   Year Died ▼

Was this contribution to the work a "work made for hire"? □ Yes □ No

AUTHOR'S NATIONALITY OR DOMICILE
Name of Country
OR { Citizen of ▶ _____
Domiciled in ▶ _____

WAS THIS AUTHOR'S CONTRIBUTION TO THE WORK
Anonymous? □ Yes □ No
Pseudonymous? □ Yes □ No
If the answer to either of these questions is "Yes," see detailed instructions.

NATURE OF AUTHORSHIP Briefly describe nature of the material created by this author in which copyright is claimed. ▼

3

YEAR IN WHICH CREATION OF THIS WORK WAS COMPLETED This information must be given in all cases. ◄ Year

DATE AND NATION OF FIRST PUBLICATION OF THIS PARTICULAR WORK Complete this information ONLY if this work has been published.
Month ▶ _____ Day ▶ _____ Year ▶ _____ ◄ Nation

4

COPYRIGHT CLAIMANT(S) Name and address must be given even if the claimant is the same as the author given in space 2.▼

See instructions before completing this space

TRANSFER If the claimant(s) named here in space 4 are different from the author(s) named in space 2, give a brief statement of how the claimant(s) obtained ownership of the copyright.▼

DO NOT WRITE HERE / OFFICE USE ONLY
APPLICATION RECEIVED
ONE DEPOSIT RECEIVED
TWO DEPOSITS RECEIVED
REMITTANCE NUMBER AND DATE

MORE ON BACK ▶
• Complete all applicable spaces (numbers 5-9) on the reverse side of this page
• See detailed instructions
• Sign the form at line 8

DO NOT WRITE HERE
Page 1 of _____ pages

Figure 8.1 (cont'd.)

EXAMINED BY	FORM PA
CHECKED BY	

☐ CORRESPONDENCE
  Yes

☐ DEPOSIT ACCOUNT
  FUNDS USED

FOR
COPYRIGHT
OFFICE
USE
ONLY

DO NOT WRITE ABOVE THIS LINE. IF YOU NEED MORE SPACE, USE A SEPARATE CONTINUATION SHEET.

PREVIOUS REGISTRATION Has registration for this work, or for an earlier version of this work, already been made in the Copyright Office?
☐ **Yes** ☐ **No** If your answer is "Yes," why is another registration being sought? (Check appropriate box) ▼
☐ This is the first published edition of a work previously registered in unpublished form.
☐ This is the first application submitted by this author as copyright claimant.
☐ This is a changed version of the work, as shown by space 6 on this application.
If your answer is "Yes," give: **Previous Registration Number** ▼   **Year of Registration** ▼

5

DERIVATIVE WORK OR COMPILATION Complete both space 6a & 6b for a derivative work; complete only 6b for a compilation.
a. Preexisting Material Identify any preexisting work or works that this work is based on or incorporates. ▼

See instructions
before completing
this space.

b. Material Added to This Work Give a brief, general statement of the material that has been added to this work and in which copyright is claimed. ▼

6

DEPOSIT ACCOUNT If the registration fee is to be charged to a Deposit Account established in the Copyright Office, give name and number of Account.
Name ▼   **Account Number** ▼

7

CORRESPONDENCE Give name and address to which correspondence about this application should be sent. Name/Address/Apt/City/State/Zip ▼

Area Code & Telephone Number ▶

Be sure to
give your
daytime phone
◀ number

CERTIFICATION* I, the undersigned, hereby certify that I am the
Check only one ▼
☐ author
☐ other copyright claimant
☐ owner of exclusive right(s)
☐ authorized agent of
  Name of author or other copyright claimant, or owner of exclusive right(s) ▲

of the work identified in this application and that the statements made
by me in this application are correct to the best of my knowledge.

Typed or printed name and date ▼ If this is a published work, this date must be the same as or later than the date of publication given in space 3.

_____ date ▶ _____

Handwritten signature (X) ▼

8

**MAIL
CERTIFI-
CATE TO**

Name ▼

Number/Street/Apartment Number ▼

City/State/ZIP ▼

**Certificate
will be
mailed in
window
envelope**

Have you:
• Completed all necessary spaces?
• Signed your application in space 8?
• Enclosed check or money order for $10 payable to *Register of Copyrights*?
• Enclosed your deposit material with the application and fee?
MAIL TO: Register of Copyrights. Library of Congress. Washington. D.C. 20559

9

* 17 U.S.C. § 506(e). Any person who knowingly makes a false representation of a material fact in the application for copyright registration provided for by section 409, or in any written statement filed in connection with the application. shall be fined not more than $2,500.

U.S. GOVERNMENT PRINTING OFFICE 1986–491-560 40 007

July 1986–200.000

ly, since each is considered a distinct work for copyright purposes. It is permissible, however, to group the segments on a single PA form, as long as you list each item that is being registered. However, if you are registering a multimedia kit, you should list the types of materials that comprise the kit (e.g., "multimedia kit, including videotape and workbook").

Section 2 of Form PA is where you designate who owns the media materials that you are registering. If the entire production was created as a work-made-for-hire, as is the case with most corporate productions, the employer or client for whom the work was created should be listed as the sole author and should file the registration form. But what if the production was not created as a pure work-for-hire? For example, what if one or more individuals are claiming a legitimate ownership interest in the work? If this is the case, you should list each of the individuals in the slots labeled "name of author." Section 2 of Form PA has slots for listing three authors, and you can list more on separate sheets. In addition, in the slots labeled "nature of ownership," you should indicate what each individual contributed to the work (script, original music, animated sequences, the novel on which the script was based, etc.).

Section 3 of Form PA asks you to indicate when the work was completed and when it was first published. Although the completion and publication of media productions can occur almost simultaneously, these dates are usually different. Under U.S. copyright law, the date of completion is defined as the point at which the work first appears in fixed form. For a video production, for example, this would typically be the point at which you have completed the tape that you will use as the master for creating copies. The date of publication is defined, in most cases, as the point at which you actually begin distributing the copies.

In the case of a production created over an extended period of time, it is possible to register preliminary versions of the production that are fixed at a particular point in time. Just be sure to file a separate Form PA when the production is complete and indicate, in Section 5 of the form, that previous versions of the work had been registered. Along similar lines, it is also possible to register a completed work that has not yet been published. In this instance, simply leave the date of publication blank.

In Section 4 of Form PA, you must designate who is claiming the copyright for the work that is being registered. The copyright claimant is either the author of the work (which, in the case of a work-made-for-hire, is the employer or client for whom the work was created) or the individual or group to whom the original author has transferred the copyright. If the copyright was transferred to an individual or group that is now claiming ownership of the work, Form PA requires you to indicate how the transfer took place. For example, if the transfer occurred through a written contract with the original owner, as is often the case with media productions, you would simply type or write "by written contract" in the space provided.

As mentioned above, Section 5 is where you indicate whether the work has been registered before. If the work was registered previously, you must check the appropriate box to explain why you are seeking another registration. Legitimate candidates for re-registration include productions that were registered in unpublished form and that are now published, productions for which the copyright claimant may have changed through a transfer of ownership following the original registration, and productions that are changed versions of a previously registered work. If the latter is the case, you must explain how the work has changed in Section 6.

Section 6 of Form PA applies to productions that are derivative works or compilations. It also applies to works that were registered in one or more previous versions. When completing Section 6, you must begin by identifying the preexisting copyrighted or public domain materials on which the work is based. Then you must explain what new material you have added to justify a claim of originality and the need for a new registration. For example, if your work is a television production based on a short story, you would begin by providing the name of the story in item 6a. Then, in item 6b, you would explain that your production is a "dramatization for television." Similarly, if you are registering a new version of a previously registered production, you would begin by providing the name of the previous version—even if it is the same as the name for the new version. Then, in item 6b, you would explain how the version that you are currently registering differs from the previous version (e.g., "revisions to more than 10 scenes," "revisions to many scenes and three new scenes added," etc.).

Sections 7, 8 and 9 ask you to supply some additional information that will help the Copyright Office process your application. Be sure to indicate the correct address to which correspondence about your application and the registration certificate should be sent. This will typically be your business address or, if you use an attorney on copyright matters, your attorney's address. If you have an account with the Copyright Office and you want the $10 copyright fee to be charged to that account, complete the deposit account item in Section 7 of the application form.

Filing for Registration

Once you have completed Form PA, you are ready to file for registration with the Copyright Office. Along with Form PA, you must submit a check or money order for $10 as a processing fee (unless you have indicated on Form PA that you are charging the fee to your deposit account). You must also submit the required "deposit materials."

Deposit Requirements

Under the Copyright Act of 1976, producers of motion pictures and videotapes that are published with a copyright notice are required to send the Copyright Office both one complete copy of the film or tape and a written description of the contents. You must submit these deposit materials within three months of publication (the date at which you begin distributing copies of the work) regardless of whether you plan to register the work. However, since you must make the deposit anyway, it makes sense to submit the required materials along with Form PA and your registration fee. If you submit the materials outside of the registration process and then decide to register the production at a later date, you will have to deposit an additional copy.

The Written Description

The written description submitted for deposit should be a shooting script or some other complete production document that provides a full accounting of the work. At a minimum, the description should include:

1. The title of the work. If the work is part of a series, both the continuing title and the episode title and/or number, if any, of the particular episode, installment, or segment should be given;

2. A statement of the nature and general theme of the work and the summary of its plot or contents;

3. The date when the motion picture was "fixed" (that is, generally when the filming or video recording was completed). If the motion picture consists of an authorized video recording of a live television program made simultaneously with the telecast, the description should make this clear and should contain information about the telecast;

4. If the work has been transmitted on television, the date of the first telecast;

5. The running time; and

6. The credits appearing on the work, if any.[3]

Of course, you are also free to include other information that will help identify and distinguish your production.

---

[3]"Copyright Registration for Motion Pictures including Video Recordings," Circular R45, Copyright Office, Library of Congress, 1980, 13.

Submitting a Copy of the Work

Along with the written description, you must submit a copy of the production to the Copyright Office. Under the rules for registering copyright, there are separate requirements for depositing copies of unpublished and published works. If the work is unpublished, you have a choice. You can go the full route and deposit one complete copy of the production that contains all of the visual and aural elements that you want the registration to cover, or you can opt to deposit what the Copyright Office calls "identifying material." The identifying materials for motion pictures and video recordings can include either an audio recording (cassette, reel tape, etc.) that reproduces the entire soundtrack or a set of prints (stills) consisting of one-frame enlargements from each 10-minute segment of the work. If you choose not to deposit a complete copy and instead go with the identifying materials option, the Copyright Office requires that your written description include all six of the elements listed above.

If you are registering a published motion picture or videotape, or if you have published the production and are submitting the required copy outside the registration process, you do not have a deposit option. You must submit both the written description and a complete copy that represents the best edition of the production. The Copyright Office defines the terms "Complete Copy" and "Best Edition" for the producer:

A copy is "complete" if the reproduction of all of the visual elements comprising the copyrightable subject matter in the work is clear, undamaged, undeteriorated, and free of splices, and if the copy itself and its physical housing are free of splices, and if the copy itself and its physical housing are free from any defects that would interfere with the performance of the work or that would cause mechanical, visual, or audible defects or distortions....

The "best edition" is that edition published in the United States at any time before the date of deposit that the Library of Congress determines to be most suitable for its purposes. The criteria, listed in order of importance, are:

1. Film
    a. Preprint material, by special arrangement
    b. Most widely distributed film gauge
    c. 35 mm rather than 16 mm
    d. 16 mm rather than 8 mm
    e. Special formats (for example, 70 mm) only in

> **exceptional cases**
> **f. Open reel rather than cartridge or cassette.**
> **2. Videotape**
>   **a. Most widely distributed tape gauge**
>   **b. 2-inch tape**
>   **c. 1-inch tape**
>   **d. 3/4-inch tape cassette**
>   **e. 1/2-inch tape cassette** [4]

If it is not practical to submit the deposit (for example, a 1-inch videotape) in the same package with Form PA and the registration fee, you can send the deposit separately. If you do this, make sure that the package contains a clear request that the deposit materials be held in connection with an application for registration that is being filed under separate cover.

Exceptions to the Deposit Rule

If fulfilling the deposit requirements will present severe problems for a producer, it is possible to apply for a waiver or exception under two provisions of the regulations: the *Motion Picture Agreement* and a procedure called *Special Relief*.

The first option, the Motion Picture Agreement, helps if you are able and willing to submit the deposit copy but you would like to get it back. By requesting and signing the Motion Picture Agreement, you can have your deposit returned to you, at your expense, after the copyright registration is complete. However, the deposit is subject to recall for addition to the permanent collection of the Library of Congress for a period of two years, and you must agree to resubmit a copy of archival quality if the Library of Congress exercises that option. For more information about the Motion Picture Agreement, write to:

> The Deposits and Acquisitions Section
> Acquisitions and Processing Section
> Copyright Office, Library of Congress
> Washington, DC 20559

The second option, special relief, is worth looking into if extenuating circumstances prevent you from submitting a deposit that satisfies the "complete copy" and "best edition" standards described above. Special relief is

---

[4]"Copyright Registration for Motion Pictures Including Video Recordings," Circular R45, Copyright Office, Library of Congress, 1980, 13-14.

considered on a case-by-case basis. To be considered, write to the Chief of the Examining Division of the Copyright Office. In you correspondence, indicate that you are requesting special relief and provide a detailed description of the reasons for the request. The correspondence must be signed by or on behalf of the person applying for copyright registration.

The Film Collection of the Library of Congress

Although producers tend to view the copyright deposit requirements as burdensome, they do result in one significant, and generally unrecognized, benefit for media professionals. Most of the materials obtained through the deposit requirements are placed in the Library of Congress's film and video collection. Once they are entered into the collection, the materials can be screened by individuals who are conducting research for a publishing or production project. There are some restrictions governing access to the collection, however. Works from the collection can only be viewed at the library, and reproduction or loaning of materials is not permitted without the prior, written consent of the copyright owner. In addition, access to the collection must be arranged in advance. For more information, contact the Motion Picture and Television Reading Room, Library of Congress (202-707-1000).

The Certificate of Registration

You have submitted a completed, signed Form PA to the Register of Copyrights. You have also submitted the $10 filing fee and the required deposit materials. Now what happens?

The Register of Copyrights will review and, if everything is in order, approve your application. Then the Copyright Office will send you a Certificate of Copyright Registration. Although this piece of paper may not look like much, it will prove very valuable if you ever find yourself involved in an infringement action or some other dispute over ownership of the registered materials. For this reason, the Certificate of Registration should be stored in secure place with your other production documents.

It is important to note that, in registering materials, the Copyright Office is not certifying their authenticity or originality—only that they existed on the date specified in the Certificate of Registration and that the ownership information from Form PA has been entered in the copyright records. If a production that you have submitted for registration includes material stolen from other works, for example, the Register of Copyrights will not know that, and it will go ahead and issue a Certificate of Registration anyway. At a later point, however, the owners of the materials that you have stolen may come after you with proof of their own, including their own Certificate of

Registration and copies of the original materials, to show that you have used their work illegally. If they prove their case, the Copyright Office may also come after you for failing to disclose your use of previously copyrighted materials on the registration form—an offense for which you can be fined up to $2500.

PROTECTING TITLES THROUGH TRADEMARKS

As you know, copyright law protects the content of your production—the sounds and images that comprise the program—from unauthorized use. But what about the title of the production? For example, if you produced an executive exercise program called "The No-Sweat Workout," would copyright law prevent someone else from using the same name for another production?

First the bad news. Under copyright law and the U.S. Copyright Office rules, "names, titles, and short phrases or expressions are not subject to copyright protection." In other words, nothing in the copyright statute or the copyright office regulations would prevent other producers else from stealing your terrific title. Now for the good news. Although copyright law cannot help, you may be able to protect your title by turning to another area of intellectual property law: trademark law.

What Is a Trademark?

A trademark is a "word, symbol, design or combination word and design... which identifies and distinguishes the goods or services of one party from those of another."[5] In other words, a trademark is a name or logo that helps establish an identity for a product and that serves to distinguish the product from the competition. Examples of well-known trademarks include Xerox® (for copiers and other office equipment), Kodak® (for film and photographic equipment), Dolby® (for a noise reduction system used in audio equipment), and Coppertone® (for suntan lotion). When the mark distinguishes a service rather than a product (for example, AutoExpress℠ for a fast check-out service for rental cars), it is called a service mark.

When a trademark appears in print, it is usually accompanied by the ™ or ® symbol. The ™ indicates that the mark is in the process of being registered or that the owner intends to register it. The ® indicates that registration has been secured and that the mark is now a registered trademark. If the name is a service mark, the ℠ symbol is used.

---

[5] "Basic Facts About Trademarks," U.S. Department of Commerce: Patent and Trademark Office, 1989.

What Are the Sources of Trademark Law?

In the United States, trademark law is governed by a mix of common law and state and federal statutes. This contrasts significantly with copyright law, which is governed by a single federal statute—the Copyright Act of 1976 (as modified by the United States adherence to the Berne Convention). The difference derives from the U.S. Constitution, which specifically gives Congress the power to grant and govern copyrights and patents, but which includes no comparable provision for trademarks. As a result, Congress has had to approach trademarks less directly, through its constitutional power to regulate interstate commerce. This has limited federal jurisdiction to regulating the interstate use of trademarks, a limitations that has left the door open for the courts and state legislatures to play a continuing role in shaping trademark law.

The major federal trademark statute is the Trademark Act of 1946, known as the Lanham Act. The Lanham Act defines the types of names that can benefit from federal trademark protection, the scope and duration of that protection, and procedures for federal registration of trademarks. In the United States, registration and other federal trademark procedures are administered by the Patent and Trademark Office (PTO) of the U.S. Department of Commerce.

On November 16, 1988, Congress passed the Trademark Law Revision Act of 1988, the first comprehensive revision of the Lanham Act. One of the major changes introduced by the 1988 legislation is its provision for registering a trademark before the mark has actually been used in interstate commerce. For more information, see the section on the trademark registration process that appears later in this chapter.

Individual states also have their own trademark laws. In most cases, the state laws and registration procedures parallel the federal trademark provisions, with trademark status being granted on a "first use" basis to qualified names. In other words, on both the federal and state levels, the first person or company that uses a product name has the right to claim the name as a trademark—as long as that name is sufficiently distinct from other marks. However, the courts have been kept busy over the years trying to sort out exactly what constitutes first use and a "distinct" mark. Through their involvement in these and related issues, the state and federal courts have created a considerable body of case law in the areas of trademarks and unfair competition.

Trademark registration at the state level can play a significant role in establishing the first use of a product name and in protecting products that are distributed within a particular state. However, because most products, including media productions, are distributed across state lines, anyone who is serious about trademarking a name or title should probably pursue federal registration. Most of the discussion that follows focuses on the federal trademark regulations and registration procedures. Information about a state's trademark laws can usually be obtained from the agency responsible for registering corporations or regulating commerce within that state.

Trademarking the Titles of Creative Works

What types of names can be registered for federal trademark protection? For manufactured goods, the rules are quite clear and straightforward. With few exceptions, almost any name that distinguishes a company's manufactured products is eligible for federal trademark registration—as long as the product has been sold in interstate commerce, and as long as the mark is not similar enough to an existing trademark in the same category of products (clothing, games and playthings, medical apparatus, etc.) to cause confusion.

The trademark rules are less clear when it comes to registering the titles of books, media productions and other creative works. One intent of trademark law, as it has evolved, is to protect the names of goods and services that are likely to have a lasting lifespan in the marketplace. In other words, the trademark regulations assume that there is a need to protect the titles of products and services as they attempt to establish and maintain an identity in a marketplace that is often crowded with competing goods and services. There is also a recognized need to protect marks that are used to label entire lines of products (Macintosh® computers, Bic® pens, etc.), so companies can have a reasonable opportunity to recover the investments that they have made in developing and establishing a product line.

As products go, most creative properties are fairly ephemeral. For example, most books and media productions go into and out of distribution in a matter of a few years. This means that, if you went ahead and tried to register the title of a book or production as a trademark, it might well be on its way out of distribution by the time that the registration was issued. This is significant, because continued use of the mark in commerce is a requirement of continued trademark protection. Once you have registered a trademark, you must continue to use it or you will lose it.

Also, although a good title can help sell a creative work, the title is usually not the essential feature that distinguishes one creative product from another in the marketplace. For example, if you produced a film and called it *Casablanca*, it is unlikely that many people would buy a ticket to your film assuming that they were going to see the Humphrey Bogart original—unless you were also guilty of some serious false advertising. However, if you manufactured a washing machine and distributed it under the Maytag or Westinghouse label, you might well cause considerable confusion in the marketplace for major appliances. In other words, media productions and other individual creative properties are not like washing machines, microwave ovens or any other type of product for which brand name recognition often plays a major role in the purchasing decision. As result, since there is less of a threat of confusion in the marketplace for media productions, there is less perceived need to protect the names of creative properties through trademark registration.[6]

For these reasons, the PTO is usually reluctant to grant federal trademark protection to the titles of individual media productions or other creative works. It generally is willing, however, to trademark the name of a series of media productions, books or other intellectual properties. This means, for example, that although you probably would not be allowed to trademark the title *No Sweat Workout* if it was attached to just one exercise video, you probably could trademark the title if it covered a series of programs that would have an extended lifespan in the marketplace (*The No Sweat Workout: Original, Classic Edition, The No Sweat Workout: Low Impact Edition, The No Sweat Workout: No Impact Edition*, etc.). It would also be possible to protect the title by trademarking it in connection with its use on manufactured merchandise (a possibility if, for example, you are marketing a line of executive exercise clothing called *No Sweat Sweats* alongside your "No Sweat Workout" videos).

For most media productions, then, registering the title as a trademark is not really an option unless the production is part of a series of programs sold under the same title, or unless you are also planning to use the name on manufactured products. However, even if your title is not eligible for federal trademark registration, it might still qualify for protection under state statutes and case law governing trademarks and unfair competitive practices. In addition, you may be able to register a particular design or logo that is used in connection with a production or title, and you might want to register the name of your production company. For more information about the criteria that determine whether it makes sense to try to register for federal trademark protection, see the section that follows.

---

[6]The preceding paragraph is not meant to suggest that it is safe or acceptable to use *Casablanca* or any other existing and known title as the name for your production. While doing so would not be considered a trademark violation, you could leave yourself open to unfair competition or "false designation of origin" challenges. In addition, if your production is a film, you could also run into trouble with the Motion Picture Association of America (MPAA), the industry group that gives films audience ratings (G, PG, PG-13, etc.) and that operates a title registration service. The MPAA will not give a rating to or allow its members to distribute a motion picture whose name is likely to be confused with that of a film that is already in distribution.

The Federal Trademark Registration Process

You have decided that the title "No Sweat Workout" is catchy and potentially valuable enough to be worth protecting, and you would like to register it as a trademark. How do you go about it? As a first step, you should stop and evaluate whether trademark registration is really worth the effort. As the next step, assuming that you decide to proceed, you will need to conduct a search to determine if the name, or a similar name, is already trademarked or being used by someone else. Then, if you find that your title is unique, you will need to fill out and file the appropriate registration forms with the PTO (Patent and Trademark Office).

Once you file for trademark registration, be prepared to wait. It can take six months or more for an initial ruling from the PTO, and two years or more for the full registration process to run its course.

Step 1: Determining if Trademark Registration Is Worth the Effort

Earlier in this chapter, the section on Copyright Registration warned that, for some productions, copyright registration might be more trouble than it's worth. This is even more true for trademark registration. First, compared to copyright registration, the trademark registration process is more complicated and costly. Second, once you complete the application process, the PTO may rule against your request for registration. As discussed earlier, only titles that cover a series of productions or that are used in connection with merchandised materials are eligible for trademark protection.

For these reasons, you should begin by asking if your title meets the minimum eligibility requirements for registering the title of a creative work. Does the title cover a series of programs? Is it used on merchandised materials? If neither is the case, you should probably forget about proceeding with trademark registration, since your title is probably not eligible for federal trademark registration. If you feel that yours is a special case and you would still like to proceed, it would pay, at this point, to pause and discuss matters with an attorney who specializes in trademark law. The attorney should be able to tell you if yours is a special enough case to stand a chance of being made an exception to the Patent and Trademark Office's general rules.

Even if your title meets the minimum eligibility requirements, trademark registration may not necessarily be the right route for you. If you proceed with registration, you will need to take the time or spend the money to conduct a trademark search. You will also need to determine whether your title is distinct and "protectable" enough to withstand both the scrutiny of the PTO and challenges from other trademark holders. This determination is best made with counsel from a trademark attorney—and counsel costs money.

Finally, once you have registered the mark, you will need to make sure that you follow all of the proper procedures to guarantee that the trademark retains its protected status.

To decide whether registration is worth this effort and expense, you need to assess what the title is truly worth to you. Do you have definite plans to continue developing programs or materials that use the title? Will the programs or materials enter a market in which a "brand name" is important? In other words, how much do you stand to gain from trademarking the title, and what do you stand to lose if you do not register it?

As you are making this assessment, keep in mind that federal trademark registration is not the only way to protect a title. You can look into registering the mark at the state level, for example, and many states have passed unfair competition laws that will prevent others from simply stealing your mark. In fact, you do not have to register the trademark to enjoy many of the protections provided by federal trademark law. However, registration with the PTO does provides several advantages, including the following:

• The right to sue in federal court for trademark infringement, and the right to recover profits, damages and costs (including the possibility of recovering treble damages and attorney's fees) through a federal court infringement action.

• *Prima facie* evidence of the validity of the registration, the registrant's ownership of the mark and the registrant's exclusive right to use the mark in commerce in connection with the goods or services specified in the certificate.

• "Constructive" notice of a claim of ownership (which eliminates a good faith defense for a party adopting the trademark subsequent to the date of registration).

•The right to deposit the registration with Customs in order to stop the importation of goods bearing an infringing mark, and a basis for filing trademark applications in foreign countries.

Because other prospective trademark users will usually check the federal trademark listings before adopting a mark, registering your title with the PTO will also put out the word that the title is already in use. Getting the word out in this way will help deter others from adopting the same or a similar mark.

If you have determined that your title is eligible for federal trademark protection and if the benefits of registration listed here outweigh the costs, proceed to step 2. If you decide not to proceed, you may still want to consider speaking with a trademark attorney to determine what protection might be available outside the federal registration process.

Step 2: Determining the "Protectability" of Your Title

Your title *No Sweat Workout* covers a series of programs, so you know that it satisfies one of the key criteria for registering the titles of creative works. You have also decided that the title is valuable enough to justify the time and expense involved in registering the title with the PTO. The next step is to determine whether the title, in its present form, is distinct enough to be protected against challengers under U.S. trademark regulations.

In evaluating protectability, prospective trademarks are usually classified in one of four categories: generic marks, descriptive marks, suggestive marks, and arbitrary or "coined" marks. Under trademark law, generic marks receive the least protection, arbitrary marks receive the most protection, and descriptive and suggestive marks fall in between.

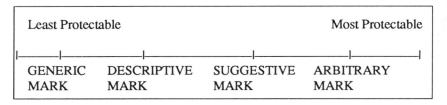

Generic marks are terms such as *automobile* and *computer* that encompass entire classes of goods and services. Common sense dictates that generic marks cannot be trademarked by any one company, since doing so would prevent all other companies from using the generic term in describing their products. Think, for example, of what would happen if IBM were allowed to trademark the term "computer." Not only would companies such as Apple Computer, Inc., and Prime Computer, Inc., be forced to change their corporate names, they would also would be reduced to calling their products "data processing units," "automatic calculating and display devices," or something similarly awkward. If your title is a generic name or a very general term such as *Management Training* or *The Workout*, the PTO will not allow you to register it as a trademark.

Descriptive marks are names such such as one "One Coat" for house paint or "Quick Stop" for convenience stores that describe the product or service in some manner. If a title is purely descriptive, it is usually ineligible for trademark protection. However, descriptive titles can qualify for trademark protection if they acquire a secondary meaning in the minds of customers.

Examples of descriptive marks that have acquired secondary meaning (and that, as a result, have qualified for trademark registration) include "Superglue" for a brand of adhesive and "Computer Factory" for a chain of computer stores.

Suggestive marks are names that, although they may include descriptive elements, do not directly describe the product or service. Instead, suggestive marks use language that suggests some connection between the product and an image that the company would like to convey. Irish Spring soap and Arid antiperspirant are examples of suggestive trademarks. Most suggestive marks are strong candidates for trademark protection, with no requirement that the mark acquire secondary meaning in the marketplace before registration is allowed to proceed.

As you might suspect, the exact boundary between descriptive and suggestive marks is difficult to define. In fact, the question of just where this boundary lies has been the basis of a continuing series of disputes between trademark applicants, who insist that their name or title is eligible for protection because it is suggestive, and the PTO or trademark challengers, who argue that the mark cannot be protected because it is descriptive. For example, the PTO might argue that your title *The No Sweat Workout* is purely descriptive, while you might argue that the title is cute, clever and poetic enough to be protectable as a suggestive mark.

The best way to guarantee that your name is eligible for protection is to invent an arbitrary or coined mark—a name that carries little or no natural connection to the good or services that it identifies. Although arbitrary and coined marks are usually considered together as a single classification, they are different. An arbitrary mark is a real word that acquires new meaning when it is applied to a product or business, as when Apple was applied to a line of computers. In contrast, a coined mark is an invented word that has no meaning except when it is used in connection with a product or business, as when Xerox was applied to an office equipment company or, more recently, when UNISYS was coined as the name for the new company created by the merger of Burroughs and Sperry Rand. Because they are based on invented words or connections, there is little chance that the public would confuse one arbitrary or coined mark with another. As a result, arbitrary and coined marks are the most protectable of all trademarks.

What do these definitions and distinctions tell a media producer who is attempting to trademark a title? First, if your title falls into the generic or descriptive category, it is probably not worth proceeding to the next step in the trademark registration process. However, if the title is a suggestive or an arbitrary/coined term, it probably is worth proceeding. If you believe that your title might fall on the boundary between descriptive and suggestive marks, or if you believe that you have a descriptive title that has acquired secondary meaning, consider running the title by a trademark attorney. An attorney can tell you whether your title is likely to pass the protectability test and, if it may not, how you might modify it to make it more protectable.

Step 3: Conducting a Trademark Search

You have determined that your title is eligible for federal trademark registration and that it is protectable. The next step in the registration process is to make sure that no one else is already using your title, or a title that is close enough to yours to cause confusion. To find this out, you must conduct a trademark search.

Although you can conduct a trademark search yourself, the more common practice is to hire a professional search firm to do the job, or to hire a trademark lawyer who will take care of the search for you. If you prefer to complete some preliminary research on your own before investing in an attorney or a trademark search firm, you can check your title against those listed in *The Trademark Register of the U.S.*, a directory from a private publisher that is available in most large libraries. Even though *The Trademark Register of the U.S.* is updated annually, you should also check the *Trademark Official Gazette*, a weekly publication of the PTO, to see if any potentially conflicting marks have been registered since the last edition of *The Trademark Register*. Another operation is to check the records of all active and pending registrations maintained by the Trademark Search Library of the PTO. The library is located at Crystal Plaza 2, 2nd Floor, 2011 Jefferson Davis Highway, Arlington, VA 22022.

This sort of preliminary research can help rule out titles that are in obvious conflict with existing marks registered with the PTO. However, if your research indicates that there is no conflicting mark, you should still plan to proceed with a full trademark search. Conducting the search through an attorney or directly with a trademark search firm[7] is advisable, since you can be reasonably sure that a professional search will cover all of the relevant records, including:

•The files at the PTO, which include records of all pending, issued, abandoned, expired, and cancelled federal trademark registrations;

---

[7]If you want to work directly with a trademark search firm, rather than through a lawyer, you can ask a lawyer to recommend a firm, you can look in the phone book under Trademark Search Services, or you can call Research on Demand at 800-227-0750. Research on Demand provides a number of computerized research services, including a trademark search service.

• The trademark registers in each state;

• Trade directories and telephone books (which will turn up uses of the mark that may not be covered by federal or state registration, but that may be protected by common law rights.)

The report that results from a trademark search is simply a list of the known names that may conflict, in some way, with your title. Significantly, the report itself will include no recommendation as to whether the title is safe for you to use. Although you can review the report and decide on your own, this is one point where it almost always pays to talk to an experienced trademark attorney. An attorney will be able to examine the report for you, evaluating any conflicting titles, pointing out any potential problems that you might have missed and recommending ways that you could change your title to avoid trouble.

Step 4: Filing the Trademark Registration Form

Your preparatory research is complete. You have determined that your title is eligible for federal trademark registration and that it is protectable. You have also determined, through a trademark search, that there appear to be no conflicting titles in use. Does this mean that you are finally ready to register the trademark? Almost. To file the registration forms with the PTO, you will need one more item—proof that you have either shipped your product across state lines or that you have a "bona fide intent" to do so.

Under the original Lanham Act, you could not file to register a product name as a trademark until the name had been used in interstate commerce. This meant that you had to wait until you had sold the product across state lines before you could even begin the trademark registration process—a wait that could be very scary if you had invested heavily in the production, packaging and marketing of a new product.

The Trademark Law Revision Act of 1988 changed this by establishing a two-track trademark application system based on either "intent to use" or "actual use" of the mark. Under the new system, trademark applicants who have a "bona fide intent" to register a product name as a trademark can, in effect, reserve the name by filing a trademark application before the product is actually released.

How will the PTO know if your application is based on a bona fide intent to use the mark? In most cases, the PTO will simply take your word for it once you sign and file the appropriate forms. However, once the PTO approves your intent-to-use application, you will need to show that you have gone ahead and used the mark in interstate commerce or that you still have

Figure 8.2

TRADEMARK/SERVICE MARK APPLICATION, PRINCIPAL REGISTER, WITH DECLARATION	MARK (Identify the mark)
	CLASS NO. (If known)

TO THE ASSISTANT SECRETARY AND COMMISSIONER OF PATENTS AND TRADEMARKS:

APPLICANT NAME:

APPLICANT BUSINESS ADDRESS:

APPLICANT ENTITY: (Check one and supply requested information)

☐ Individual - Citizenship: (Country) _____

☐ Partnership - Partnership Domicile: (State and Country) _____
   Names and Citizenship (Country) of General Partners: _____

   _____

☐ Corporation - State (Country, if appropriate) of Incorporation: _____

☐ Other: (Specify Nature of Entity and Domicile) _____

   _____

GOODS AND/OR SERVICES:
   Applicant requests registration of the above-identified trademark/service mark shown in the accompanying drawing in the United States Patent and Trademark Office on the Principal Register established by the Act of July 5, 1946 (15 U.S.C. 1051 et. seq., as amended.) for the following goods/services: _____

BASIS FOR APPLICATION: (Check one or more, but NOT both the first AND second boxes, and supply requested information)

☐ Applicant is using the mark in commerce or in connection with the above identified goods/services. (15 U.S.C. 1051(a), as amended.) Three specimens showing the mark as used in commerce are submitted with this application.
   • Date of first use of the mark anywhere: _____
   • Date of first use of the mark in commerce which the U.S. Congress may regulate: _____
   • Specify the type of commerce: _____

        (e.g., interstate, between the U.S. and a specified foreign country)
   • Specify manner or mode of use of mark on or in connection with the goods/services: _____

        (e.g., trademark is applied to labels, service mark is used in advertisements)

☐ Applicant has a bona fide intention to use the mark in commerce on or in connection with the above identified goods/services. (15 U.S.C. 1051(b), as amended.)
   • Specify intended manner or mode of use of mark on or in connection with the goods/services: _____

        (e.g., trademark will be applied to labels, service mark will be used in advertisements)

☐ Applicant has a bona fide intention to use the mark in commerce on or in connection with the above identified goods/services, and asserts a claim of priority based upon a foreign application in accordance with 15 U.S.C. 1126(d), as amended.
   • Country of foreign filing: _____   • Date of foreign filing: _____

☐ Applicant has a bona fide intention to use the mark in commerce on or in connection with the above identified goods/services and, accompanying this application, submits a certification or certified copy of a foreign registration in accordance with 15 U.S.C. 1126(e), as amended.
   • Country of registration: _____   • Registration number: _____

   Note: Declaration, on Reverse Side, MUST be Signed

Figure 8.2 (cont'd.)

DECLARATION

The undersigned being hereby warned that willful false statements and the like so made are punishable by fine or imprisonment, or both, under 18 U.S.C. 1001, and that such willful false statements may jeopardize the validity of the application or any resulting registration, declares that he/she is properly authorized to execute this application on behalf of the applicant; he/she believes the applicant to be the owner of the trademark/service mark sought to be registered, or, if the application is being filed under 15 U.S.C. 1051(b), he/she believes applicant to be entitled to use such mark in commerce; to the best of his/her knowledge and belief no other person, firm, corporation, or association has the right to use the above identified mark in commerce, either in the identical form thereof or in such near resemblance thereto as to be likely, when used on or in connection with the goods/services of such other person, to cause confusion, or to cause mistake, or to deceive; and that all statements made of his/her own knowledge are true and all statements made on information and belief are believed to be true.

Date	Signature
Telephone Number	Print or Type Name and Position

INSTRUCTIONS AND INFORMATION FOR APPLICANT

To receive a filing date, the application must be completed and **signed by the applicant** and submitted along with:

1. The prescribed fee for each class of goods/services listed in the application;
2. A drawing of the mark in conformance with 37 CFR 2.52;
3. If the application is based on use of the mark in commerce, three (3) specimens (evidence) of the mark as used in commerce for each class of goods/services listed in the application. All three specimens may be the same and may be in the nature of: (a) labels showing the mark which are placed on the goods; (b) a photograph of the mark as it appears on the goods, (c) brochures or advertisements showing the mark as used in connection with the services.

Verification of the application - The application must be signed in order for the application to receive a filing date. Only the following person may sign the verification (Declaration) for the application, depending on the applicant's legal entity: (1) the individual applicant; (b) an officer of the corporate applicant; (c) one general partner of a partnership applicant; (d) all joint applicants.

Additional information concerning the requirements for filing an application are available in a booklet entitled **Basic Facts about Trademarks,** which may be obtained by writing:

U.S. DEPARTMENT OF COMMERCE
Patent and Trademark Office
Washington, D.C. 20231

Or by calling: (703) 557-INFO

This form is estimated to take 15 minutes to complete. Time will vary depending upon the needs of the individual case. Any comments on the amount of time you require to complete this form should be sent to the Office of Management and Organization, U.S. Patent and Trademark Office, U.S. Department of Commerce, Washington D.C., 20231, and to the Office of Information and Regulatory Affairs, Office of Management and Budget, Washington, D.C. 20503.

definite plans to do so. The PTO will not actually register a mark that was filed under the intent-to-use procedure until you submit proof that the product bearing the name has been sold in interstate commerce.

Of course, you can still register the old, "actual use" way, waiting until your product has actually shipped in interstate commerce and then applying to the PTO. In either case, you will need to file the form shown in Figure 8.2. Along with the application form, the filing must include the following:
• a drawing of the mark

• three specimens of the mark showing actual use in connection with goods and services (assuming that you are filing based on actual use of the mark); and

• the $175 filing fee.

Notice that the application form requires you to indicate whether you are filing based on actual use of the mark in interstate commerce or your intent to use the mark. If you are filing an intent-to-use application, you do not need to provide specimens at this time. However, as discussed below, you will need to include the specimens when submitting the follow-up form required by the PTO.

The drawing of the trademark that accompanies your application must show the mark as it is actually used in interstate commerce or as you intend it to be used. The PTO has fairly strict rules for formatting the drawing, particularly if you want to protect a specific depiction (type treatment, logo, design elements, etc.) of the trademark rather than simply the words that comprise the mark. Those rules are described in detail in the instructions that accompany the application form.

The PTO rules state that the five specimens included with your application (or, in the case of an intent-to-use application, included with the follow-up forms filed later) should be "actual labels, tags, containers, displays, etc. as long as they are capable of being arranged flat and of a size not larger than 8 1/2 x 13 inches."[8] This means that, if the mark is displayed on packaging that can be made to lie flat, you should submit the packaging as your specimen, rather than copies of actual videotapes or other bulky program materials. If packaging is not available, you should submit five copies of a photograph or photocopy that shows the trademark displayed on your product.

---

[8]"Basic Facts About Trademarks," U.S. Department of Commerce: Patent and Trademark Office, 1989.

Step 5: Inside the PTO

Once you have submitted your actual use or intent-to-use application, a PTO employee will check to make sure it is complete. If it is not, it will be returned to you with a request to provide the missing information or materials. If the application is complete, it will be passed on to a Trademark Examining Attorney, who will issue what in PTO parlance is called an "initial determination of registrability." This document will indicate either that the mark is eligible for registration or that it is being refused on procedural or statutory grounds. If the registration is refused for statutory reasons, it will probably be because the mark:

1. Does not function as a trademark to identify the goods or services as coming from a particular source; for example, the matter applied for is merely ornamentation;

2. Is immoral, deceptive or scandalous;

3. May disparage or or falsely suggest a connection with persons, institutions, beliefs or national symbols, or bring them into contempt or disrepute;

4. Consists of or simulates the flag or coat of arms or other insignia of the United States, or a State or municipality, or any foreign nation;

5. Is the name, portrait or signature of a particular living individual, unless he has given written consent; or is the name, signature or portrait of a deceased President of the United States during the life of his widow, unless she has given her consent;

6. So resembles a mark already registered in the PTO as to be likely, when applied to the goods of the applicant, to cause confusion, or to cause mistakes, or to deceive;

7. Is merely descriptive or deceptively misdescriptive of the goods or services;

8. Is primarily geographically descriptive or deceptively misdescriptive of the goods or services of the applicant;

9. Is primarily merely a surname.[9]

---

[9]"Basic Facts About Trademarks," U.S. Department of Commerce: Patent and Trademark Office, , 1989, 2-3.

If the Examining Attorney refuses your application on these or other grounds, you have six months to respond with clarifications or additional information. If the Examining Attorney is still not convinced, you may appeal the decision to the Trademark Trial and Appeal Board, an administrative tribunal within the PTO.[10]

Once the Examining Attorney has approved your application, or once you have successfully appealed a refusal of registration, your mark is published in the Trademark Official Gazette. At this point, any party that wants to challenge your registration of the mark has 30 days to do so or to indicate its intent to do so and to request an extension. If the mark is challenged and you are not able to reach an accommodation with the opposing party, the matter must be resolved in a proceeding before the Trademark Trial and Appeal Board.

If there is no opposition to your mark, or if you defeat the opposition before the Trademark Trial and Appeal Board, the PTO will proceed to register your trademark. Assuming that you did not get caught up in a procedure before the Trial and Appeal Board, the PTO should issue the registration 12 weeks following the date that your mark was first published in the *Official Gazette*.

Keep in mind that, if you have filed an intent-to-use application, the PTO will not actually register the trademark until you submit proof that you have used the mark in interstate commerce. You provide this proof by filing either the Amendment to Allege Use form (PTO Form 1579), if the actual use occurred before the PTO approved the mark for publication in the Official Gazette, or the Statement of Use form (PTO Form 1580) if the actual use occurred after the mark was published in the *Official Gazette* and the PTO has issued a Notice of Allowance that no opposition was filed. In either case, the form must be accompanied by the three specimens described earlier and an additional $100 filing fee.

What if you have run into delays and are having trouble proving actual use? Once the Notice of Allowance is mailed from the PTO, you will have six months to use the mark and file the Statement of Use form. If the six months expire and you have still not used the mark, you must file form 1581, Request for Extension of Time. When you submit form 1581, you are

---

[10]If your application is rejected for reasons 7, 8, or 9 listed above, and if your appeal fails, your mark may still be eligible for registration on the Supplemental Register. While this does not carry all of the benefits of being listed on the Primary Register, it does provide you with some significant rights, including the right to sue for trademark infringement in Federal courts. For more information about the distinction between the Primary and Supplemental Registers, consult a trademark attorney.

required to include a $100 fee and a description of your continuing efforts to move the mark into use in interstate commerce. Working in six-month increments, you can keep extending the deadline in this manner for up to three years from the point that the Notice of Allowance was issued.

Care and Feeding of Your Trademark

When you receive your certificate of registration, file it in the same safe place as your other production documents. If you have used the services of a trademark attorney, the attorney's office should also receive a copy of the registration certificate.

A trademark registration used to be good for 20 years. The Trademark Law Revision Act of 1988 reduced this to 10 years. At the end of the 10 year term, you can file to renew the trademark for another 10 years. The renewal process can continue indefinitely, as long as the trademark owner can show that the mark is still in use.

Both the original Lanham Act and the Trademark Law Revision Act of 1988 also have a "sixth year provision" that requires trademark holders to show actual use of the trademark during the sixth year of registration. To satisfy this requirement, you must file an affidavit affirming continued use, a specimen of the mark, and evidence affirming that the mark is still in use in connection with all of the goods and services indicated in the registration. The sixth year provision and the reduced registration period are both designed to help weed out abandoned trademarks from the registration roles.

When you display your registered trademark in the production or on packaging or marketing materials, it should always be followed by the ® symbol. You should also include a trademark line that identifies who owns the mark, as in "The No Sweat Workout is a registered trademark of Workmate Productions, Inc." This warns others of the registered status of the mark, and the materials that carry these notices provide evidence for you to use in renewing the registration and establishing continued use. If registration is still pending, use the ™ symbol and say that the mark is "a trademark of Workmate Productions, Inc."

If the trademark appears more than once, you do not have to keep repeating the ® or ™ symbol and trademark line. Instead, you can use the symbol and trademark line the first time that the mark appears, and the title alone after that point.

PATENTS

There are three major types of protection available for intellectual properties—copyright, trademarks, and patents. Of the three, copyright is of the greatest concern and interest to media producers, because copyright law affects both how you use existing materials in putting your production together and how you protect the production once it is finished. That is why copyright has received the greatest amount of attention in this book. Trademarks are of lesser interest to media producers, because trademark registration applies only to names and titles and because only certain types of titles can be trademarked. That is why trademark law has received less attention than copyright law in this book.

The third type of intellectual property protection, patent protection, is of the least interest and relevance to media producers. That is because patents apply to inventions, not to media productions or other creative properties. In addition, to be eligible for patent protection, the invention usually must be either a process (for example, a new method for manufacturing paper), machine or manufactured item. In other words, you can forget about patents unless you have a sideline as an inventor of, say, video equipment or new editing processes.

Even if you are an inventor, you may want to think twice before attempting to patent your latest breakthrough. Patent registration is a lengthy, costly and often unsuccessful process. Because a patent awards a monopoly to an inventor for a 17-year period, the PTO does not simply hand out patents to everyone who applies. Instead, the burden is on you to prove that your invention falls into one of the categories of products or processes that is eligible for patent protection and that it meets the PTO's strict criteria for "novelty" and "lack of obviousness."

Although it is possible to complete the rigorous patent registration procedure yourself, most applicants work with an attorney throughout the process. And because the process can take two years or more with no guarantee of success, patent applicants often end up with a large legal bill and nothing to show for it. With this in mind, many independent inventors choose to forego applying for a patent and choose, instead, to rely on some combination of copyright, trademark, trade secret, and unfair competition law to protect their creations.

BROADCAST LAW

If you produce programs intended for broadcast distribution, you should be familiar with several provisions of broadcast law that affect program content. Those provisions include the Fairness Doctrine and Personal Attack Rule; the Equal Time Provision; and the rules affecting sponsor identification and the broadcast of obscene material.

Sources of Broadcast Law

In the United States, the fundamental source of broadcast law is the Communications Act of 1934, the legislation that established the Federal Communications Commission (FCC) and the system for allocating and regulating radio and television stations that the FCC administers. Under that system, the FCC grants a broadcaster a license to use a specific channel assignment for a defined period—currently five years for television stations. During the license period, the broadcaster is responsible for any program material transmitted on its station. At the end of the period, the broadcaster can renew its license, provided that it can show that the station has operated in the public interest by adhering to the rules established by the Communications Act of 1934 and extended and enforced through subsequent FCC rulings.

Because broadcast channels are very valuable commodities, television station owners stand to lose a great deal if their licenses are not renewed. For that reason, most are extremely careful about the programming that they carry. Keep in mind that, if a television station decides to buy and broadcast a program that in some way violates broadcast regulations, it is the station owner rather than the producer of the program who is at risk. The FCC can only regulate program producers indirectly, through its power to influence station owners and the type of programs that they tend to purchase.

Do state and local governments play a role in regulating television stations? Not really. Because broadcast signals carry across state lines, broadcast regulation is almost exclusively a federal matter, a manifestation of Congress's constitutional authority to regulate interstate commerce. However, state and local governments can and often do assume an active role in regulating cable television. Because cable systems do not use the public airwaves to transmit signals across state lines, and because most cable systems are franchised locally, the federal government has only a more limited ability to regulate cable system operators. Many state and local governments have stepped in to fill this void, passing regulations or writing local franchise contracts that require cable operators to provide services such as government and public access channels free of charge and to seek government approval for rate increases.

The Fairness Doctrine

Since its inception in 1934, the FCC has issued a number of rulings aimed at ensuring that broadcasters cover issues of public importance in a fair, balanced manner. Over the years, these rulings and various restatements of the Commission's position have come to be known as the Fairness Doctrine.

The Fairness Doctrine carries a two-fold responsibility for television broadcasters. First, each TV station must devote a reasonable portion of its air time to covering controversial issues that are important to the community that the station serves. Second, the coverage must be fair and balanced, presenting different sides of an issue rather than simply a single point of view. This does not mean that the station must give exactly equal air time to every viewpoint on every issue that it covers, or that advocates of each opposing position automatically receive free air time. However, it does mean that the station must be able to show the FCC that, overall, it has covered controversial issues of local importance and that it has done so in a fair manner.

The Fairness Doctrine also includes a provision called the Personal Attack Rule. This rule states that when, during the coverage of controversial issues, an attack is made upon the character, integrity, or personal qualities of an identified individual or group, the station must both notify the individual or group and give them the opportunity to respond. Significantly, this rule does not apply when the person being attacked is a public official, or when the attack is made while the station is covering or reporting a bona fide news event.

It is important to note that, despite some supporting language in a 1959 amendment to the Communications Act of 1934, the Fairness Doctrine is not formally a part of U.S. statutory law. As a result, the manner in which the doctrine is interpreted and enforced has varied over the years, depending on the mood of the FCC and the status of case law in this area. Broadcasters have always been very vocal opponents of the doctrine, claiming that it violates their constitutional rights under the First Amendment and that it actually works to discourage TV stations from covering controversial issues. In the current era of deregulation, the FCC has tended to agree with this argument, even going so far as to tell Congress that it would refrain from enforcing the doctrine. But many members of Congress have gone the other way, expressing support for the intent of the doctrine by sponsoring several legislative initiatives to add a formal fairness amendment to the Communications Act of 1934.

Until this legislative and bureaucratic wrangling is resolved (and beyond that point if the resolution involves a reinstatement or codification of the Fairness Doctrine), broadcasters must continue to be concerned about the fairness implications of the programming that they carry. For media producers, this means that broadcasters will look very carefully and cautiously at programs that cover controversial issues, particularly if the manner in which the issues are presented may obligate the station to provide air time to opposing points of view. For example, assume that you are a producer in the video department of an industrial company that is one of the major employers in a community, but that is also the target of protests by environmentalists who oppose the manner in which the company disposes of its waste products. In conjunction with the public relations department, you have put together a 10-minute video about a new manufacturing process that, when fully implemented at the plant, promises to create 500 new jobs and to cut the amount of waste product that the plant produces. You approach a local television station about using the video as part of a weekly program that covers business developments in the area. The producer of the program likes what you have done but, after consulting with the station's lawyers, decides to decline your offer because airing the video could open the station up to a fairness complaint from environmental groups who feel that your company is not going far enough in cleaning up its disposal problems.

Would you receive the same response if you had tried to show your video on the local cable system? That depends. In the past, the Fairness Doctrine has been applied to local origination cable channels—the channels that are actually operated by the cable company—but not to public or leased access channels. The reasoning here is that the cable company controls the program content on local origination channels but has little or no control over the programming on public or leased access stations. However, because the federal government does not formally license cable operators, the FCC's authority to apply the Fairness Doctrine to local origination stations has also been called into question. The answer to this and related questions awaits the resolution of the great Fairness Doctrine Debate.

The Equal Time Rule

If you have ever produced promotional materials for candidates running for public office, you are probably already familiar with the Equal Time Rule. Unlike the Fairness Doctrine, which has yet to be made part of U.S. statutory law, the Equal Time Rule has its own section in the Communications Act of 1934. Section 315(a) of the Communications Act states that:

> **If any licensee shall permit any person who is a legally qualified candidate for any public office to use a broadcasting station, he shall afford equal opportunities to all other such candidates for that office in the use of such broadcasting station....**

This does not mean that station owners must give away air time to candidates—only that they must make equivalent air time available to all candidates for the same office on equivalent terms. For example, if a station offers one candidate for sewer commissioner (the Equal Time Rule applies to any legitimate candidate for *any* elected office) a 30-second slot in prime time for $5000, it must make 30-second slots in prime time available to all other candidates for sewer commissioner for $5000. In this sense, the Equal Time Rule is really the "Equal Time at Equal Cost" rule.

If your production will feature a performer who happens to be running for public office, be careful. The equal time provision applies not just to political commercials but to any recognizable appearance by a candidate in any type of program or context. That is why President Gerald Ford's role in a television campaign for the United Way created equal time concerns, as did the airing of Ronald Reagan's movies during his election campaigns. And that is why using an actor who is running for, say, dog catcher in a commercial intended for local broadcast during the election period could also cause problems.

Sponsor Identification

A consumer electronics company has hired your company to produce a program about the future of home entertainment systems. The company gives you a big budget and creative control of the production. It does, however, request that you feature its products in the program.

You deliver the program, and the sponsoring company loves it. The company shows the production to its employees and distributors, and they love it, too. Excited by the response, the company decides to offer copies free of charge to any TV station that wants to air the program, either in its entirety or in excerpts. Several stations indicate they do intend to broadcast the program.

Is there a problem here? No, not as long as the stations that broadcast the production avoid a practice commonly called "plugola" by identifying the program as sponsored material. The FCC requires broadcasters to tell viewers when a program is commercial material and to identify the sponsor. The rules are particularly stringent for commercial spots that are designed to advocate a particular position while disguising the identity of the sponsor. For example, when a pharmaceutical company creates a series of "infomercials" that advocate a particular approach to treating high blood pressure—an approach that happens to involve a drug that the company manufactures—the stations airing the ads better be sure that the pharmaceutical company is identified as the sponsor. Otherwise, the stations may be subject to FCC sanctions, and the pharmaceutical company may find that is the subject of an investigation by the Federal Trade Commission.

Obscene Content

If your productions tend toward the risque´, do not plan on seeing them aired on broadcast television in the United States. This is particularly true if the programs include language that could be considered profane or obscene. Section 326 of the Communications Act of 1934 gave the FCC the power to act against broadcasters who air programs containing "any obscene, indecent, or profane language." In 1948, this provision was made part of general U.S. criminal law, which provides for penalties of up to two years and fines not to exceed $10,000 for each infraction.

Of course, the standards that define what is obscene have changed over the years, and broadcast television today often seems more risque´ than it was even a few years ago. Still, broadcasters tend to be very sensitive about this issue, particularly since they must be concerned about the reactions of local parent, church and community groups. In addition, the FCC has indicated that it will be increasingly willing to take action against material that it considers indecent, especially when that material is broadcast during family viewing hours.

These rules do not apply to cable television networks (including basic cable, pay cable, or pay-per-view services) or local cable operators because they are not considered broadcasters. However, cable system operators must be sensitive to the standards of the community in which they are franchised, and many cable systems provide "lock out" boxes that parents can use to prevent—or at least to try to prevent—minors from viewing adult programming.

DISTRIBUTION LICENSE AGREEMENTS

Chapters 2 and 3 discussed how contracts can help you define relationships with the performers, crew members and subcontractors who will help you produce a program. Now that you have completed production, you may be thinking of entering into an arrangement with a distributor or publisher who will sell the finished program. This section discusses how contracts can help make sure that you cut the right distribution deal.

If you are a producer working within a corporate video department, you may never need to worry about distribution contracts. Once you finish a program, it will simply be displayed or distributed internally according to the plan that was worked out as part of original production agreement. This also holds true for independent production companies who produce programs as works-made-for-hire for corporations. However, as the home and business video markets have flourished, many corporate video departments have begun to look to outside distribution of productions as a way to build their operating budgets and perhaps even to turn a profit for the company. And many independent production companies have begun either to retain the copyright to their corporate video productions or to look for production deals that permit them to profit from sales to supplemental markets. In these cases, both corporate and independent producers would do well to become wise in the ways of distribution license agreements.

The Components of a License Agreement

A distribution license agreement should include the three main components that comprise all contracts: the offer, consideration, and acceptance. Of course, the boundaries between these different components often become blurred in the actual contract, and most contracts include a number of additional provisions and guarantees.

A distribution contract should begin by establishing in clear, nonambiguous terms just what it is that you are offering the distributor (distributor is used here as a generic term that encompasses both distributors and publishers) to distribute and what rights the distributor will have in the materials. What sort of program is this? Will you retain the copyright in the work (almost always the preferable option for the producer), or are you transferring the copyright to the distributor?

In a distribution license, it is especially important to establish the term and scope of the offer. How long will the distributor retain the rights to sell the program? In which markets? Is this an exclusive agreement, or will you have the right to enter into similar contracts with other distributors? In the sample contract shown in Figure 8.3, all of this is spelled out in a separate Grant of Rights section.

The sections of the contract that deal with consideration should detail the compensation that you will receive for granting the distributor the privilege of selling your program. Is the deal being done on a royalty basis, or will you receive a lump sum payment? If this is a royalty deal, will there be an advance against royalties (an advance payment to the producer that is then recouped by the distributor from royalty payments due to the producer)? Will the rights granted in the contract revert back to you if the distributor either ceases selling the program or fails to meet specified minimum sales levels? How many free or reduced-price copies is the distributor allowed to provide to reviewers or for promotional purposes? Even more important, what will the royalty percentage be, and how will it be calculated? Will the calculations be based on gross sales or, more typically, net sales following returns? Is there a minimum guaranteed royalty, even if the program does not sell well? How and when will royalty checks be issued? What accounting records will the distributor be required to keep, and what rights will you have to

Figure 8.3: Sample Video Licensing Agreement

License Agreement dated November 5, 1990, by and between Workmate Productions, Inc. (Grantor), a Connecticut corporation with offices at 253 Myrtle Rd., Stamford, CT 06905, and Davis Video, Inc. (Distributor), a New York corporation with offices at 1630 Broadway, New York, NY 10019, with respect to the video program "The No Sweat Workout."

1. Definitions

As used herein, the following terms shall have the following definitions:

(a) The "Term" shall mean the period from January 1, 1991, through December 31, 1994.

(b) The "Territory" shall mean the United States, including its possessions and territories, Canada, the United Kingdom, and Australia.

(c) The "Program" shall mean "The No Sweat Workout," a 30-minute exercise video program or copies of the video program made under this Agreement.

(d) "Royalty" shall mean the consideration more fully described in Section 6 below.

(e) "Master Tape" shall mean a complete version of the final, edited Program in 1-inch or 3/4-inch videotape format delivered to the Distributor for use as a duplicating master.

2. Grant of Rights

(a) Grantor hereby grants to the Distributor and its licensees the exclusive right during the Term to duplicate videocassette and video disc copies of the Program from the Master Tape and to sell, rent, or otherwise distribute the copies throughout the Territory. The foregoing grant of rights shall include all rights necessary to distribute copies of the Program on videocassette or video disc.

(b) Further, Grantor hereby grants Distributor the right to use the name of the Program and the voice and likeness of any party who rendered services in connection with the

Figure 8.3: Sample Video Licensing Agreement (cont'd.)

Program in the packaging, advertising, promotion, and publicizing of the Program.

(c) All rights not specifically granted herein to the Distributor shall be reserved to the Grantor. Such reserved rights shall include all merchandising rights to the Program and the right to transmit the Program via broadcast, cable, or satellite channels or to grant others the right to do the same.

3. Delivery of Master Tape

Grantor agrees to deliver the Master Tape to the Distributor on or before December 17, 1990.

4. Copyright

Copyright in the Program shall be retained by the Grantor. Grantor shall be responsible for placing an appropriate copyright notice on the Master Tape. Distributor agrees to reproduce such copyright notice on all copies of the program and related packaging.

5. Editing: Prior Consent

Distributor agrees that it shall not edit the Program without Grantor's prior consent.

6. Consideration: Advance Against Royalties and Royalty Payments

(a) In consideration for the foregoing grant of rights, Distributor agrees to pay the Grantor an advance against royalties of Eight Thousand Dollars ($8000) payable as follows: Four Thousand Dollars ($4000) upon execution of this agreement and Four Thousand Dollars ($4000) upon Grantor's compliance with Section 3 above. This advance against royalties will be applied against royalties payable to the Grantor under this agreement. In no event, however, will the advance against royalties be repayable in whole or in part, regardless of royalties due under this agreement.

(b) Distributor further agrees to pay Grantor royalties of ten

Figure 8.3: Sample Video Licensing Agreement (cont'd.)

percent (10%) of net receipts from distribution of copies of the Program. "Net Receipts" shall mean the gross receipts

actually received by Distributor (exclusive of sales, use, excise, and other taxes, packing, insurance, shipping and similar charges reimbursed by customers) from the sale, rental, and licensing of the Program, less the amount of any credits or refunds for returns, taking into account any reserves previously established by Distributor.

(c) Distributor may withhold a reasonable portion of royalties due as a reserve against returns, providing that reserve shall not exceed twenty percent (20%) of royalties otherwise due to Grantor for a particular accounting period. Any such reserve shall be liquidated no later than with the rendition of the third accounting statement following the accounting statement in which the reserve was established.

7. Accounting and Payments

(a) Distributor shall account to Grantor for royalties based on Net Receipts received by Distributor during each six month period ending on June 30 and December 31 of each year. Within 90 days after the end of each such accounting period, Distributor shall furnish Grantor a report showing the Net Receipts received and a calculation of the royalties payable for such period.

(b) At the time of each such report, Distributor shall pay Grantor the amount of royalties due, after deducting the amounts of: (a) any unrecovered advances, with respect to the Program in question, (b) any other costs incurred by Distributor which are expressly deductible hereunder; (c) reasonable reserves for returns in accordance with section 6; and (d) any taxes, duties or other amounts required by law to be withheld by Distributor.

(c) Grantor may designate a certified public accountant who may audit and copy Distributor's books and records concerning the sale and distribution of the Program. Said examination shall be at the Grantor's sole cost and expense, conducted during normal business hours and

Figure 8.3: Sample Video Licensing Agreement (cont'd.)

upon reasonable notice, and may not be conducted more than once annually. The books and records for a particular

accounting period may be audited only during the three (3) years following rendition of the statement for such period.

8. Replacement and Promotional Copies

Net Receipts shall not include any receipts from copies of the Program that are distributed by Distributor to customers as replacements for defective copies, and no amount shall be credited or paid to Grantor with respect to any receipts from copies distributed for promotional purposes to the press, trade, sales representatives or potential customers, so long as no more than 1500 copies of the Program are so distributed and so long as no payments are received by Distributor for such promotional copies. If more than 1500 copies of the Program are so distributed, then Grantor shall receive a royalty payment of 10% of the latest advertised retail price for each copy in excess of 1500 that is so distributed.

9. Commencement of Marketing and Minimum Level of Sales

(a) Distributor agrees to make a reasonable and substantial effort to commence public distribution of the Program through Sales and/or Licenses within six (6) months after Distributor's receipt of the Master Tape. If Distributor fails to distribute the Program within such six (6) month period, Grantor may give written notice of its intent to terminate this Agreement, and if Distributor fails to commence public distribution of the Program within six (6) months after receipt of such notice, this Agreement shall terminate as set forth in Section 10, and Grantor shall retain any payments previously received under this Agreement in full settlement of all claims against Distributor.

(b) Distributor makes no representations or warranties that the Program will be successfully marketed or that any minimum level of sales or licensing will be achieved. If, however, the total of all Net Receipts for the first four six-month accounting periods described in Section 7.a do not exceed

Figure 8.3: Sample Video Licensing Agreement (cont'd.)

$200,000, Grantor shall have the option to give written notice of its intent to terminate this Agreement as set forth in Section 10.

10. Termination

Upon the expiration of the Term, or upon receipt of a written termination notice as described in Sections 9.a and 9.b, Distributor shall cease manufacturing the Program and all rights granted in this Agreement will revert to the Grantor. For a period of six months thereafter, however, Distributor shall have the non-exclusive right to sell and/or rent the inventory of copies of the Program remaining as of the expiration or termination date. At the end of this period, Distributor shall at its election erase or destroy any remaining copies of the Program and, upon request, furnish Grantor an affidavit thereof.

11. Representations and Warranties

Grantor represents and warrants that it has the right to enter into and fully perform this agreement and grant the rights granted herein; that Grantor owns or controls or is the authorized representative of the party that owns or controls the right to distribute videocassette or video disc copies of the Program; that Grantor has not entered into or shall not enter into any agreement that would affect or impair the rights granted herein; and that the exercise of any of the rights granted hereunder will not infringe upon any rights (including but not limited to contract, copyright, trademark, privacy and publicity rights) of any third party.

12. Indemnification

Grantor and Distributor shall each at all times indemnify and hold the other harmless from and against any and all charges, claims, damages, costs and expenses, including reasonable attorney's fees, incurred in connection with the breach of any representation, warranty, or other provision hereof. The indemnitee will promptly notify the indemnitor of any claim. The indemnitor will adjust, settle, defend, or otherwise dispose of such claim at its sole cost. If the indemnitor has been so notified and is not pursuing such matter, the indemnitee may take such action on behalf of

Figure 8.3: Sample Video Licensing Agreement (cont'd.)

itself and/or as attorney-in-fact for the indemnitor to adjust, settle, defend or otherwise dispose of such claim in which case the indemnitor shall, upon being billed therefor, reimburse the indemnitee in the amount thereof.

13. Notices

All notices, requests, consents, demands and other communications hereunder shall be in writing delivered by hand or mailed by first class mail to the respective parties to this agreement set forth above or to such other person or address as a party hereto shall designate to the other party hereto from time to time in writing forwarded in like manner. Any notice, request, consent, demand, or communication given in accordance with the provisions of this paragraph shall be deemed to have been given or made seven (7) days after deposit in the mail, postage prepaid, or when hand delivered provided that communications with respect to a change of address shall be deemed to be effective when actually received.

14. Execution of Contract

Grantor shall have a period of thirty (30) days from receipt of this Agreement to sign and return the Agreement to the Distributor. If the signed Agreement is not returned to the Distributor within that period, Distributor shall have the option to withdraw its offer of agreement.

15. Miscellaneous

Grantor shall execute or cause to be executed any and all documents needed to effectuate the purposes and intents of this Agreement. This agreement contains the entire understanding and supersedes all prior understandings between the parties hereto relating to the subject matter herein, and this agreement cannot be changed or terminated orally. Grantor waives any right to purport to terminate any rights herein or to pursue any remedies in connection with this agreement other than a suit for money damages. Grantor will, upon Distributor's request, promptly furnish to Distributor copies of such agreements or other documents as Distributor may desire in connection with any provisions

Figure 8.3: Sample Video Licensing Agreement (cont'd.)

of this agreement. This agreement and all matters or issues collateral thereto shall be governed by the laws of the State of New York applicable to contracts and executed and performed entirely therein.

IN WITNESS WHEREOF, the parties hereto hereby execute this Agreement as of the date first specified above.

Grantor   Distributor
WorkMate Productions, Inc.   Davis Video, Inc.

By: _____   By: _____

Date: _____   Date _____

---

examine those records? Also, if the production involved union performers, who will be responsible for figuring and making residual and supplemental market payments?

Finally, toward the end of the contract, there should be language that indicates how much time both parties can take to respond to the agreement and how the parties will indicate that they have accepted the terms of the agreement.

In addition to these core categories, the license agreement should include language that defines the procedures for terminating the deal, the representations and warranties that cover the arrangement, and a number of other contract specifics—all of which are covered in the sample agreement.

Sample Video Distribution Agreement

Figure 8.3 is a sample distribution agreement for the "No Sweat Workout" video. Note that this contract covers an arrangement in which the video program is already completed and the production company is placing it with a distributor. For a sample agreement in which a distributor is commissioning a company to produce a program, see the Project Contract (Figure 3.5) in Chapter 3.

Note, also, that this is one sample contract that was designed to fit one type of distribution deal. Because each publishing and distribution deal is unique, you should make sure that each of your contracts is custom-fitted to the deal at hand.

Negotiating the Agreement

Like most distribution agreements, this sample was drawn up by the distributor based on its standard contract and offered to the production company as the basis for their deal. The production company then reviewed the contract, marking any sections that required clarification or negotiation. Figure 8.3 shows the finished contract after all areas of dispute have been resolved to the satisfaction of both parties.

As the producer who is being asked to accept an agreement offered by a distributor, you should anticipate having to negotiate and even eliminate some sections of the contract. In fact, the negotiating process should start before the contract is even drawn up, in discussions with the distributor through which you define the core components of the deal. What rights will you be granting to the distributor? For how long? How much will the distributor be paying you for the rights?

When you receive the written contract, think of it as a draft that must be proofread, studied and discussed. First check to make sure that the core components of the deal, as detailed in the contract, match the understanding that you had reached in your discussions with the distributor. Then make sure that the rest of the agreement contains no other definitions or provisions that may present problems.

At this point, as a matter of policy, many producers pause to have a lawyer review the contract. A lawyer can help to translate any legal language that you might not understand and to locate any hidden terms and fine print that will work to your disadvantage. If you are not adept at figuring financial details, you may also want to have an accountant or other finance-type examine the consideration part of the deal. If you work within a corporate setting, company regulations may require you to have the contract reviewed and approved by the legal department.

One contract provision that distributors will sometimes try to sneak by you and that you will almost always want to reject is the "option on next work" clause. This provision gives the distributor the right of first refusal on your next production. Since this does not buy you anything (you could always give them the right of first refusal at a later date if you wanted to), the advantage is all to the other party. Because experienced producers recognize this, distributors almost expect to have the contract returned with this clause crossed out. Do not disappoint them.

Most distributors also expect that there will be some negotiation over the basic terms of the agreement. Do not disappoint them here, either. You will not offend a distributor by asking to have a provision in the contract clarified or by requesting changes. Of course, the extent to which the distributor will be willing to comply with your requests for changes will depend on how reasonable the changes are and how highly the distributor prizes your production. But you should never be afraid to ask. You should also not be afraid to back away from a deal if the distributor insists on terms that simply will not work for you.

Reviewing the Sample Agreement

As distribution agreements go, the sample shown in Figure 8.3 is relatively clean and simple. The major areas that tend to create problems in this sort of contract—delimiting the territory and defining the rights granted to the distributor and the royalties to be paid to the producer—are all fairly straightforward.

In Section 2.a of the agreement, WorkMate Productions, Inc. (the "Grantor") grants Davis Video, Inc. (the "Distributor") the right to make and distribute videocassette and video disc copies of "The No-Sweat Workout" (the Program) throughout the territory defined in Section 1.b for the term defined in Section 1.a. Given the definitions that the contract provides for Territory and Term, this means that Davis Video will have the right to sell the program on videocassette and disc in the U.S., United Kingdom and Australia for the four year period beginning January 1, 1991, and ending December 31, 1994. However, as described in Section 2.c, WorkMate Productions is retaining the merchandising rights to the program (the right to sell "No Sweat" sweatsuits and any similar spinoff items) and the right to distribute the program on broadcast, cable and satellite channels—as well as any other rights that are not specifically granted to Davis Video through this agreement. As stated in Section 4, the copyright for the program will remain with WorkMate.

Section 6 specifies the consideration that WorkMate Productions will receive in return for the rights granted to Davis Video. Upon signing the agreement, WorkMate will receive a non-refundable advance against royalties of $8000. Over the term of the agreement, WorkMate will also be paid a royalty of 10% of the Net Receipts from sales of copies of the Program. Of course, WorkMate will not actually see a royalty check until the $8000 advance against royalties has been earned out. Given the royalty rate of 10%, this will happen when Davis Video's Net Receipts from sales of the work reach $80,000.

The royalty section of every distribution or publishing contract must be examined very carefully. In particular, distributors can have very peculiar ways of defining "Net Receipts" and the other terms that determine just how much money you will make from the deal. The definition in this sample contract is simple and fair. It gives Davis Video the right to withhold a reasonable amount as a reserve against returned copies (Section 6.c), but does not give Davis the right to deduct any of the other marketing or packaging expenses that some publishers and distributors sometimes try to tack onto an agreement. In addition, in some agreements, the royalty arrangements can get very complex, with the royalty rate changing based on the number of copies sold and where and how they are sold. If you find that you do not fully understand these financial details, consult with an attorney or accountant who can explain them to you.

How did Davis Video and WorkMate Productions come up with $8000 as the figure to use for the advance against royalties that will be paid to WorkMate? In most cases, the advance figure is the result of negotiations between the two parties. From its side, if Davis is like most publishers and distributors, it started by running some numbers through a not very scientific formula that figures in a number of factors, including what its break even point will be on the project and how many copies it could reasonably expect to sell over the term of the agreement. Even more important, since a nonrefundable advance like this one is essentially a guarantee to WorkMate Productions, Davis Video probably tried to figure how small an advance it could get away with paying WorkMate. From the other side, WorkMate had to determine how much of an advance it needed to make the deal worthwhile and how much it could reasonably expect Davis Video to pay. The result of these calculations and negotiations is the $8000 advance specified in the contract.

In publishing and distribution agreements based on a royalty arrangement, it is important to build a way for the grantor to get the rights to the materials back in the event that the distributor or publisher does not perform as promised. As described in section 10, the agreement between WorkMate and Davis Video can be terminated in either of two ways: it can simply run its course and expire at the end of the term, or WorkMate can end it by submit hose terms allow WorkMate to terminate the agreement if Davis fails to market the program within a reasonable time period or if Davis fails to achieve the minimum sales level specified.

Most of the other sections of the sample distribution agreement should be familiar to you from the sample contracts in Chapter 3. Like all of the sample contracts in this book, this one is meant serve as a model that suggests the structure and scope of a typical agreement. However, you should not assume that you can use this sample as the basis for your own contract, or that you can simply pick and mix provisions from this agreement to build a contract that meets your needs. When in doubt, talk to a contract attorney who is familiar with your particular situation.

SUMMARY

What are the steps that you should take to protect your completed production?

The first step to protecting your finished production is to make sure that all of your production records are stored in a secure place. Then you should consider registering the copyright with the U.S. Copyright Office and, for some productions, the title with the U.S. Patent and Trademark Office. If you will be making distribution arrangements with a third party, you will also need to consider how to protect your rights through a distribution contract. If your production will be broadcast, you should also be aware of several federal regulations affecting the content of programs broadcast on U.S. television stations.

How does copyright registration help to protect your production?

Registration with the Copyright Office is not required for copyright protection. However, registration with the Copyright Office does confer a number of important benefits, including the right to sue infringers for statutory damages. Even more important, registration establishes an official record for the work that the courts will accept as evidence supporting the validity of your copyright.

How do you register the copyright of a media production with the Copyright Office?

To register the copyright of a media production, you must complete and file a copy of Form PA, along with $10 processing fee. You must also deposit a copy and written description of the production.

What is a trademark?

The U.S. government defines a trademark as a "word, symbol, design or combination word and design. . . which identifies and distinguishes the goods or services of one party from those of another."

What are the sources of U.S. trademark law?

U.S. trademark law is governed by a mix of common law and state and federal statutes. The major federal trademark statute is the Trademark Act of 1946, known as the Lanham Act. In 1988, Congress passed the Trademark Law Revision Act of 1988, the first comprehensive revision of the Lanham Act. In the United States, trademark registration and other federal trademark procedures are administered by the Patent and Trademark Office (PTO) of the U.S. Department of Commerce.

Can you register the title of a media production as a trademark?

Generally, you can trademark the titles of creative works only when the title covers a series of works or when the title is used in conjunction with manufactured products.

What are the benefits of trademark registration?

You do not have to register the trademark to enjoy many of the protections provided by federal trademark law. However, registration with the PTO does provides several advantages, including: the right to sue in Federal court for trademark infringement; *prima facie* evidence of the validity of the registration and the registrant's ownership of the mark; and the right to deposit the registration with Customs in order to stop the importation of goods bearing an infringing mark. Also, registering your title with the PTO will put out the word that the title is already in use. This will help deter others from adopting the same or a similar mark.

How do you register a trademark with the Patent and Trademark Office?

Before you try to register a title with the PTO, you must first determine if the title meets minimum eligibility requirements for registration. You must also conduct a trademark search to determine if the title is already in use as a conflicting mark. To file for registration, you submit the appropriate form, a drawing of the the mark, the $175 filing fee, and three specimens of the mark showing actual use. The specimen requirement assumes that you are filing based on actual use of the mark in interstate commerce. Under the revised trademark law, it is also possible to file for registration before you have actually used the mark, as long as you can show that you have a *bona fide* intent to use the mark.

What federal laws and regulations affect the content of broadcast television programming?

The federal laws and regulations affecting the content of broadcast programming include the Fairness Doctrine and Personal Attack Rule; the Equal Time Provision; and the rules affecting sponsor identification and the broadcast of obscene material.

What are the main components of a video distribution license agreement?

A video distribution license should include the three major components that comprise all contracts: the offer, consideration, and acceptance. In distribution agreements, you should pay particular attention to defining the term (duration) of the agreement; the exact rights that you are assigning through the agreement; the territory in which the distributor will be able to sell the production; how royalties, if the deal involves royalties, or other consideration will be computed and paid; and who will hold the copyright to the production. It is also important to include a provision for terminating the agreement if the distributor fails to bring the production to market or to meet minimum sales levels. Conversely, it is important that the agreement not include language that gives the distributor the right of first refusal to market your next production.

Appendix A: State and Provincial Film and Television Office

Note: In some states and provinces, there are also local film and television offices that serve specific areas. The state or provincial office listed here should be able to refer you to the appropriate local agency.

Alabama Film Office
340 N. Hull St.
Montgomery, AL 36130
(205) 261-4195 (800) 633-5898

Alaska Motion Picture and
Television Production Services
3601 C St., #722
Anchorage, AK 99503
(907) 563-2167

Alberta Film Industry Development
Office
Sterling Place
9940 106 St. 10 Fl.
Edmonton, AB, T5K 2P6 Canada
(403) 427-2005

Arizona Film Commission
1700 W. Washington
Phoenix, AZ 85007
(602) 255-5011 (800) 528-8421

Arkansas Motion Picture Development
Office
1 State Capitol Mall
Little Rock, AR 72201
(501) 682-7676

British Columbia Film Commission
British Columbia Enterprise Center
770 Pacific Blvd. S.
Vancouver, BC, V6B 5B7 Canada
(604) 660-2732

California Film Commission
6922 Hollywood Blvd., #600
Hollywood, CA 90028
(213) 736-2465

Colorado Motion Picture & TV
Commission
1313 Sherman St., #500
Denver, CO 80203
(303) 866-2778

Connecticut Film Commission
210 Washington St.
Hartford, CT 06106
(203) 566-8458

Delaware Development Office, Film
Division
99 Kings Hwy.
Dover, DE 19903
(302) 736-4254

Florida Motion Picture and Television
Bureau
107 W. Gaines St.
Tallahassee, FL 32301
(904) 487-1100

Georgia Film and Videotape Office
230 Peachtree St. N.W.
Atlanta, GA 30303
(404) 656-3591

Hawaii Film Industry Branch
220 S. King St.
Honolulu, HI 96813
(808) 548-4535

Idaho Film Bureau
Commerce Department
700 W. State St.
Boise ID 63720
(208) 334-2470 (800) 942-8338

Illinois Film Office
State of Illinois Center
100 W. Randolph
Chicago, IL 60601
(312) 917-3600

Indiana Film Commission
1 N. Capitol
Indianapolis, IN 46204
(317) 232-8829

Iowa Film Office
200 E. Grand Ave.
Des Moines, IA 50309
(516) 281-8319

Kansas Film Commission
400 W. 8 St.
Topeka, KS 66603
(913) 296-2009

Kentucky Film Office
Berry Hill Mansion
Louisville Rd.
Frankfort, KY 40601
(502) 564-3456

Louisiana Film and Video Commission
P.O. Box 94361
Baton Rouge, LA 70804
(504) 342-8150

Maine Film Commission
State House Station, #59
Augusta, ME 04333
(207) 289-5710

Manitoba Cultural Industries
Development Office—Film Office
93 Lombard Ave.
Winnipeg, MB, R3B 3B1 Canada
(204) 947-2117

Maryland Film Commission
217 E. Redwood St.
Baltimore, MD 21202
(301) 333-6633

Massachusetts Film Bureau
10 Park Plaza, #2310
Boston, MA 02116
(617) 973-8800

Michigan Office of Film and TV
Services
1200 6 St.
Detroit, MI 48226
(313) 256-2000

Minneapolis (Minnesota) Office of
Film, Video, and Recording
City Hall, #323-M
Minneapolis, MN 55415
(612) 348-2947

Mississippi Film Office
Economic Development Department
P.O. Box 849
Walter Sillers Bldg.
Jackson, MS 39205
(601) 359-3449

Missouri Film Commission
P.O. Box 118
Jefferson City, MO 65102
(314) 751-9049
(800) 647-6724

Montana Film Promotion Division
Commerce Department
1424 9 Ave.
Helena, MT 59620
(406) 444-2654 (800) 548-3390

Nebraska Film Commission
301 Centennial Mall S.
P.O. Box 95143
Lincoln, NE 68509
(402) 471-3368

Nevada Motion Picture and TV Division
McCarran International Airport
Las Vegas, NV 89158
(702) 486-7150

New Brunswick Film and Video
Commission
P.O. Box 12345
Fredericton, NB, E3B 5C3 Canada
(506) 453-2555

Newfoundland and Labrador
Development and Tourism
Department—Film Division
P.O. Box 4750
St. John's, NF, A1C 5T7 Canada
(709) 576-2800

New Hampshire Film and TV Bureau
105 Loudon Rd.
P.O. Box 856
Concord, NH 03301
(603) 271-2598

New Jersey Motion Picture and TV
Commission
Gateway 1, #510
Newark, NJ 07102
(201) 648-6279

New Mexico Film Commission
1050 Old Pecos Trail
Santa Fe, NM 87501
(505) 827-8580 (800) 545-9871

New York State Governor's Office for
Motion Picture and TV Development
1515 Broadway, 32 Fl.
New York, NY 10036
(212) 575-6570

North Carolina Motion Picture
and TV Development Office
430 N. Salisbury St.
Raleigh, NC 27611
(918) 733-9900

North Dakota Film Office
Tourism and Promotion Department
Liberty Memorial Bldg.
Bismark, ND 58505
(701) 224-2525 (800) 437-2077

Nova Scotia Film Office
Station M, P.O. Box 2287
Halifax, NS, B3J 3C8 Canada
(902) 422-3402

Ohio Film Bureau
P.O. Box 1001
Columbus, OH 43266
(614) 466-2284

Oklahoma Film Office
6601 Broadway Extension
Oklahoma, OK 73116
(405) 841-5135 (800) 443-6552

Ontario Film Development Corporation
81 Wellesley St. E.
Toronto, ON, M4Y 1H6 Canada
(416) 965-8393

Oregon Film and Video Division
595 Cottage St. N.E.
Salem, OR 97310
(503) 373-1232 (800) 547-7842

Pennsylvania Film Bureau
449 Forum Bldg.
Harrisburg, PA 17120
(717) 783-3456

Quebec Film Office
1755 Rene-Levesque Blvd. E.
Montreal, PQ, H2K 4P6 Canada
(514) 873-5027

Rhode Island Film Commission
150 Benefit St.
Providence, RI
(401) 277-3468

Saskatchewan Film Development Office
Cultural Industries Department
1942 Hamilton St.
Regina, SK, S4P 2C5 Canada
(306) 787-8148

South Carolina Film Office
P.O. Box 927
Columbia, SC 29202
(803) 737-0400

South Dakota Film Office
Tourism Department
Capitol Lake Plaza
Pierre, SD 57501
(605) 773-3301 (800) 843-800

Tennessee Film, Entertainment, and
Music Commission
320 6 Ave. N., 7 Fl.
Nashville, TN 37219
(615) 741-3456 (800) 251-8594

Texas Film/Music Office
P.O. Box 12728
Austin, TX 78711
(512) 469-9111

Utah Film Commission
State Office Bldg., #6220
Salt Lake City, UT 84114
(801) 538-3039 (800) 453-8824

Vermont Film Bureau
134 State St.
Montpelier, VT 05602
(802) 828-3236

Virginia Film Office
Economic Development Department
1000 Washington Bldg.
Richmond, VA 23219
(804) 786-3791

Washington DC Mayor's Office of
Motion Picture and TV Development
1111 E. St. N.W.
Washington, DC 20004
(202) 727-6600

Washington State Film and Video Office
3121 Ave. N
Seattle, WA 98109
(206) 464-7148

West Virginia Commerce Department
Film Commission
State Capitol Bldg., MB-33
Charleston, WV 25305
(304) 348-3670

Wisconsin Film Office
Tourism Development Division
123 W. Washington Ave., Box 7970
Madison, WI 53707
(608) 267-3456

Wyoming Film Office
Travel Commission
I-25 and College Dr.
Cheyenne, WY 82002
(307) 777-7851 (800) 458-6657

Yukon Film Production Office
Box 2703
Whitehorse, YT, Y1A 2C6 Canada
(408) 667-5400

APPENDIX B: RESOURCES FOR LICENSING MUSIC

Performing Rights Societies

American Society of Composers,
Authors, and Publishers (ASCAP)
1 Lincoln Plaza
New York, NY 10023
(212) 595-3050
-or-
6430 Sunset Boulevard
Los Angeles, CA 90028
(213) 466-7681

Broadcast Music Inc. (BMI)
320 W. 57th St.
New York, NY 10019
(212) 586-2000
-or-
87830 Sunset Boulevard
Hollywood, CA 90069
(213) 659-9109

Society of European Songwriters,
Authors, and Composers (SESAC)
156 W. 56th St.
New York, NY 10019
(212) 586-3450

Selected Rights and Permissions Agencies

BZ Rights and Permissions
125 West 72nd St.
New York, NY 10023
(212) 580-0615

Mary Williams Music Clearance
Corporation
6223 Selma Ave.
Suite 211
Hollywood, CA 90028
(213) 462-6575

The Clearing House, Ltd.
6605 Hollywood Boulevard
Hollywood, CA 90028
(213) 469-3186

Selected Music Libraries

Associated Production Music
6255 Sunset Boulevard
Hollywood, CA 90028
(213) 461-3211

Capitol Production Music
1750 N. Vine St.
Hollywood, CA 90028
(213) 461-2701
(800) 421-4163

DeWolfe Music Library, Inc.
25 West 45th St.
New York, NY 10036
(212) 382-0220

Dimension Music Library
PO Box 1561
Jupiter, FL 33468
(395) 746-2222

Omnimusic Production Music Library
52 Main St.
Port Washington, NY 11050
(516) 883-0225

Soper Sound Music Library
PO Box 498
Palo Alto, CA 94301
(415) 321-4022
(800) 227-9980

TRF Production Music Libraries
40 E. 49 St.
New York, NY 10017
(212) 753-3234

APPENDIX C: GUILDS, UNIONS, AND ASSOCIATIONS

This appendix provides addresses and phone numbers for the major national television and film guilds, unions and associations in the United States. Most entries include information for both a New York and California office. Many unions and guilds also have local offices in other cities. For information about these locals, call the New York or California office listed here.

Guilds, Unions, and Alliances

Actor's Equity Association (AEA)
165 West 46th St.
New York, NY 10036
(212) 869-8530

6430 Sunset Boulevard
Hollywood, CA 90028
(213) 462-2334

Alliance of Motion Picture and
Television Producers (AMPTP)
14144 Ventura Blvd.
Sherman Oaks, CA 91423
(818) 995-3600
(For information in New York, contact
the Motion Picture Association of
America.)

American Federation of Musicians
(AFM)
1501 Broadway
New York, NY 10036
(212) 869-1330

1777 North Vine St.
Hollywood, CA 90028
(213) 461-3441

American Federation of Television and
Radio Artists (AFTRA)
260 Madison Ave.
7th Floor
New York, NY 10016
(212) 532-0800

1717 North Highland Ave.
Hollywood, CA 90028
(213) 461-8111

American Guild of Musical Artists
(AGMA)
1841 Broadway
New York, NY 10023
(212) 265-3687

12650 Riverside Dr.
North Hollywood, CA 91607
(213) 877-0683

American Guild of Variety Artists
(AGVA)
184 Fifth Avenue
New York, NY 10010
(212) 675-1003

4741 Laurel Canyon Blvd.
North Hollywood, CA 91607
(818) 508-9984

Director's Guild of America (DGA)
110 West 57th St.
New York, NY 10019
(212) 581-0370

7920 Sunset Blvd.
Hollywood, CA 90046
(213) 289-2000

International Alliance of Theatrical
Stage Employees (IATSE)
1515 Broadway
New York, NY 10036
(212) 730-1770

14724 Ventura Blvd.
Sherman Oaks, CA 91403
(818) 905-8999

International Brotherhood of Electrical
Workers (IBEW)
230 W. 41st St.
New York, NY 10036
(212) 354-6770

5643 Vineland Ave.
North Hollywood, CA 91601
(213) 877-1171

International Brotherhood of Teamsters,
Chauffeurs, Warehouse Men, and
Helpers (IBTC)
1 Hollow Lane
Lake Success, NY 10019
(516) 365-3470

PO Box 6017
North Hollywood, CA 91603
(818) 985-7374

National Association of Broadcast
Employees and Technicians (NABET)
322 8th Avenue
New York, NY 10001
(212) 757-7191

1800 North Argyle Ave.
Hollywood, CA 90028
(213) 462-7484

Screen Actors Guild (SAG)
1515 Broadway
New York, NY 10036
(212) 944-1030

7065 Hollywood Blvd.
Hollywood, CA 90028
(213) 465-4600

Screen Extras Guild
3629 Cahuenga Blvd. West
Los Angeles, CA 90048
(213) 851-4301

Writer's Guild of America (WGA)
555 West 57th St.
New York, NY 10019
(212) 767-7800

8955 Beverly Blvd.
Los Angeles, CA 90048
(213) 550-1000

**Professional Associations and
Industry Groups**

Academy of Motion Picture Arts and
Sciences
8949 Wilshire Blvd.
Beverly Hills, CA 90211
(213) 278-8990

Association of Independent Commercial
Producers (AICP)
100 E. 42nd St.
New York, NY 10017
(212) 557-2900

2121 Avenue of the Stars
Los Angeles, CA 90067
(213) 557-2900

Association of Independent Video and
Filmmakers (AIVF)
625 Broadway
New York, NY 10012
(212) 473-3400

Independent Producers Association
1604 Vista Del Mar
Hollywood, CA 90028
(213) 461-6966

International Television Association
(ITVA)
6311 North O'Conner Road
Irving, TX 75039
(214) 869-1112

Motion Picture Association of America
(MPAA)
1133Ave. of the Americas
New York, NY 10036
(212) 840-6161

14144 Ventura Blvd.
Sherman Oaks, CA 91423
(818) 995-3600

National Academy of Television Arts
and Sciences
110 W. 57th St.
New York, NY 10019
(212) 586-8424

National Association of Broadcaters
(NAB)
1711 North St. N.W.
Washington, DC 20036
(202) 429-5489

National Association of Television
Program Executives (NATPE)
10100 Santa Monica Blvd.
Los Angeles, CA 90067
(213) 282-8801

National Cable Television Association
(NCTA)
1724 Massachusetts Ave. N.W.
Washington, DC 20036
(202) 775-3550

Glossary

Note: Words in italics are defined elsewhere in the glossary.

acceptance: The section of a *contract* where each *party* indicates that they agree with and consent to be bound by the terms of the contract. Also the act of agreeing to the terms of a contract.

actual damages: See *damages*.

administrative law: Laws created by government agencies through the issue and enforcement of rules, regulations, orders and policies. See also *statutory law*.

affidavit: A sworn statement of fact often filed as a document in legal proceedings.

arbitration: A means of settling a dispute in which the matter is submitted to an independent person or agency for resolution. Arbitration is often used as an alternative to *litigation*.

appellate (appeals) court: A court that reviews previously judged cases to determine if the case was properly presented and the law was properly applied.

breach of contract: The failure of one or more parties to abide by the terms of a contract. See also *remedy*.

case law: See *common law*.

circuit court: A court whose jurisdiction covers several districts, counties or regions.

civil law: In the term's most common use, the body of law concerned with non-criminal matters. In civil cases, the dispute is generally a private matter between two parties, rather than between an accused criminal and the state. Compare to *criminal law*.

code: An indexed compilation of laws arranged around specific subjects (the penal code, the motor vehicle code, etc.)

collective bargaining agreement: An agreement between an employer and a group of employees, usually organized and represented by a union, that establishes and regulates the terms of employment.

common law: In its most general use, law based on judicial precedents. The body of common law on a particular legal subject consists of all of the previous judgments and judicial decrees on that subject. Contrast with *statutory law*.

consideration: The part of a *contract* that defines what compensation will be paid or detriment incurred under the terms of the contract. See also *acceptance* and *offer*.

constitutional law: In the United States, the body of law based on the articles and amendments that comprise the U.S. Constitution. The supreme law of the United States, as interpreted and enforced by the federal courts, particularly the U.S. Supreme Court.

contract: A legally binding agreement that creates obligations between two or more parties. See also *offer, consideration* and *acceptance*.

copyright: The right of ownership in an item of intellectual property such as a book, film or television program. The exclusive right to reproduce and sell an intellectual property.

copyright infringement: Using copyrighted material without the consent of the copyright holder, an illegal act under U.S. copyright law.

criminal law: The body of laws intended to protect society. Criminal cases include fraud, burglary, murder and other crimes that threaten the safety or well-being of society. Contrast with *civil law*.

damages: Compensation, usually monetary, awarded by a court or arbitrator to an individual or group injured by the actions of another. "Actual damages" compensate the injured party for financial losses that it can specifically prove are due to the actions of the wrongdoer. "Punitive damages" are extra compensation beyond actual damages awarded to punish the wrongdoer.

defamation: Making untrue, derogatory statements that injure or bring into disrepute the good name of another. When the statements are made verbally, the defamation is "slander." When they are made in writing or in any recorded medium (e.g., videotape, film or audiotape), the defamation is "libel."

defendant: In civil law proceedings, the person who is responding to the complaint brought by the plaintiff. In criminal law proceedings, the person who has been accused of the crime.

diversity jurisdiction: The authority of federal courts to hear cases and disputes between citizens of different states or between a U.S. citizen and a foreigner.

Equal Time Provision: The statutory provision established in section 315(a) of the Communications Act of 1934 that requires broadcasters who provide political candidates with advertising opportunities or other air time to do so on an equal basis to all candidates running for the same office.

express contract: A contract that is declared at the time that it is made. A contract in which the terms are made explicit and in which all parties are clearly aware that they are agreeing to those terms. Contrast with *implied contract.*

Fairness Doctrine: A body of rules promulgated by the Federal Communications Commission (FCC) to ensure that broadcasters cover issues of public importance in a fair, balanced manner. Under the Fairness Doctrine, each TV station must devote a reasonable portion of its air time to covering controversial issues of public importance, and the coverage must be fair and balanced. Over the years, the FCC has enforced the Fairness Doctrine with varying degrees of diligence.

fair use: A provision of U.S. copyright law that allows certain individuals and groups to use certain copyrighted materials without obtaining permission from or paying compensation to the copyright owner. Whether a particular use is considered fair use depends on purpose of the use (with fair use usually being reserved for non-profit purposes), the nature of the copyrighted work, the amount of the work used, and the effect of the use on the market for the work.

felony: A serious crime. Usually, a crime that is punishable by imprisonment or death. Contrast with *misdemeanor.*

implied contract: A contract that is not made explicit but that is instead implicit in a transaction between parties. Contrast with *express contract.*

indemnity: A contractual provision in which one party agrees to compensate another for any loss or damage that it causes in fulfilling or failing to fulfill its obligations under the contract. See also *warranty*.

infringement: See *copyright infringement*.

intellectual property: Materials such as books, inventions, paintings, films and television programs that are products of the intellect and imagination and that can be protected as property under U.S. copyright, trademark, and patent laws. Also, the category of law that includes copyright, trademark and patent law.

judge made law: See *common law*.

libel: See *defamation*.

litigant: An individual or group involved in a lawsuit.

litigation: A lawsuit or, more generally, any legal action or contest for which a court is the primary forum.

mechanical rights: The rights to reproduce and sell copies of a sound recording. See also *performance rights* and *synchronization rights*.

misdemeanor: A relatively minor crime. Usually, a crime that is punishable by a fine or by brief imprisonment in a local jail or facility other than a penitentiary. Contrast with *felony*.

offer: The fundamental proposal that forms the core of any contract. The section of the contract where the parties promise to do or to refrain from doing some specified act in return for some specified consideration. See also *consideration*.

oral contract: A contract that is made and agreed to vocally rather than in writing. Although oral contracts are valid in many circumstances, it is preferable to place all business contracts in writing. See also *written contract*.

party: An individual or group that play a direct role in a legal matter or who enters into a contract or other legal relationship. In litigation, there are two primary parties: the plaintiff and the defendant.

patent: A government grant that gives an individual or group the right to own and control an invention or design for a specified period of time. A patent gives the owner, in essence, a legal monopoly over the invention. In the U.S., patents are administered by the Patent and Trademark Office.

performance rights: For media producers, the rights that allow the public display or distribution of a recording of a copyrighted music piece that has been included in the soundtrack of a production. This assumes that synchronization rights to the music piece have already been secured. Performance rights are usually licensed through a performing rights society such as the American Society of Composers, Authors, and Publishers (ASCAP) or Broadcast Music Inc. (BMI).

plaintiff: The person or party who initiates a lawsuit. Contrast with *defendant*.

precedent: A previously decided case that serves as an example for later cases that involve the same or similar issues of law. Also, a rule of law that is established in a certain case and that carries authority in deciding subsequent cases. See also *common law*.

prima facie: Literally, "at first view." Evidence of a legal matter that can be taken at face value and that is presumed valid.

public domain: Creative properties such as written materials or video or film footage that are free from copyright protection. Public domain materials are properties that cannot be copyrighted (such as government publications) or for which the copyright has expired or been abandoned. Once a work falls into the pubic domain, it an be used freely, with no requirement that the user notify or compensate the creator or original copyright owner.

punitive damages: See *damages*.

regulatory law: See *administrative law*.

release: The act of giving up of a right or claim, such as the *right of privacy*. Also, the written contract that verifies that an individual has given up a right or claim. Media producers should obtain releases from all performers and property owners whose images and property appear in a production and who are not covered by some other contract.

remedy: In a contract, the section that defines the compensation that a party will receive or the actions that it can take if the other party breaks the terms of the agreement. Also, more generally, any compensation that a court or arbitrator provides to an injured party. See also *breach of contract* and *damages*.

residuals: The commissions or royalties that a party receives on the sales of a production, generally payable in accordance with the terms of an applicable collective bargaining agreement.

right of privacy: The legal right to be left alone, free from unwarranted publicity or interference. The right of privacy includes the right not to be portrayed in a media production unless other factors such as the newsworthiness of an event outweigh the right of privacy. To protect themselves from privacy challenges, media producers should obtain a release from each individual who is depicted in a production.

right of publicity: An individual's right to control and to profit from the commercial use of his name and likeness.

signatory: A party that has agreed to and signed a treaty or collective bargaining agreement.

slander: See *defamation*.

statute: A law that is enacted through legislative action. A law that is created by the U.S. Congress, a state or local legislature, or some other legislative body that is acting upon constitutional authority. Compare to *common law* and *constitutional law*.

statutory law: Law that is based on statutes rather than precedents or interpretations of the constitution.

summary judgment: A decision rendered by a judge before the case has been referred to a jury or, in some cases, before the case has been brought to trial. Summary judgments usually occur only when the facts in a case are beyond dispute.

synchronization rights: In a media production, the right to add a copyrighted musical piece to a production and to conform it to the video track. See also *performance rights*.

term: In a contract, the duration of the agreement or a specific section of the agreement. Also, a word or phrase that has a specific meaning within the context of a contract.

tort: Any wrong other than a breach of contract in which a party claims injury by another party and for which a court can provide compensation. See also remedy.

trademark: A word, symbol, design or combination word and design that identifies and distinguishes the goods or services of one party from those of another. In the U.S., trademarks can be registered through the Patent and Trademark Office.

warranty: In a contract, assurances by one party with respect to the subject of the contract on which the other party to the contract may rely. For example, the party that will be delivering materials under a media production contract might warrant that it is the sole owner of the materials. Usually, the party making the warranty will indemnify the other party against any losses that occur if the warranties prove untrue. See also *indemnity*.

work-made-for-hire: A book, media production or other creative property that is owned by the party that commissioned the work or the employer for whom the work was made, rather than by the creator of the work. In most cases, U.S. copyright law confers the right of ownership on the party that creates a work. The exceptions are instances in which an employee creates the work during the course of employment, in which case the work is owned by the employer, or instances in which the work was created under a written contract that specifies that it is "made for hire," in which case it is owned by the party that is paying for the work to be created.

written contract: A contract that is placed in writing and that the parties sign to indicate their acceptance. See also *oral contract*.

Bibliography

Bezanson, Randall P. et al. *Libel Law and the Press: Myth and Reality.* New York: Free Press, 1987.

Black, Henry Campbell. Edited by Joseph R. Nolan et al. *Black's Law Dictionary (5th edition),* St. Paul, MN: West Publishing, 1983.

Bremer, Daniel L. and Monroe E. Price. *Cable Television and Other Nonbroadcast Video: Law and Policy.* New York: Clark Boardman Callaghan, 1992.

Bunnin, Brad and Peter Beren. *Author Law and Strategies.* Berkeley, CA: Nolo Press, 1983.

Carter, T. Barton; Marc A. Franklin; and Jay B. Wright. *The First Amendment and the Fourth Estate: The Law of Mass Media* (4th Edition). Mineola, NY: The Foundation Press, 1988.

Chickering, Robert B. and Susan Hartman. *How To Register a Copyright and Protect Your Creative Work.* New York: Charles Scribner's Sons, 1987.

Copyright Office, Library of Congress. *Copyright Basics (Circular 1).* Washington, DC: U.S. Government Printing Office, 1987.

Copyright Office, Library of Congress. *How to Investigate the Copyright Status of A Work* (Circular R22). Washington, DC: U.S. Government Printing Office, 1987.

Crawford, Tad. *Legal Guide for the Visual Artist.* New York: Allworth Press, 1989.

Degan, Clara (ed). *Understanding and Using Video.* White Plains, NY: Longman Inc., 1985

Dill, Barbara. *The Journalist's Handbook on Libel and Privacy.* New York: Free Press, 1986.

Gifis, Steven. *Law Dictionary.* Woodbury, NY: Barron's Educational Services, 1984.

Henn, Harry G. *Henn on Copyright Law.* New York: Practising Law Institute, 1991.

Jacobs, Bob. *How To Be An Independent Video Producer.* Boston, MA: Focal Press, 1986.

Kane, Siegrun D. *Trademark Law: A Practitioner's Guide.* New York: Practising Law Institute, 1987.

Lewis, Anthony. *Make No Law: The Sullivan Case and the First Amendment.* New York: Random House, 1991.

Lindey, Alexander. *Lindey on Entertainment, Publishing, and the Arts, Agreements and the Law (Four Volumes). (2nd Edition).* New York: Clark Boardman, Ltd. 1982.

Marlow, Eugene. *Managing Corporate Media.* Boston, MA: Focal Press, 1989.

Nimmer, Melville B. *Nimmer on Copyright.* New York: Matthew Bender, 1992.

_____ . *Cases and Materials on Copyright and Other Aspects of Entertainment Litigation Including Unfair Competition, Defamation, Privacy. (3rd Edition).* St. Paul, MN: West Publishing, 1985.

Prelinger, Richard and Celeste R. Hoffnar (eds.). *Footage 91: North American Film and Video Sources.* New York: Prelinger Associates, Inc., 1991.

Rosden, George Eric and Peter Eric. *The Law of Advertising* (4th Edition). New York: Matthew Bender, 1989.

Taubman, Joseph. *In Tune with the Music Business.* New York: Law Arts Publishers, 1980.

U.S. Department of Commerce, Patent and Trademark Office. *Basic Facts About Trademarks.* Washington, DC: U.S. Government Printing Office, 1989.

U.S. Department of Commerce, Patent and Trademark Office. *General Information Concerning Patents.* Washington, DC: U.S. Government Printing Office, 1989.

About the Author

Philip Miller is a writer and editor who specializes in communications and legal topics. His publications include "Licensing Footage: Copyright and Other Legal Considerations," which appeared in *Footage 91*, and *Portable Video*, a book written with John LeBaron and published by Prentice Hall.

Previously, Mr. Miller was director of product development in the software group of Scholastic Inc., a telecommunications specialist at Massachusetts Educational Television, and a high school English teacher in New Hampshire. He has also taught courses in media and communications policy at Tufts University, the University of British Columbia, and the New School for Social Research.

Mr. Miller received a bachelor's degree from the University of Vermont and a master's degree from the Harvard Graduate School of Education.

Index

346·048/ MIL